CITIES IN RELATIONS

T0335356

Studies in Urban and Social Change

CITIES IN RELATIONS

TRAJECTORIES OF URBAN DEVELOPMENT
IN HANOI AND OUAGADOUGOU

Ola Söderström

WILEY Blackwell

This edition first published 2014
© 2014 John Wiley & Sons, Ltd

Registered Office
John Wiley & Sons, Ltd, The Atrium, Southern Gate, Chichester, West Sussex, PO19 8SQ, UK

Editorial Offices
350 Main Street, Malden, MA 02148-5020, USA
9600 Garsington Road, Oxford, OX4 2DQ, UK
The Atrium, Southern Gate, Chichester, West Sussex, PO19 8SQ, UK

For details of our global editorial offices, for customer services, and for information about how to apply for permission to reuse the copyright material in this book please see our website at www.wiley.com/wiley-blackwell.

The right of Ola Söderström to be identified as the author of this work has been asserted in accordance with the UK Copyright, Designs and Patents Act 1988.

Library of Congress Cataloging-in-Publication Data

Söderström, Ola.
Cities in relations : trajectories of urban development in Hanoi and
Ouagadougou / Ola Soderstrom.
     pages cm
   Includes bibliographical references and index.
   ISBN 978-1-118-63281-9 (cloth) – ISBN 978-1-118-63280-2 (pbk.)   1. Urbanization–
Vietnam–Hanoi.   2. Urbanization–Burkina Faso–Ouagadougou.   3. Ouagadougou
(Burkina Faso)–Relations.   4. Hanoi (Vietnam)–Relations.   5. Transnationalism.
6. Human geography.   I. Title.
   HT384.V52H3674 2014
   307.7609597′3–dc23
                                               2013045081

A catalogue record for this book is available from the British Library.

Cover image: © Ola Söderström
Cover design by Simon Levy Associates

Set in 10.5/12pt NewBaskerville by SPi Publisher Services, Pondicherry, India
Printed in Malaysia by Ho Printing (M) Sdn Bhd

1   2014

Contents

Figures

Tables

Acronyms

ADB	Asian Development Bank
AFD	Agence Française de Développement
ASEAN	Association of Southeast Asian Nations
CBF	Centre pour le Bien-être des Femmes
CDS	City Development Strategy
CIGC	Centre International des Grandes Conférences
CNR	Comité National de la Révolution
EAMAU	Ecole Africaine des Métiers de l'Architecture et de l'Urbanisme
EU	European Union
FDI	Foreign Direct Investment
GaWC	Globalization and World Cities Research Network
HAIDEP	Hanoi Integrated Development and Environment Programme
HCMC	Ho Chi Minh City
HPC	Hanoi People's Committee
IMF	International Monetary Fund
JICA	Japanese International Cooperation Agency
KOF	Konjunkturforschungsstelle
NCC	National Convention Center
NGO	Non-Governmental Organization
ODA	Official Development Assistance
OMA	Office for Metropolitan Architecture
PPJ	POSCO Engineering & Construction
SAP	Structural Adjustment Program
SOE	State Owned Enterprises
UCLG	United Cities and Local Governments
UN HDI	United Nations Human Development Index

UNDP	United Nations Development Programme
VINACONEX	Vietnam Construction and Import, Export Corporation
VNCC	Vietnamese Construction Consultant Cooperation
WTO	World Trade Organization
ZACA	Zone d'Activités Commerciales et Administratives

Series Editors' Preface

The Wiley Blackwell Studies in Urban and Social Change series is published in association with the *International Journal of Urban and Regional Research*. It aims to advance theoretical debates and empirical analyses stimulated by changes in the fortunes of cities and regions across the world. Among topics taken up in past volumes and welcomed for future submissions are:

- Connections between economic restructuring and urban change
- Urban divisions, difference, and diversity
- Convergence and divergence among regions of East and West, North and South
- Urban and environmental movements
- International migration and capital flows
- Trends in urban political economy
- Patterns of urban-based consumption

The series is explicitly interdisciplinary; the editors judge books by their contribution to intellectual solutions rather than according to disciplinary origin. Proposals may be submitted to members of the series Editorial Committee, and further information about the series can be found at www.suscbookseries.com.

Jenny Robinson
Neil Brenner
Matthew Gandy
Patrick Le Galès
Chris Pickvance
Ananya Roy

Preface and Acknowledgements

This book has grown out of my regular travels to Palermo in Italy during the 1990s and 2000s and experiencing the changes to the city during that time. These changes were first experienced in my imagination: in the first years it felt like traveling to an insular and isolated city; with time this impression dissolved but I did not really know why. As a cultural geographer, I then started looking at places and practices in the city, seeing how their design, their atmosphere, their users were morphing into places and practices I had seen elsewhere – in Milan, Berlin or London. In 2006, I wrote a research application and embarked on a study with a group of scholars from Palermo on the city's cosmopolitanization. This study eventually became a book (Söderström et al., 2009). As I explain in Chapter 1, this current book on "cities in relations" is an extension of the research in Palermo. Here I explore in much the same way, but with a comparative focus, how the cities of Hanoi in Vietnam and Ouagadougou in Burkina Faso have shaped, and been shaped by, their relations with elsewhere.

All the books we write – at least this is my motivation for doing it – are learning processes. I write to investigate new fields, new places, and work with new people. Until the Palermo project I was not "into world city literature": I had worked on more specific themes, such as politics of heritage (Söderström, 1992), urban design processes (Söderström et al., 2000) or visuality in planning (Söderström, 1996; Söderström, 2000). Neither was I equipped when I started my research on Ouagadougou and Hanoi with the sophisticated rationale of political science scholars (Savitch and Kantor, 2002) or urban political geographers (Robinson, 2004) for developing urban comparisons. Rather, with my background in cultural geography, my initial perspective was elaborated in dialogue with global urban anthropology (Appadurai, 1996; Burawoy, 2000; Hannerz, 1996) and transnational cultural economy

(Crang et al., 2003). Thus, during the preparation of this book, I have learnt a lot from venturing into other types of theoretical literature on cities, from talking with colleagues in other fields, and from working in new contexts.

In my experience of UK and North American academia, this type of research nomadism is not at all usual. Scholars tend to work in "research silos" and remain in their subfield. In Switzerland – where I work – and in many universities in continental Europe – where departments are smaller and scholars cannot be overly specialized – this is somewhat more frequent. For better and for worse: for better, because new ideas, new ways of seeing often emerge from stepping into new knowledge domains; for worse, when intellectual nomadism leads to superficiality. I hope you will think when reading this book that in this case it is for the better. How successful I have been in learning more about cities, I cannot say myself. But what I can say is that here I have brought together my different interests: in urban change, in urban planning, in material culture, and in the everyday experience of cities. By combining these different perspectives that rarely coexist within urban studies, my aim is to provide a comprehensive understanding of how transnational and translocal relations shape the development of "ordinary cities" (Robinson, 2006) in the Global South.

Providing the empirical material necessary for these different perspectives on urban change in Ouagadougou and Hanoi by myself would have been impossible. The research on which this book is based has been highly collective, and I would like to thank here everyone who worked on this project: Blaise Dupuis who coordinated the fieldwork in Hanoi and Ouagadougou, who drew the maps, and gave precious comments on the manuscript; Stephanie Geertman who led the research team in Hanoi, and Pierrick Leu who led the team in Ouagadougou. Stephanie's and Pierrick's research expertise in each city, their capacity to access people and information, their competence, and their patience with often difficult working conditions have been crucial for the project and this book. It was particularly important to work with two team leaders living in Ouagadougou and Hanoi and working continuously on the project for a full year. In Hanoi, I would like to thank Le Quynh Chi, who co-authored the research report (Söderström et al., 2010) with Stephanie Geertman; Pham Thuy Loan (University of Civil Engineering), Nguyen Quoc Thong (Ministry of Construction), and Trinh Duy Luan (Institute of Sociology), who worked as advisors during the research. Special thanks also to Dao Ngoc Nghiem, the former chief architect of Hanoi, from whom we often solicited his unique knowledge of the city. In Ouagadougou, I would like to thank Léandre

Guigma (architect-planner in Ouagadougou) and Benoît Sawadogo (Department of Geography, University of Ouagadougou) for their work on the research and knowledge of the city; Alexandra Biehler (CNRS, Paris) for her advice at different stages of the project; and Adama Zerbo (Municipality of Ouagadougou) for rich discussions on the city's international networks.

This research is typical of what Collier et al. (2007) describe as a "human science laboratory" where work is distributed across different sites and collectively constructed. It led to a voluminous report comprising the case-studies and an initial comparison (Söderström et al., 2010). However, the present book is single-authored because I have synthesized and reframed the results of the research I conceived in 2008. I have also consistently developed a relational comparison of urban development in Hanoi and Ouagadougou, which was absent from the initial research. Other research results have taken the form of papers written in collaboration (Söderström et al., 2012; Söderström and Geertman, 2013). Other collectively authored publications targeting a more specific readership – such as Vietnamese planners and architects (Geertman et al., 2014) – are in preparation.

Several chapters are based on previously published texts. I am grateful for permission to reuse large parts of the following: "Loose threads: the translocal making of public space policy in Hanoi," *Singapore Journal of Tropical Geography*, 2013 (co-authored with Stephanie Geertman); "Translocal urbanism: how Ouagadougou strategically uses decentralised cooperation," in B. Obrist et al. (eds.), *Living the City in Africa*, Berlin: LIT (co-authored with Blaise Dupuis and Pierrick Leu), 2013; "Exploring geographies of architectural design beyond 'starchitecture' and global cities," in J.M. Jacobs and S. Cairns (eds.), *Architecture/Geography: Inter-disciplining Space, Re-imagining Territory*, London, Routledge, 2014; "What travelling urban types do. Postcolonial modernization in two globalizing cities," in O. Söderström et al. (eds.), *Critical Mobilities*, London, Routledge, 2013.

I would also like to thank friends and colleagues who provided helpful comments on the project of this book, on specific chapters, or on the entire manuscript. In particular: Jenny Robinson, Margo Huxley, Jane Jacobs, Stephen Cairns, Didier Ruedin, Francesco Panese and Blaise Dupuis. The thoughtful comments by anonymous referees of Wiley-Blackwell's Studies in Urban and Social Change series have also helped me to push further some of my arguments. The research was made possible by a generous grant from the Swiss National Science Foundation, the efficient and non-bureaucratic agency supporting research in Switzerland. The book was partly written during a sabbatical spent in Singapore, thanks to a generous fellowship from the Faculty of Arts and Social Sciences at the National University of Singapore. Many thanks to Brenda Yeoh and Tim Bunnell for their generous help in getting me over to the Asia Research Institute at NUS, which offered me a very stimulating and friendly milieu for writing this book.

As ever, my research and this book would not have been possible without the support, advice, benevolence, calm, and love of Ariane.

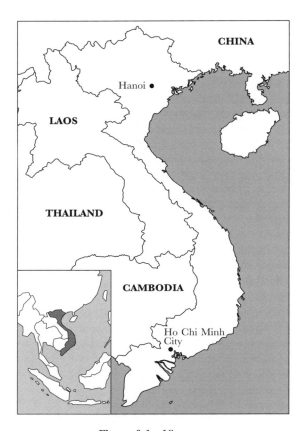

Figure 0.1 Vietnam

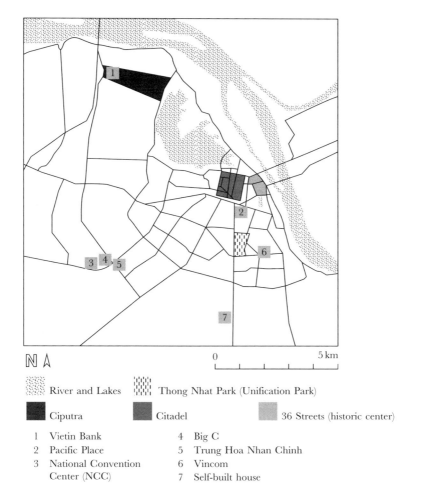

Figure 0.2 Hanoi, with the location of places analyzed in the book. Created by Blaise Dupuis.

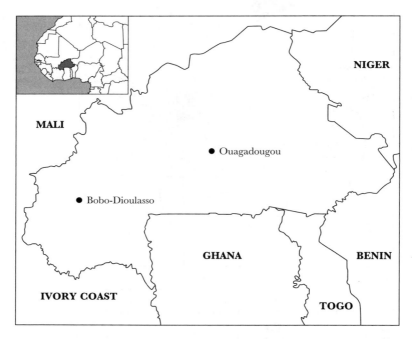

Figure 0.3 Burkina Faso

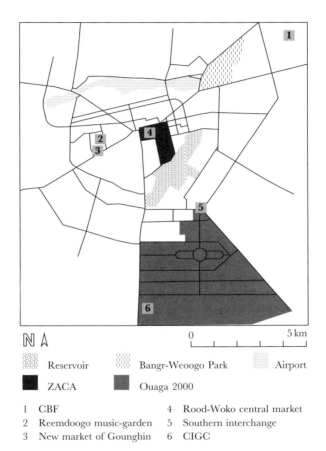

Figure 0.4 Ouagadougou, with the location of places analyzed in the book. Created by Blaise Dupuis.

1
Comparing Cities in Relations

On June 26 2008, Burkina Faso's first large road interchange was inaugurated in the capital Ouagadougou. Partly financed by Libyan funds, it was celebrated by the president as a symbol of the country's modernization. Three days later, the breaking news in local media was that a truck was trapped under the bridge of the interchange. The unfortunate truck driver had not checked the height of the new bridge and realized too late that his vehicle was too high to pass under it. A few months later, a friend in Ouagadougou told me about her cousin who had fallen from the same bridge on her motorbike and was badly hurt. Later, a taxi driver told me about his sophisticated tactics for avoiding the celebrated new infrastructure. These are some of the numerous "interchange stories" that have been circulating in Ouagadougou since the summer of 2008.

In October 2011, after having participated in a workshop on public space policy in Vietnam, I was walking at night with a group of other participants and organizers in the streets of Hanoi. At one point, one of us – the former director of Bogotá's Parks and Sports Department, now an international consultant – burst out criticizing the invasion of sidewalks by motorbikes. "It's easy though," he said, "we should do here what we did in Bogotá: reclaim the sidewalks for pedestrians and put obstacles that will make motorbike parking impossible."

A few days later, I was sitting in the office of one of Vietnam's largest construction companies interviewing a Hanoi architect on the recently

Cities in Relations: Trajectories of Urban Development in Hanoi and Ouagadougou,
First Edition. Ola Söderström.
© 2014 John Wiley & Sons, Ltd. Published 2014 by John Wiley & Sons, Ltd.

emerging "starchitecture" in the city. My interviewee was explaining how he had contacted Foster and Partners on behalf of the CEO of a large Vietnamese bank to build their new headquarters. At that point two "Foster" engineers entered the room for a videoconference with their London office on technical aspects of this building, in construction at the time.

What these three stories about two cities have in common is probably not immediately obvious, but this is precisely what this book is about. These stories each tell us something different about how transnational relations feed into the ways of life of two globalizing cities of the South. The truck trapped under the Ouagadougou interchange shows how "imported" built forms shape new ways of getting around the city. The solutions of the Colombian consultant for Hanoi's sidewalks show how an increasingly dense web of inter-urban policy connections influences local urban policies. And, finally, the examples of the Hanoi "broker in iconic architecture" as well as the "Foster" videoconference with London, point to the processes through which urban landscapes are increasingly shaped by design processes that stretch across space, moving ideas, built forms, and symbolic capital from place to place. So, to put it succinctly, this book is about *cities in relations*. It looks at how relations across borders, rather than resources in place or in cities' hinterlands, make cities the way they are today.

In order to explore these different dimensions of urban relatedness, I look at two cities which, not long ago, were "relation-poor." Cities have, of course, always been in relation with distant elsewheres, but in some periods of their development, they can be more isolated, more marginal. This happened to Hanoi during the Cold War and Ouagadougou during Burkina Faso's revolutionary socialist regime in the 1980s. In the 1990s, both of these cities became re-connected to a variety of global flows. As a result, the pace and intensity of change in different aspects of urban life have been very spectacular in the period during the past two decades both in Burkina Faso's and in Vietnam's capital. Hanoi and Ouagadougou are therefore interesting places – real laboratories – in which the role of transnational relations in urban development can be observed.

There is second reason why these two cities are particularly interesting to research and compare: since 1990 they have followed different trajectories of globalization. In Ouagadougou, a city very dependent on foreign donor countries and city-to-city relations, political connectedness has been central, whereas in Hanoi economic connectedness, through foreign investments, international trade, and migrant remittances, has been the major factor of urban change. Moreover, the orientation of their cross-border relations is different: Ouagadougou looks to Europe, North Africa and other West African cities, whereas Hanoi has increasingly developed its connections with its Asian neighbors (Indonesia, Japan, South Korea). This means that the two cities differ not only in specific variables, such as economic productivity, but also in their relatedness with "elsewhere" and in how this has evolved through time. This is what this book proposes – a relational comparison: it takes relations, their evolution, form, intensity, and orientation as the elements of comparison.

By doing this, on one hand, the book tries to advance theoretical and methodological debates about relationality and comparative urbanism and, on the other, it makes an argument about the increasingly transnational and translocal dimensions of urban development.

First, *Cities in Relations* argues that a relational analysis of cities requires that we abandon abstract conceptions of relations as "swirls of flows" to consider them as historical products, moored in material forms and generating change through power-mediated processes. I also argue that we need to widen our imagination regarding what city relations are made of. Drawing on the distinction in French between *globalisation* (economic globalization) and *mondialisation* (the different aspects and effects of global interconnectedness), this book thus moves beyond the economic reductionism of most world-city literature. It looks at how policies, urban forms, and people's urban practices are shaped by relations with elsewhere according to distinct logics. I thereby develop a set of grounded narratives of urban *mondialisation* – staging for instance the role of traditional chiefdoms in Ouagadougou or the Communist party in Hanoi – that are not easily captured by the mantra of neoliberalization.

Second, I bring an innovative way of seeing and making urban comparison. Pushing further recent discussions on relational comparison I focus on cities' worlds of relations – defined by their type, intensity, and orientation. This book shows that if we want to understand the role of city relations, we need to compare not only cities but how they are inscribed in worlds of relations and how these relations shape urban development in different ways. This comparative strategy results in the cases of Hanoi and Ouagadougou in the identification of distinct trajectories of urban globalization where we would normally describe quite similar "transitions from socialism to free market."

Third, this book shows how these relations are appropriated and what their effects are on the ground. On the one hand, this brings to the fore the mediating role of state or non-state actors and the fact that urban politics today is often a battleground where different transnational relations (and their "embedded" political programs) are played against each other. On the other hand, it highlights that traditional categories of analysis – city branding, capital accumulation, domination, resistance – quite often do not suffice to make sense of urban development, notably in cities of the Global South. In my narratives about Hanoi and Ouagadougou I therefore borrow or develop a set of concepts and methodologies – object biographies, ethopower, design in the wild, script, affordance, etc. – in order to enlarge the lexicon of world-city literature.

Finally, on a political level, I argue that relations are not only pervasive in cities today but that they also constitute important resources for urban development. Here as well, a wider imagination regarding city relations is called for. In order to conceive development strategies that do more than try to imitate cities at the top of world-city rankings, cities need to use the full potential of the dense web of relations in which they are situated today. I believe that exploring the *mondialisation* of cities is necessary not only for the advancement of urban studies but in order to mobilize relational resources for context-relevant policies, or, what I call, drawing on Friedmann (2007), an assets-based politics of city relatedness.

Relating Hanoi, Ouagadougou ... and Palermo

When I chose to work on Hanoi and Ouagadougou, I was finishing a book on the city of Palermo in Sicily (Söderström et al., 2009).[1] Together with a team of Italian colleagues I had studied how the city had "cosmopolitanized" since the early 1990s. In 1993, in the wake of the assassination of the two anti-Mafia judges Giovanni Falcone and Paolo Borsellino, a new (anti-Mafia) mayor, Leoluca Orlando, was elected. As a result, the city opened up in many ways: more tourists arrived, a young cultural elite was attracted by the city's unusual charm, and new models of urban development were "imported" from abroad. To grasp the logic of these changes, we studied the recent history of urban policies and focused on a sample of twelve places created after the regime change. We wrote the "biography" of these places by studying, on the one hand, the transnational relations embedded in their design and, on the other, the discourses and practices of their users. Because the new local government had developed a progressive program breaking with decades of Mafia domination, writing this geo-history of Palermo since 1990 led us to produce a narrative of urban globalization that was more complex than the account of a simple conversion of the city to the neoliberal urban *doxa*.

Building on the experience of this research and wanting to expand the understanding of globalization in cities rarely studied in urban research, I decided to apply a similar methodology in two cities of the

South having a similar recent history of re-connection to global flows. In order to confront trajectories of urban change in very different contexts, I chose two cities situated in countries in economic transition since the early 1990s: Hanoi, the capital of a fast-growing Asian country, and Ouagadougou, the capital of Burkina Faso in Africa, one of the world's poorest countries.

A Brief Introduction to Two Distant Cousins

There are striking parallels in the recent history of Burkina Faso and Vietnam, where the two cities are situated. First, they are both former French colonies (until 1960 for the former, 1945 for the latter), maintaining important relations with the former metropole. Second, their landscape and legal apparatus have been deeply influenced during the second half of the 20th century by revolutionary socialist regimes: Vietnam became (and still formally is) a socialist republic in 1945; while Burkina Faso had a (much shorter) revolutionary phase during the government of Thomas Sankara (1983–1987). Land property was nationalized under these regimes and the urban built environment was largely state produced, with the purpose of creating a new form of society. Third, in the early 1990s, land ownership was progressively privatized and the economy deregulated under external pressure (mainly the end of USSR support in Vietnam and the conditional aid of the International Monetary Fund and the World Bank in Burkina Faso).[2] Fourth, Vietnam and Burkina Faso are experiencing intensive urban transition. According to the United Nations' Department of Economic and Social Affairs, the estimates of urban growth are 3 percent for the period 2010–2015 for Vietnam and 6 percent for Burkina Faso. However, in 2009, the Vietnamese Ministry of Construction predicted 6 percent growth over the next 25 years (Labbé, 2010). Lastly, both countries are also close in terms of globalization indexes. For instance, according to the indexes calculated in 2012 by the Swiss Institute of Technology in Zurich – which I discuss in more detail in the following chapter – Vietnam is ranked 130th and Burkina Faso 140th out of 208 countries in the world. Although geographically very distant, these two countries share a series of common features, and these family resemblances at national level are partly to be found also at city level, as we will now see in this brief introduction to the two cities (a more detailed comparison is provided in Chapter 2).

With 6.56 m inhabitants in 2010, Hanoi is Vietnam's second largest city (after Ho Chi Minh City (HCMC) with 7.39 m). It is the capital of a poor country, ranked 127th (out of 186 countries) on the United

Nations' 2013 Human Development Index (UN HDI), but with one of
the world's fastest-growing economies. Hanoi's population more than
doubled in 2008 when the government decided to extend its boundaries, including different adjacent areas, among which was the entire
Ha Tay Province.[3] The city is situated in Northern Vietnam's interior at
the head of the Red River Delta, a mainly flat area of rice-fields subject
to flooding (Figure 0.1). It was founded in 1010 when the Emperor
Ly Thai To defeated the Chinese – who had dominated the region
for a thousand years – and established the capital of his empire next
to the Red River. The city was initially organized around the imperial
citadel and the trading streets, comprising what is today the historic
center (Figure 0.2). From this time on, with the exception of the period
between 1802 – when the capital was moved to Hue by the Nguyen
dynasty – and 1945, Hanoi was the small capital of an agrarian country.
When the French seized the city in 1874, it was a modest city of less
than 100,000 inhabitants. Colonization had a deep impact on Hanoi:
the French expanded it, and between 1902 and 1953 planned a modern
regional capital for French Indochina. They constructed infrastructures
(the railway, a tram, a bridge across the river) and built a new area south
of the historic center, in the form of a grid of wide streets, administrative
buildings, housing blocks, and villas (now the French quarter) (Logan,
2000). On September 2 1945, Ho Chi Minh declared independence and
made Hanoi the capital of the Democratic Republic of Vietnam. This
declaration, rejected by the colonial power, led to the First Indochina
war (1945–1954). Two years later, the Vietnam War began (1956–1975).
Twenty-eight years of war, consuming a large part of the country's
resources, combined with a strict regulation of rural–urban migration,
severely limited the city's post-World War II development.

The economic reforms (*Doi Moi*) that started in 1986, together with
the ability of people to move freely within the country, led to important
transformations. Hanoi's population grew rapidly, the city was renovated
and began to sprawl outwards. As there were pressing housing needs
and little alternative for investment in the 1990s, private capital accu-
mulated by the emerging middle and the upper classes was invested in
real estate, either through self-construction for households' own needs
or for the purpose of speculation. In a second post-*Doi Moi* phase of
urban development, after 2000, the Vietnamese state created the institutional conditions for large national and foreign companies to develop
vast residential or mixed-use developments on the periphery of the city
(Labbé and Boudreau, 2011). In 2005, Hanoi thus had "137 new urban
areas, responsible for 2.1 million square meters of new dwelling space
in the city" (ibid.: 282). Since the end of the Vietnam War and the
reunification of the country, there has been an urban division of labor:

Ho Chi Minh City (HCMC) was Vietnam's largest city and its economic center, while Hanoi was its political center. Thus, the output of HCMC's industry represented 25 percent of the country's total in 2008, compared to Hanoi's 13 percent, while 9 percent of Hanoi province's workforce was employed by the government, compared to 6 percent in HCMC (Labbé, 2010: 8). However, this situation might be changing. First, because the economic growth of the city has been very strong (10 percent GDP growth in average between 2000 and 2010); second, because the government aims, with the creation of a metropolitan region and a knowledge-based development strategy, at making Hanoi a competitive world city (Logan, 2009).

The question, as in many other cities across the world, is to what extent this growth strategy will be compatible with the resolution of the city's old and new problems. Old problems are: a housing shortage, which continues to be a major problem for the poor for whom no affordable housing is produced and who continue to live in very densely populated areas and precarious conditions (UN-Habitat, 2008: 11); infrastructure such as piped water – inaccessible for 22 percent of the city's population in 2003 (UN-Habitat, 2009: 273); waste water treatment and solid waste collection; and in addition, an inefficient and corrupt system of urban governance. New problems are: rapidly increasing levels of sprawl; socio-economic inequalities; traffic congestion; and water and air pollution. Many of these problems are shared by the other city I study in this book and to which I now turn.

Ouagadougou is the capital of the African country of Burkina Faso, one of the world's poorest countries, ranked 183rd on the 2013 UN HDI. The city is situated on a flat plateau roughly in the center of the country, in the province of Kadiogo (Figure 0.3), and in 2010 had a population of 1.91m inhabitants. There are only oral historical sources concerning the city's precolonial history. According to these sources, it was founded in the 11th century AD and then became the capital of the Moaga kingdom in 1441. The city, organized around the royal palace and the market, gained in importance from the 18th century onward, when it became the place where the new king was enthroned and buried (Fourchard, 2001). The first map, drawn in 1887 by the French captain and explorer Binger, shows a settlement that resembles a village more than a city (Dekeyser, 1998). Ouagadougou had some 5,000 inhabitants at the time and the residence of the king, the *Mogho Naaba*, consisted of three rather modest houses (Binger, 1892). The region was colonized in 1896 by the French, who settled in the city in 1904 and made it the capital of a newly created territory, the Haute-Volta, in 1919. The city's nickname until the 1950s was "Bancoville" in reference to the predominance of buildings constructed with dry mud bricks ("banco" in Francophone Africa). As they did in Hanoi during the same period, although with far less financial and technological investment, the French applied a segregated and rationalist urban development: next to the old center, they created a new European sector with large orthogonal boulevards, villas and infrastructures (schools, a hospital, a new market) (Fournet et al., 2009). After a period of decline before World War II, the city developed in the 1950s with the construction of transport infrastructures: the airport in 1952 and the opening of a train connection to the coastal Abidjan in the Ivory Coast two years later.

When the country gained its independence in 1960, Ouagadougou numbered 57,000 inhabitants. During the half-century since then, rural migrations, accelerated by two severe droughts in 1973–1974 and 1983–1984, have caused rapid demographic growth – up to 12.5 percent per year. The population grew to 172,000 in 1975 and to 441,000 inhabitants in 1985 (Jaglin, 1995). During this period, because of a weak system of governance torn between municipal power and customary chiefdoms, the city sprawled without following any coherent plan (Biehler, 2010). As a consequence, large zones of settlements were created beyond the colonial grid system. The socialist regime of Thomas Sankara (1983–1987) tried to break the power of chiefdoms, to democratize access to land ownership, and provide housing for all. The allocation of a land plot to each household formalized the development of the periphery but also favored a system of land speculation based on the reselling of plots. Modern social housing as well as new infrastructures were built by the socialist regime, but this development policy ended with the coup by the present head of state, Blaise Compaoré, against his former ally Sankara in 1987. Since 1991, the government's entrepreneurial development strategy has involved the creation of a business-oriented city center, the development of a new urban area for the elite to the south, and the construction of conference facilities (Figure 0.4). This strategy is complemented by (and, as I show in Chapter 3, sometimes in contradiction with) the initiatives of the mayor, Simon Compaoré,[4] elected in 1995.

Today, the city is the political and economic center of the country, and is where 70 percent of its industrial activity is concentrated. Present-day Ouagadougou comprises three main residential zones: one of modern housing, with villas; a second of formal popular housing; and a third of informal, "spontaneous" housing. Large parts of the second and third zones – which together accounted for 73.8 percent of the city's total population in 2005 – are under-equipped in terms of access to drinkable water, sewage, drainage of rain water, roads, and energy (Biehler, 2010: 181). In 2003, a quarter of the population did not have access to drinking water (UN-Habitat, 2007: 10). These inequalities follow (apart from two exceptions in the east and south of the city) a clear center–periphery pattern, with the comparatively well-off in the center. The city faces problems that are characteristic of a city of the Global South: lack of infrastructure, inequality, poverty, and pollution due to the increase of motorized traffic (Beall and Fox, 2009). The government and the municipality consider, for good reasons, demographic growth and sprawl as particularly important urban problems: between 1996 and 2006 Ouagadougou's population grew at an average of 7.6 percent and, in 2008, the city covered 268 square km – 50 percent more than in 1990 (Boyer and Delaunay, 2009: 31).

The two cities I have briefly introduced above have low to insignificant citation indices in world-city literature and do not appear to be given much attention in literature that purports to examine, and make general claims about, global urbanization processes. Studying their recent transformations, I choose to look at cities beyond the too-narrow focus in world-city literature on large economic and political centers, or beyond "metrocentricity" (Bunnell and Maringanti, 2010). In what follows, I situate this book within a broader field of urban research and explain my approach.

World-city Research Beyond the West

The first 15 years of research on world cities since Friedmann's (1986) path-breaking work primarily dealt with cities of the Global North and had a strong ethnocentric bias. This important body of work focused on cities that are the main command centers of the world economy and largely equated urban globalization with what happened within and between them (Sassen, 1991; Taylor, 2004). Cities in the South were "off the map" of urban studies (Robinson, 2002). Since then, there has been a growing literature on urban globalization in the South (Gugler, 2004b; Segbers et al., 2007); "other" global cities (Mayaram, 2009); the specific Asian ways of being global (Roy and Ong, 2011); interconnected everyday lives in African and Southeast Asian cities (Simone, 2010); and urban theory beyond the West (Edensor and Jayne, 2011). It is not my intention to review in detail this now vast body of research, but instead I focus on a series of volumes that help to explain and position my approach in this book.

The volume edited by Josef Gugler (2004b) is important as it is the first to systematically study 12 cities in the South that can be characterized as world cities across four continents (Bangkok, Mumbai, Cairo, Hong Kong, Jakarta, Johannesburg, Mexico City, Moscow, São Paulo, Seoul, Shanghai, and Singapore). It is innovative as well in that it moves beyond economic reductionism by paying attention to the role of the state and civil society in the processes of urban change. The three main findings of this collection of studies are that: these cities do not converge around a unique mode of development but, on the contrary, display an extraordinary diversity; their centers tend to become elite enclaves; and the role of the state, though little discussed in the classics of world-city literature, is important everywhere. Similarly, focusing on the making of global city-regions in the South – Johannesburg, Mumbai, São Paulo and Shanghai – the volume edited by Segbers et al. (2007) focuses on the role of political elites. Its most interesting, and for the editors "unexpected", finding concerns the role of world-city discourses in these political strategies, both "to mobilize the city internally and to create an identity for the city vis-à-vis the outside world" (Segbers et al., 2007: 11).

Both volumes are heavily influenced by the categories and hierarchies of Sassen (1991; 2002) and Taylor (2004): Gugler (2004a), for instance, justifies the choice of cities by stressing the importance of studying "second-tier" world cities. In contrast, my work in this book follows King's (1990: 82) formula that "all cities are world cities." *Cities in Relations* is not about a specific category of places playing a major role in world economy or polity, but about globalization happening in quite "ordinary cities" (Robinson, 2006). Moreover, it is not interested in questions of ranking (except as an emic category of local actors) and focuses, as I develop below, on the role of different forms of relatedness rather than on specific indicators of globalization and processes of change.

Beside such economic and political analyses of urban transformations in the South, we also witness an "ethnographic turn in global metropolitan studies" (Roy and Ong, 2011: XV) with work focusing on everyday practices and discourses. Simone's work (2004a; 2010) in particular, focusing on informality and livelihood in African and Southeast Asian cities, looks at relations beyond the much-discussed financial flows between global cities. Refusing to rehearse once again the dystopian accounts regarding the failure of urban development in rapidly urbanizing contexts, his street-level analyses rather show how people develop coping or survival strategies and how, despite the lack of infrastructure and state services, they make cities work. However, Simone studies social relations within these cities rather than inter-urban relations. Although he speculates in interesting ways on "which connections between cities across Asia and Africa could be envisioned" (Simone, 2010: 267), he does not examine in detail the forms of actual transnational and translocal relations to which my analysis is devoted. So, while I share Simone's (postcolonial) principle that we should look at those cities as spaces of everyday life beyond the gloomy reports of international organizations, I have chosen here to pay less attention to informality and survival strategies and to focus instead on how such connections with elsewhere generate changes in urban practices (see Chapter 6).

Finally, within this ethnographic turn, I am sympathetic to the perspective developed in the collection edited by Roy and Ong (2011) on practices of "worlding" in Asian cities. Drawing on Gayatri Spivak, Ong (2011: 13) defines worlding practices as "constitutive, spatializing, and signifying gestures that variously conjure up worlds beyond current conditions of urban living. They articulate disparate elements from near and far; and symbolically re-situate the city in the world." I share with Roy and Ong an interest in how "elements from near and far" are articulated, and in the different ways of being global by investigating the following in this book: transnational urban policy making (Chapters 3 and 4); transnational architectural design (Chapter 5); and the mundane practices and discourses of city dwellers (Chapter 6). I also share, as I explain below, Ong's (2011) desire to narrate urban change in the South without being confined to the two dominant tropes of political economy, with its focus on the diffusion of neoliberalism, and postcolonialism, with its focus on resistance.[5] However, while drawing on these approaches, in this book I take an explicitly comparative perspective. In sum then, this book looks at cities beyond the West, beyond the large metropoles and beyond economicism to show that transnational relations matter even in marginal cities in the South but each time in quite specific ways.

So, what is precisely the meaning of a comparison between Hanoi and Ouagadougou? If I compare the two cities according to different variables, I can of course situate their respective levels of economic productivity, levels of revenue, and so on. However, this is of limited interest and necessitates little more than retrieving tables from online resources. More interesting is to compare processes of economic and political transition in order to understand how, with similar points of departure – a socialist revolution – but in quite different contexts and during the same period of time, two cities are managing a transition to liberalism. This processual comparison is what I briefly carry out in Chapter 2 in order to provide a background for my analysis. But what I principally aim at in this book is to compare the two cities' relations with elsewhere, or, in other words, a *relational comparison*. The idea of relational comparison builds on recent discussions on comparativism in urban studies. Therefore, I now first turn to the idea of relational geographies, and then to relational urban comparisons. I argue first for a relational geography that, on the one hand, does not evacuate history, the relative boundedness of places and regions and the role of power and, on the other, emphasizes the innovations brought by geographical relatedness. I secondly develop a relational comparative framework that takes cities' worlds of relatedness as bases of comparison.

Relational Geographies

The conceptualization of geography (my disciplinary "*port d'attache*") as dealing with relations between different entities is premised on a specific understanding of space. Departing from conceptions of space as either absolute, in which space is a container of phenomena; or relative, in which space is relative to the objects considered in space and time, a relational concept of space, in its broadest sense, conceives space as the product of relations. In philosophy, such a relational view is generally considered as having been pioneered by Leibniz (but see Malpas, 2012). It "implies the idea of internal relations; external influences get internalized in specific processes or things through time [...] an event or a thing at a point in space cannot be understood by appeal to what exists only at that point" (Harvey, 2006b: 124–125).

In geography, there are various ways of considering space as a relational construct. For the Swiss geographer Raffestin (1986), territory and human territoriality rather than space are the objects of geographical knowledge. Territory is the product of the appropriation of space by human territoriality, itself made of relationships with others and with exteriority mediated by labor, territory, and language (Klauser, 2012; Raffestin, 1986). Inspired by Raffestin and extending his perspective, the Italian geographer Angelo Turco (2010) has developed a theory of the sociohistorical process of territorialization. In this tradition, relational geography, indebted to Foucault, Deleuze, and the semiotics of Juri Lotman, focuses on the role of mediators, such as linguistic codes, in the production of geographical space.

In Anglophone geography, different variants of a relational view have been articulated around flows, movements, and connections rather than around mediators (Amin, 2002; Massey, 2005; Thrift, 2006). Developing a view that is closer to Leibniz than Raffestin, they share an insistence on the mutual constitution of spatial objects through their relations. Drawing on authors such as Deleuze and Latour, the project of relational geography is here, as Jones (2009: 412) puts it succinctly, "to replace topography and structure-agency dichotomies with a topological theory of space, place and politics as encountered, performed and fluid." Attempting to reconstruct the discipline's ontology and vocabulary, this perspective emphasizes networks instead of territories and scales (Marston et al., 2005); openness instead of boundedness (Amin, 2004); topology instead of topography (Allen and Cochrane, 2010); and redefines places as nodes in complex networks and flows (Massey, 1991). Under the impulse of authors such as Massey (2005), Allen (2008), Amin (2002) and Thrift (2008), this theoretical stance has become very popular since the 1990s in Anglophone human geography and beyond.

As a consequence, geographical space, long seen as a nested hierarchy of different containers of phenomena, subjects, and objects, is now seen as "a swirl of flows, networks and trajectories, as a chaotic ordering that locates and dislocates, and as an effect of social process that is itself spatially dispersed and distributed" (Malpas, 2012: 228).

However, not all Anglophone relational human geography is captured by Malpas's nearly apocalyptic description in the quote above. It rather corresponds to one of its poles, the poststructuralist one. There is also, as Jacobs (2012) points out regarding urban geography, a neo-structuralist relational geography examining the urban as a hierarchically ordered world system of city-networks (Derudder et al., 2011; Taylor, 2004). In this second version, we find the same emphasis on networks (of service firms in particular), connectivity (of the same firms), and flows (such as airport passengers), but instead of conceiving space as being in continuous becoming and re-ordering, these authors retain the idea of an underlying "architecture" of space produced by the location and connections of economic activities. This is particularly clear in Taylor's arguments (2004: 57) about the four "key agencies" producing world-city networks and in his central thesis that cities in "the new global pattern of inter-city relations are ultimately the result of the recent rise of large numbers of global service firms" (Taylor, 2004: 60). Still other forms of relational geography can be located between the structuralist and poststructuralist pole, such as the proposal by Jessop et al. (2008) to move beyond uni-dimensional approaches that focus either on networks, or places, or scales, or territories. Jessop et al. argue that instead of being opposed these different dimensions of geographical space, related to different conceptions of what makes the geography of societies, should be seen as mutually constitutive and articulated in systematic ways.

Thus, if we look at this complex theoretical landscape, we have to observe that "there are urban geographies making claims to relational thinking that are radically incompatible, and live not in relation but in parallel universes" (Jacobs, 2012: 1). I need therefore to explain how I envisage the relational character of cities. The best way to do so is to discuss recent critiques of this perspective.

Critiques of relational geographies

Critics argue that relational thinking "insufficiently problematizes boundedness, inertia, power and time" (Jones, 2009: 499). Let me unpack these different points. For Malpas (2012: 233), the problem lies in a lack of serious engagement with the concept of space itself. On the basis of a historico-philosophical interpretation of the concept, he contends that any thinking of space and place should refer to three fundamental aspects: boundedness, openness, and emergence. A relational geography celebrating openness and the disappearance of boundaries is problematic, he argues, as "all relations presuppose boundaries while the boundary is properly that on which the possibility of relation is dependent" (Malpas, 2012: 238). This fundamental argument – that entities in relation need to be limited in some way in order to be considered and studied as being in relation – is well-taken. And indeed, when geographical research moves from abstract ontological discussions to empirical work, relational approaches always necessarily study connections between territorialized actors, administrations, or things. The study of mobile policies – to take an example of poststructuralist geographical analysis – looks at phenomena that, even though they "change in the movement" and might originate from a number of different places, always create relations between locales defined by their boundaries (McCann and Ward, 2010). This argument on boundedness is also taken up and expanded by Jessop et al. (2008) in their previously mentioned critique of uni-dimensional geographies and their call "for a more systematic recognition of polymorphy – the organization of sociospatial relations in multiple forms and dimensions – in sociospatial theory" (Jessop et al., 2008: 389). In other words, geographical phenomena, they argue, cannot be reduced to a view of the world centered exclusively on either networks (or relations), scales, places, or territories.

The other aspects mentioned by Jones (2009) – inertia, power, and time – are all connected in the neo-Marxist critique of radical relational thinking. The analysis of the role of place-based specificities in the making of global cities (Sassen, 2002) and of the necessity for capitalist investors to fix surplus value in specific material forms (Harvey, 2001) are two different aspects of spatial inertia contradicting a perspective putting too much emphasis on the "swirl of flows." Sassen's and Harvey's works also illustrate the power of states and capital in the production of geographical space: how, in particular, (capital) flows are channeled and constrained, and how historical legacies – time, in other words – provide a former colonial metropole like London with competitive advantages in the age of financial markets.

Although these critiques of relational thinking can at times appear as caricatures, selectively picking some of the most bombastic or provocative citations of relational geographers – such as Thrift's (2006) "there is no such thing as a boundary," (quoted in Malpas (2012: 229)) – I share the rejection of a celebration of fluidity. This is why in my analysis, I describe how flows and mobilities are related to historically evolving national and local policies (Chapters 2 and 3); how relations are productive of specific material forms (Chapter 4); and how they constrain (but also enable) ways of life in globalizing cities (Chapter 5). Moreover, in each chapter I try to discuss and balance (as I briefly develop in the following section), the relational *and* territorial dimensions of urban change. In the analysis of transnational design processes in Hanoi and Ouagadougou, for instance (Chapter 5), I show, on the one hand, how both cities are related to different spatial circuits of design, and on the other, how design is locally grounded and translated into built form. In other words, I study relations between cities as constrained, specialized and dependent on moorings in material forms and consider, therefore, that thinking cities relationally does not imply an "everything flows" perspective.[6]

Finally, there is another – and for me, quite central – aspect of the critique of relational geographies I want to address in this book. Relational thinking has been criticized for being too vague about how relations work as mechanisms of space-production and for not providing sufficient answers to the question: "What is it, exactly, that they relate?" (Jones, 2009: 495). It seems to me that the abundant recent literature on policy mobilities provides replies to this query by showing how relations generate policy change (McCann and Ward, 2011a; McCann and Ward, 2012; Peck and Theodore, 2010a; Robinson, 2013). However, as I explain in more detail below, I want to push this further by exploring different *generative* characters of relations and how different relations produce specific features of urban development. But let me first develop this general point on relations and change.

Relations, novelty and territoriality

Relations between cities can be seen as instruments of spatial standardization as well as creators of novelty. In urban studies since 1990, there has been a focus on processes of standardization and convergence as research has dealt predominantly with the spatial diffusion or transfer of neoliberal policies (Harvey, 1989; Peck and Tickell, 2002; Prince, 2010). As Brenner et al. (2010) have argued, neoliberalism is far from being immutable: it is structurally hybrid and continuously reinvents itself to thrive. Nonetheless, the focus on entrepreneurialism and neoliberalism leads research to look primarily for sameness (as a result of relations), rather than novelty, and to findings that either confirm convergence – in urban policies, landscapes, or socio-spatial structures – or identify some variations therein.[7] There is here a striking contrast with the work in global urban anthropology that developed in the 1990s, where the focus was on novelty, and culturally creative transnational and translocal connections (Appadurai, 1996; Burawoy, 2000; Hannerz, 1996). I want to reconnect urban studies with that tradition.

I am not disputing here the importance and achievements of studies of neoliberalization. In a period during which, since the late 1970s, states, cities, societies, and subjects have been profoundly reshaped by the neo-liberal *doxa* (Harvey, 2006b; Harvey, 2007), such work is, of course, cru-cial. But, as urban anthropologists have insisted, inter-urban relations cannot be reduced to that sole dimension. Therefore, I focus in this book on relations in a Deleuzian perspective in so far as all Deleuze's work from his early studies of the history of philosophy to his later work on politics and aesthetics revolved around novelty, creativity, and their conditions of emergence (Bouaniche, 2007). Deleuze's thinking, like Foucault's and Latour's, belongs to a tradition oriented towards the understanding of innovation, of how new phenomena emerge, how society transforms itself rather than – à la Bourdieu for instance – how society reproduces itself. This is what my present book is doing: studying how relations bring novelty and change to different dimensions of urban life, and how, more specifically, they reorganize urban policies, archi-tectural design, and urban practices. Continuing down the "Deleuzian path," this means looking at how relations reassemble cities. This concept of *agencement*[8] – Deleuze and Guattari's (1986; 1987) main analytic tool for dealing with relations in *A Thousand Plateaus* – has recently become the subject of vigorous debate in geography and urban studies.[9] Because it would not add anything substantial to my analysis, I will not rehearse this debate here and only very occasionally use the concept subsequently in the book. However, I want to retain the Deleuzian orientation towards (progressive) novelty. This means a curiosity and orientation towards what relations bring to globalizing cities and skepticism towards tradi-tional ways of framing the study and the interpretation of findings. Thus, in my study I focus on policy relations of policies that are not typically neoliberal (while recognizing their presence and importance); I empha-size in my examination of architectural design, transnational conception *processes* rather than only branding and logics of capital accumulation; and, finally, I look at new built environments as providers of new possibil-ities of action (*affordances*) and self-positioning for urban dwellers, and not only as sites of resistance or ways of producing neoliberal subjects.

Other geographers share this interest in relations as factors of novelty (McCann and Ward, 2011b; Robinson, 2013). In particular, studies of urban infrastructures and forms of learning in and across cities (Farías and Bender, 2010; McFarlane, 2011) have begun to change the balance within relational urban geographies between a focus on reproduction and a focus on innovation. McFarlane's (2011: 62–91) study of how Slum/Shack Dwellers International developed its reflection and action through exchanges and encounters between activists in different cities of the Global South shows, for instance, how translocal relations have been crucial for the emergence of a new type of urban social movement. This example points to the importance of studying not only novelty, but more specifically *progressive* forms of novelty in which relations aim at developing, for instance, fairtrade (Malpass et al., 2007), politics of asylum (Darling, 2010), or translocal solidarity (Massey, 2011).[10]

A focus on how relations generate change naturally leads to an attention to how relations are territorialized. In the abstract terms of Deleuze and Guattari (1991: 66), novelty stems both from a process of *deterritorialization* – through which people or things cease to work the way they did – and a process of *reterritorialization* – through which they come to play a new role: what was for *homo erectus* formerly a foot becomes, for instance, a hand with which she/he can grasp a branch. Translated in urban geography, this means that urban change cannot be understood by the mere observation of existing relations, say between Indonesian and Vietnamese planners, but by the analysis of how these relations end up creating a residential neighborhood in Hanoi through the mediation of territorially specific planning rules as well as political and historical circumstances (see Chapter 5 on this particular case). Urban change should thus be understood, to extend McCann and Ward's (2010: 176) argument about policy mobility, "as both relational and territorial." This is a fairly obvious statement, but necessary to make in a context where, as Malpas (2012) rightly observes, geographers have seemed overly enthralled by flows and connections *per se*. So although this book focuses on city relations, it does not evacuate the stubborn realities of territories. It pays attention to how change is embedded in place, but also to how territorial logics are dialectically related to relational ones. Indeed, a number of recent urban developments today in Hanoi and Ouagadougou, such as new national architectures, have been reactions to a greater global connectivity of the two cities.

Studying relations and their territorialization can be done from the point of view of a single or of several cities. Here, I compare the relatedness of two cities. I look at how, from a starting point in 1990 that was similar in many respects, they evolved through developing and orienting their relations in different ways. This is a specific way of understanding comparativism and relational comparisons to which I now turn, arguing that we need to move beyond theoretical positioning and propose a methodology of relational urban comparativism.

Comparing Cities

Comparing cities has always been a discursive means of putting them in relation. Comparison is, for instance, one of the rhetorical tools for explaining the diversity of the ecumene and its cities in Herodotus's *Histories* (Jacob, 1991). There is also a long history of pragmatic or "actually existing" urban comparativism developed by municipalities in order for them to situate their achievements and to learn from others. As Clarke (2012a) remarks "this activity has been heightened since at least the 19th century when European colonialism placed cities as sites of encounter between different planning cultures or sites of production for new planning knowledge and techniques."[11]

On a global scale, such action-oriented comparisons have been promoted since 1990 by different bilateral and multilateral agencies, local authorities, and NGOs: since 1997, the creation of UN-Habitat's Best Practices and Local Leadership Program has developed South–South partnerships; while in 2004, the creation of United Cities and Local Governments (UCLG),[12] which brings together already-existing city networks, has opened up new routes for decentralized North–South cooperation. These are the forms of comparison that municipalities do through being in relation. But of course, the type of comparison I develop is a strategy aiming at understanding urban development rather than producing it.

Comparative strategies

As a series of authors have noted, there has been a renaissance of comparative studies and especially a development of reflection on comparative urbanism in recent literature on urban policies (Boudreau et al., 2007; Clarke, 2012a; Nijman, 2007; Ward, 2008). In this context, political scientists Kantor and Savitch (2005) have provided interesting guidelines for a systematic comparison of urban politics. Comparison, they argue (2005: 136), should: (a) be governed by an explicit theoretical framework; (b) use common categories; and (c) make comparisons throughout the work. Their own comparative study looks at cities' bargaining strategies aimed at getting political support for, and capital investment in, their development (Savitch and Kantor, 2002). The cities they compare are all situated in Western liberal democracies (UK, France, Italy, Canada, US) and they identify variations between what are – seen from a global perspective – similar types of cities.

If we broaden the scope, we can situate this form of comparison within a typology of different comparative strategies. Brenner (2001), Ward (2010) and Robinson (2011a) have all used and reworked Tilly's (1984) typology of ways of comparing in the context of urban studies, distinguishing between individualizing, universalizing, variation-finding, and encompassing strategies. Both Ward (2010) and Robinson (2011a) have offered an important critique of these traditional ways of envisaging comparativism. For Ward, they present three weaknesses: first, an insufficient problematization of scale, which is generally taken for granted; second, the treatment of cities as "discrete, self-enclosed and analytically separate objects" (Ward, 2010: 479); and, third, a conception of causation relying on empirical regularities instead of the explanation of processes. On the basis of this critique, Ward, drawing on Hart (2002; 2004), suggests that we develop relational comparisons "stressing interconnected trajectories – how different cities are implicated in each other's past, present and future" (Ward, 2010: 480).

In a similar vein, but within a more elaborate postcolonial agenda, Robinson (2011a) suggests opening up the world of comparisons. Very often, she argues, it is considered that cities of the North and South are too different in their resources and functioning to be compared in any significant way. But, "with growing assertions of convergence and connections across urban experiences in a globalized world [...] the argument that there are few commonalities to explore across certain kinds of cities would be hard to support" (Robinson, 2011a: 5). She therefore encourages the comparison of very different cases, in order to develop a "revitalized and experimental international comparativism that will enable urban studies to stretch its resources for theory-building across the world of cities" and provoke "hopefully unsettling conversations about the nature and future of cities in the world" (Robinson, 2011a: 19). For Robinson (2011b: 126), there is not only a colonial past in comparative urbanism, but a colonial present "in which the structures of knowledge production grants a very few places power and authority." The issue at hand, therefore, is to develop a truly cosmopolitan comparison. Like Ward, she suggests a rethinking of the units of comparison, shifting from the supposedly bounded spatial units of cities to relations, connections, and circulations between cities. Finally, along the same lines, McFarlane (2010: 733) considers comparison across the North–South divide as a strategy of critique, whereby not only cities can be understood differently but also "the ontological and epistemological framings that inform how the world is being debated, how knowledge is being produced and questioned."

The form of urban comparison developed in this book draws on these recent discussions as it bears on two very different cities, set in very different contexts. The main aim of this comparison is, therefore, not to look for variations between similar cases or to aim at a general explanation of urban change in globalizing cities, but instead to expand our understanding of the different trajectories of globalization followed by these cities. However, I do not circumvent the benefits of traditional comparative strategies and I also establish, in Chapter 2 with a series of diachronic data, the differences and variations in time between these cities. Central to my comparative strategy is the idea of relational comparison. For Ward (2010: 481–482), in such a comparative strategy "cities have to be theorized as open, embedded and relational," "'city' scale has to be understood as a dynamic evolving scale," and "comparing cities has to be attuned to the challenges of 'theorizing back,'" in the sense of rethinking our ways of knowing the city. Entanglements, co-construction, or co-dependence become here the focus of analysis.

However, relational comparison in the work of Ward, Robinson, and McFarlane is still couched in quite general terms. There are very well-articulated reasons for redefining comparison as relational comparison, but there is little yet on where the comparison actually lies and on what to compare when it comes to empirical work. Thus, relational comparison is, in its present formulation (except for Hart's work, see below), primarily a critique of traditional comparison and as a consequence puts the weight on relation rather than comparison. I suggest here a form of relational comparison where both terms are equally addressed. While Ward proposes analyzing relations between the cities "compared," I suggest comparing the respective "world of relations" of the cities considered in general (including the possible relations between the cities considered), i.e. the numerous connections in different domains relating cities with other places abroad. Consequently, this book is not about the relations between the two cities of Hanoi and Ouagadougou but rather it compares how these cities are situated within worlds of relations and how these worlds have changed since the early 1990s.

Hart's (2002) innovative work goes in that direction. Grounded in a longitudinal empirical analysis (1994–2001) of political change in two South African towns – Ladysmith and Newcastle – her analysis focuses on the different ways Taiwanese industrialists, active in these two towns of KwaZulu Natal, operate not only in South Africa but also in places such as Southern China. Taking as a starting point the situation of these two South African towns, she compares different forms of transnational relations between Taiwan and elsewhere, as well as different histories of rural industrialization in South Africa and East Asia. While Hart's work looks at relatively small places where the Taiwanese connection stands out and is therefore the main object of inquiry, I deal with large cities shaped by a number of different transnational relations and look at the intensity, type, and orientation of their world of relations.

The underlying idea of this book is that transnational relations constitute an important dimension of cities' resources – a network capital – and are as such important factors of economic, political, and social change. It is thus necessary to analyze the *intensity* of these relations and its variation in time drawing on classical indicators of urban globalization such as FDIs (Foreign Direct Investments) or airport arrivals. However, intensity of relations alone is a crude factor for comparing cities. Relations need also to be compared in their diversity and orientation. Various *domains* of relatedness – political, social, cultural – need to be compared if we want to overcome the economic reductionism of much urban research. Finally, it is important to monitor the *orientation* of these relations: with which other cities and countries are relations established, and how does this orientation change in time? Comparing the orientation of relations brings a better understanding of the changing geopolitics of urban relatedness and how they have moved far beyond simple North–South relations. The Hanoi case shows, for instance, how since 1990 inter-Asian relations have in many domains supplanted relations with Europe and North America; while since 2000 Ouagadougou has come to play an important regional role in Africa. Through such comparative strategy, this book delineates distinct trajectories of urban globalization and shows the necessity to be specific about the forms and effects of city relations.

In summary then, the relational comparison I propose asks the following questions: How does the intensity of cities' relations vary through time? How do cities' relations to elsewhere vary across different dimensions (economic, political, social, and cultural)? What is the orientation of these relations and how does it change through time? What are the different generative characters of these relations? To answer these questions a very substantial research program is needed, requiring both quantitative and qualitative methodologies. Within this broad research program, I carve out below a series of aspects corresponding to what was feasible for us to accomplish during fieldwork and for my (far from comprehensive) interpretive competences.

What to compare

The timeframe for this comparative study is the period 1990–2010. This is determined by the fact that economic transition began in both cities in the early 1990s. However, some of the material covers 2010–2012 or, when necessary as historical background, periods before 1990.

I study first the intensity, dimensions, and orientation of Hanoi's and Ouagadougou's transnational relations by using available comparable statistical data. This allows me to describe and compare the trajectories of globalization of these two cities since 1990 (Chapter 2) and to provide a background for the following thematic chapters (Chapters 3–6), concentrating on how relations generate urban change.

Poststructuralist relational geographers have been concerned mainly with one theme: *policy* relations (McCann and Ward, 2011a; McCann, 2008; McFarlane, 2009; Peck and Theodore, 2001; Robinson, 2013; Ward, 2006). This is not surprising given that the proponents of a renaissance and rethinking of comparative urbanism are policy scholars.

This book pushes relational comparison further by looking at city relations beyond urban policy mobility. In doing this, I compare relations embedded in and generative of three aspects of urban life:

Urban policies. I compare here the two cities' transnational urban policy relations since 1990 focusing first on the role of foreign experts and expertise in master-planning and second on the more specific question of urban public space policy. This choice is motivated by the fact that most research in urban policy circulation has looked at typical neoliberal policies such as Business Improvement Districts (Ward, 2007) or "creative cities" policies (Peck, 2011a). Looking at public space policies can mean (potentially at least) looking at more progressive policies in motion.[13]

Urban forms. I draw here on the analysis of a sample of 16 newly created places (buildings, public spaces, infrastructures) in each city. As we have shown elsewhere with Michael Guggenheim (Guggenheim and Söderström, 2010a), not only policies but built forms increasingly travel as a result of processes such as increasing inter-urban competition, the globalization of architectural firms and cultural connectedness (Guggenheim and Söderström, 2010b). I more specifically focus here on transnational architectural design, or how design increasingly takes place in "stretched spaces" (Faulconbridge and McNeill, 2010).

Urban practices and discourses. Changes in urban forms take their meaning and get their efficacy only through social practice and discourse. I study here how city dwellers reposition themselves through the use of these new urban places in Ouagadougou and Hanoi. In other words, I look at what these forms do, and focus on how they work both as pedagogies of urban modernization on the one hand, and as sites of opportunities for self-chosen new urban practices on the other.

The different aspects of this relational comparison use different methodologies – the product of collective work[14] – that I explore below.

How to compare

This book combines both quantitative and qualitative methodologies, as I believe that a comparison of cities' relations with elsewhere needs to complement an extensive (and necessarily superficial) investigation with in-depth fieldwork. Quantitative data are used to capture and compare general trends and more specifically the form and evolution of cities' relations. Data generated via qualitative methods are used to understand mechanisms of urban change both at a general level – the changes in urban governance – and at the level of specific dimensions of change (urban policies, design processes, cultural change).

Which relations to observe is, of course, a crucial question for a relational comparison. By "relations to elsewhere" in this book I mean transnational relations. I use that term to describe cross-border exchanges that generally go both ways; for instance, when two architects collaborate in two different countries on the design of a building.[15] I also often use the term "translocal," when these transnational relations connect places more than countries. City networks in which two cities cooperate on a specific project, such as waste management, is a good example of such relations.[16] When dealing with data on migratory movements or policy change, therefore, I have focused on transnational migrations and circulations of ideas, though I mention intra-national relations when they are relevant.

The collection of statistical data to describe the trajectories of globalization (Chapter 2, Part 2) of both cities was done by compiling data from very different sources: international organizations; national statistical offices; municipal offices; existing studies; and newspapers. The analysis of changes in urban governance (Chapter 2, Part 1) rests on 38 interviews with professionals and others concerned with the built environment (architects, planners, city officials, government officials, officials of international organizations, social scientists, activists, artists) – 20 in Hanoi, and 18 in Ouagadougou. These rather traditional methods are useful for the study of general aspects of urban change, including changes in policy. We also used another methodology – object biography – to better grasp the generative character of transnational relations: object biographies provide the material for Chapters 4, 5, and 6, and I now examine this method in more detail.

Object biographies

There are many possible ways to show how relations shape cities anew. I have chosen to focus on urban forms, because I see them as strategic sites where the various aspects of urban change – investments, planning regulations, design processes, and urban experience – coalesce. Pivotal to my analysis is, therefore, the study of changes in urban form, and more precisely, the "biographical analysis" in each city of a sample of recent interventions representative of urban change as a whole in the two cities since 1990.[17] I do not mean that a morphological analysis of cities synthesizes processes of urban change, but that object biographies offer a means to study different dimensions of relation-generated change.

Biographies of things is not a new methodology in the social sciences. Marx's analysis of commodities, in Volume 1 of *Capital*, suggests a form of object biography that unveils the social process of the production of commodities. More recently, Appadurai's (1986: 5) influential edited book, *The Social Life of Things*, develops the spatial and anthropological dimensions of Marx's analysis, suggesting following "the things themselves, because their meaning is inscribed in their forms, use and trajectories." In contemporary human geography, to follow the trajectories of things has become a countersign for cultural economic studies (Cook, 2004; Crang et al., 2003; Freidberg, 2004).[18]

In urban studies, this interest in material forms in general and the biography of mobile forms in particular has been less sustained: the built environment is often considered as a secondary dimension, a mere reflector of societal processes. In contrast, I consider, together with some other authors (Farías and Bender, 2010; Guggenheim and Söderström, 2010b; Jacobs, 2006; King, 2004), that "urban spatial forms actually constitute as well as represent much of social and cultural existence: society is to a very large extent constituted through the buildings and spaces that it creates" (King, 1990: 1). Object biographies retracing the life of built forms are thus a powerful means to understand changing socio-economic relations across space (Blunt, 2008; Jacobs et al., 2007).

In contrast with previous work dealing with the circulation of building types and forms (Guggenheim and Söderström, 2010b), I focus here on forms as *resulting* from the mobility of people, capital, and ideas. Therefore, instead of following the forms, in the studies of Hanoi and Ouagadougou we followed the relations associated with the creation and use of forms. We selected 32 objects (buildings, public spaces, parks) built (or sometimes renovated) during the period of study, i.e. since 1990. They were selected to represent the different types of operation or program in the changes to both cities over these years. Both the types of intervention and the specific objects were chosen on the basis of the interviews carried out with "urban experts."[19]

Seven of these programs are common to both cities: housing blocks, shopping malls, small commercial structures, hotels, office towers, interventions in public spaces, and heritage preservation. For each program, we chose two to three interventions we knew had some transnational dimension, related to the building type, the origin or experience of the architect, or of the client or investors. The types of intervention are not similar in each city as the level of economic development and urban policies differ, as I show in detail in Chapter 2. New road infrastructures, studied in Chapter 6, are, for instance, a more important aspect of recent urban change in Ouagadougou than in Hanoi.

These 32 object biographies have two sides: the first concerns the process of design and the form of the object itself; the second how these objects are used. The aim of the first part of the biography is twofold: to grasp the role of transnational relations in the design process and to study how these relations are translated in the form and style of the objects. For this purpose, we conducted a total of 79 interviews with architects and their clients (30 in Hanoi, 49 in Ouagadougou). The interviews were semi-structured with a length varying between 20 minutes and two hours. We also created visual documentation of the objects (by taking photographs and collecting architectural plans).

After a first analysis of all the objects, we chose 16 objects (eight in each city) and interviewed users. We based our choice on feasibility and relevance: some objects are interesting for their design process, but, for instance, are not accessible to the wider public and were discarded. The aim of this second aspect of the biographies is to understand how new forms of social practices (like jogging in a park) and new identity positionings (such as new forms of social distinction) are articulated within these new urban places. In other words, we looked at how newly built transnational forms shape the urban culture of these two cities. In total, 137 (64 in Ouagadougou, 73 in Hanoi) user interviews were carried out based on the same interview guide. These were usually short interviews of around ten minutes, and where feasible we complemented these interviews with the observation of practices based again on a common guide.

In this book, I am only using a part of this empirical material. In Chapters 4, 5, and 6, I focus on objects relevant to developing in each case a specific argument on transnational policy connections, processes of architectural design, and changing urban cultures.

In summary, this book argues that cities' "worlds of relations" play an increasing role in contemporary logics of urban development. To substantiate this argument it analyzes the role of transnational connections in the development of the two – marginal and until recently relation-poor – cities of Hanoi and Ouagadougou between 1990 and 2012. From a theoretical point of view, I claim that we need to open up our conception of the role of these relations beyond the hypothesis of the diffusion of the same (urban policies, morphologies, or practices) and look more closely at how they bring novelty. Therefore, in terms of empirical analysis, I show how transnational connections generate change and novelty in different domains of urban life. Focusing on the generative power of relations has meant paying particular attention to how relations are territorialized through different means: planning and building regulations, power games between local actors, everyday practices of city users. From a methodological point of view, this book takes debates about comparative urbanism further by developing new forms of relational comparison. Throughout the different chapters I compare the worlds of relations of two cities through time – instead of focusing on the relations between them – and how they have generated crucial changes in both cities.

Comparing relations and how they are territorialized brings a nuanced understanding of how ordinary cities have developed during the past couple of decades, beyond rehearsed and generic narratives of "transition" and "globalization". Comparing the intensity of relations shows how quickly since the early 1990s both cities, but especially Hanoi, have been brought into a much denser "swirl of flows." Comparing the domain of these relations shows how economic connections (in the case of Hanoi) and political ones (in the case of Ouagadougou) have shaped very different trajectories of urban development. Comparing their orientation brings to the fore important geopolitical changes – the development of South–South relations and the provincialization of Europe and North America in Hanoi's case – but also an enduring dependence on old colonial links with France in a city still highly dependent on foreign development aid like Ouagadougou. Finally, the fine-grained study of transnational connections in master-planning, public space policies, and architectural design that compose the bulk of this book shows, contra a tendency to debate vaguely about flows and relations in contemporary human geography, that different politics of relatedness and territorialization are at play in these different domains.

The Structure of the Book

In each chapter of the book, I strive to balance a study of Ouagadougou's and Hanoi's relations with elsewhere with a study of their territorialization. As argued in this chapter, it is only by analyzing the relational and the territorial together that relational geographies can make sense of urban change.

In Chapter 2, I describe and compare the trajectories of urban change in the two cities. I look first at territorial aspects, analyzing shifts in urban governance since 1990 and then examining indicators of relatedness. I show that there are important similarities in their transition from socialism to a liberal economy. However, the form, intensity, and orientation of their transnational relations vary significantly: Hanoi has changed within a stable political structure, through increasing economic connectivity with the rest of Asia, whereas in Ouagadougou, transnational relatedness is primarily political and oriented towards Europe and North Africa.

In Chapters 3 and 4, drawing on recent literature dealing with policies in motion, I examine the increasing transnationalization of urban policies. I focus first (Chapter 3) on how foreign expertise and inter-municipal networks have shaped the planning agenda of Hanoi and Ouagadougou. I show that transnational policy relations are more than simple vectors of neoliberalism: they produce contradictory development options and their efficacy is highly dependent on local institutional strategies. Chapter 4 focuses on the more specific question of public space policies in order to further understand how circulating policies are territorialized. I show how both cities share difficulties related to the translation of policies developed in the context of postindustrial cities of the Global North to cities with quite different cultures of public space. I also show how they differ in their relatedness: one (Ouagadougou) being primarily connected with its former metropole, while the other (Hanoi) is the stage for competing public space policies brought by different transnational connections.

In Chapter 5, drawing on recent work on geographies of architecture, I look at how transnational relations transform the process through which urban landscapes are produced. The cases of Hanoi and Ouagadougou allow me to move beyond a traditional emphasis on global architectural firms and global cities to identify different types of transnational design processes. I thus show that Hanoi and Ouagadougou belong to different circuits of architectural design. Hanoi, more attractive for foreign capital, recently entered the circuit of "starchitecture" and master-planned neighborhoods, while Ouagadougou did not. However, I show that, especially in Ouagadougou, transnational design cannot be reduced to any straightforward logic of branding and capital accumulation. Finally, I analyze in both cities how, in an age of geographically "stretched" design processes, the state uses its control over the design of public buildings to maintain the role of architecture in the reproduction of nationalism.

In Chapter 6, I explore the relation between new urban forms and everyday life, focusing on how "traveling" urban types – such as road interchanges or shopping malls – are politically and socially appropriated. Using concepts from governmentality studies and Actor-Network Theory, I argue that built forms should be considered beyond the discipline/resistance pairing. I show that built forms make everyday urbanism more amenable to business and economic growth, but that they also provide urbanites with new affordances and possibilities for autonomous action and self-reflection.

Each chapter can be read independently: Chapter 2 provides a general background for readers interested in understanding the recent developments of the two cities, while subsequent chapters address specific dimensions of their (relational) transformation. Traversing the different chapters, there is a theoretical and methodological ambition. Every chapter is therefore introduced by a section where I situate my analysis within a specific research field, such as policy mobility studies or geographies of design. What I try to do in each case is to bring some added insight to these discussions, using my non-canonical case-studies as laboratories for thought. I use them to "think back" or think anew what we know about the different dimensions of urbanism addressed in each chapter.

In the conclusion, I pull the threads followed in the different chapters together synthesizing the analysis of the two cities' different trajectories of globalization and the different analyses regarding how transnational relations generate urban change in different domains. I argue that the different comparative strategies used in the book lead us to see these cities differently. When we compare their processes of change through time, we encounter many parallels in a path from socialism to neoliberalism. When we compare their relatedness across time and space, important differences appear in the intensity, type, and orientation of their transnational relations: Hanoi's trajectory, with its fast-growing emerging economy primarily connected to its Asian neighbors, is in clear contrast with Ouagadougou's Official Development Assistance (ODA) supported economy and political connections with Europe. Finally, when we compare what these relations actually do in different domains of urban change, the picture becomes much more complex, not reducible to simple notions such as "economic transition" or "trajectories of globalization." Because, when we observe what it is that relations generate, we are inevitably confronted with institutional strategies and human agency that territorialize these relations in often unpredictable ways. This form of comparison brings to the fore the effect of the hegemony of the Communist Party in Hanoi, the tensions within the state apparatus in Ouagadougou, as well as in both cities, the role of the agency of state officials, entrepreneurs, and ordinary citizens in the shaping of urban development.

To conclude, in reflecting on the two cities' contrasting trajectories of urban change, I return to Friedmann's (2007) plea for an endogenous urban development strategy. Hanoi's development, in particular, and especially since 2000, is "ranking-based" rather than, as Friedmann advocates, "assets-based." The Vietnamese government explicitly aims at making the capital a world-city, with the usual suspects of city rankings (London, New York, Singapore) as role models, and pays only occasional attention to Hanoi's environmental and cultural resources. A more "grounded" development strategy would avoid the present rapid destruction of its natural and cultural resources. However, drawing in particular on Ouagadougou's experience, I argue that endogenous development strategies should not be simply advocated in opposition to relation-based ones, but that we should strive for the development of assets-based "politics of relatedness."

Notes

1 The book was written in Italian. A paper in English (Söderström, 2010) presents some of the book's results.
2 Vietnam's economic reform (or *Doi Moi*) was launched in 1986, but only became effective after the 1992 reform of the Constitution and the end of the US embargo in 1994. In Burkina Faso, economic reform, imposed by IMF structural adjustment programs, took off in 1994.
3 Its territory was expanded from 900 to 3,300 square km.
4 Despite the name, he is not a relative of the president.
5 But see Young (1998) for postcolonial theory beyond resistance.
6 This discussion echoes the debate in mobility studies on mobilities and moorings and the possible romanticization and overstatement of mobile phenomena (Adey, 2006; Söderström et al., 2013; Urry, 2007).
7 I return to this discussion in the introduction to Chapter 3.
8 Poorly translated in English as "assemblage," a term that does not convey the active work implied in assembling heterogeneous elements together.
9 The frenetic publication of (often interesting) papers and theme issues around the concept of *agencement* is certainly the best recent example of the worrying extent to which Anglophone scholarship is shaped by competition and micro-distinction strategies. See, among other publications, the themed issue of *Area* (Issue 2, 2011) and the four (!) themed issues in the journal *City* (Issues 2, 3–4, 5, 6, 2011).
10 Doreen Massey's influential work on the geographies of solidarity has been recently particularly important in pushing this research agenda (Barnett et al., 2010; Massey, 2004).
11 In Europe, inter-city learning has been institutionalized since 1870 through the constitution of transnational municipal networks. Those networks have been through different phases of development (Ewen, 2012): the first (1870–1913) characterized by visits to other cities to learn about infrastructures; the second (1913–1970) during which administrative practices were exchanged through associations such as the International Union of Local Authorities; and a third (since 1970) where municipalities active in different thematic networks (around energy, sustainable development, and so on) are back as the central actors of the process.
12 The UCLG defends the interests of local governments on the world stage. Its mission is to be the world advocate of democratic local self-government, promoting its values, objectives and interests through cooperation between local governments, and within the wider international community. Over 1000 cities across 95 countries are direct members of UCLG (www.cities-localgovernments.org).
13 I discuss the literature on policy mobilities at greater length in Chapter 4.
14 See the acknowledgements in the Preface.
15 I also use the term "globalization" as a shorthand for the increasing interconnectedness and interdependence of places in the world. But I try to use it with parsimony because it is often misleading. In particular, it tends to imply two things. First (as Massey (2007) argues), that the source of

economic and social change is an external and somewhat mysterious force hovering above the world and not a set of concrete ideas, actions, and connections. Second, that "the global" is everywhere, while cities globalize unevenly: they contain highly connected "islands of globality" and also areas that are very local in the way they work. In other words, interconnections create specific networks or spheres of globality (Latour, 2009; Sloterdijk, 2004), rather than homogeneous globalized entities. This is why *relation* and not *globalization* is the keyword in this book.

16 There is a vast literature on translocalism and even more on transnationalism. Two key references are Smith (2003) and Vertovec (2009).

17 The sample was constituted through the above mentioned expert interviews.

18 See also www.followthethings.com.

19 The expertise of the research team was also important here. In Hanoi, the research leader, Stephanie Geertman, had recently completed her PhD on urban change in Hanoi when she started the project and had an excellent knowledge of the 1990–2010 period (Geertman, 2007). In Ouagadougou, Alexandra Biehler, who finished her PhD during the period of the project, was our main consultant for the choice of objects (Biehler, 2010).

2
Trajectories of Urban Change in Two Ordinary Cities

In research on world cities, as Shatkin (1998: 378) observed a few years ago, "the experience of cities in least developed countries (LDCs) [has been treated] as an unfortunate footnote to the phenomenon of globalization and economic restructuring." These cities have not seemed relevant to the process of globalization, and conversely in those contexts globalization has been considered a secondary (and purely negative) factor of urban development. Recent work, especially within the ethnographic turn in world-city research mentioned in the previous chapter, has significantly contributed to modify this point of view. Simone's (2004b: 428) work in particular has shown how the everyday life of the poor in cities of Least Developed Countries (LDCs) is organized by transnational networks that are in many ways "similar to the operations pursued by the dominant transnational economic networks of scale." However, there is a gap between work à la Shatkin's mainly focusing on economic indicators such as FDIs and street-level views à la Simone: we rarely get a view of how different aspects of globalization are shaping trajectories of change in LDC cities. This chapter tries to fill this gap for the cities of Hanoi and Ouagadougou.

In French there are two words for the English "globalization," often used interchangeably: *globalisation* and *mondialisation*. The historian of communication, Armand Mattelart (2005) was one of the first French

Cities in Relations: Trajectories of Urban Development in Hanoi and Ouagadougou,
First Edition. Ola Söderström.
© 2014 John Wiley & Sons, Ltd. Published 2014 by John Wiley & Sons, Ltd.

authors to distinguish between *globalisation*, referring to the economic
dimensions of globalization, and *mondialisation*, referring to the wide
array of processes – political, social, cultural, *and* economic – through
which the world becomes increasingly interconnected and interdepen-
dent. I find this distinction useful because it allows us to better investigate the different dimensions of globalization, their convergence or
divergence, as well as the geographically variable forms of the interconnectedness of places. For instance, some cities are very globalized
politically (Nairobi as NGO hub, for instance), but less so economically.
This distinction is important since literature on world cities and global
cities has been characterized by economic reductionism (Robinson,
2006). Although the critique of this reductionism is not new and wider
aspects are analyzed from time to time (Brenner and Keil, 2006), the
intensity of urban globalization is generally summarized by the location
and connectivity of a small (if important) part of cities' urban activities: advanced producer services. Studying the *mondialisation* of cities
means going beyond the commonsense idea that economic globalization subsumes and drives other forms of globalization, and considering
situations where the connection to global flows can be quite specialized.
These non-economic aspects are shown, for instance, in the (rare) rankings and maps produced by the specialists of world-city networks docu-
menting dimensions such as Non-Governmental Organization (NGO)
or media connectivity (Taylor, 2004).[1]

As we will see in this chapter, this is particularly relevant when studying changes in Hanoi and Ouagadougou, two cities that have followed
different trajectories of *mondialisation* since the early 1990s. In 1990,
their political and economic situation was largely similar, with state-
owned land and a state-controlled economy. They have also both been
largely re-shaped by their countries' transition from a socialist to a
liberal economy and by their increasing global connectivity. But this
chapter shows that the intensity, form, and orientation of these connections have been quite different. In particular, connections to economic
flows have been dominant in Hanoi, while connections to political ones
have been dominant in Ouagadougou. This can be explained by the
processes of political change in the two capitals and their respective
countries since the mid-20th century as well as by their situation in two
regions of the world that have experienced very different dynamics of
growth. In this chapter I therefore begin with a brief account of the
political histories of these two cities since independence and then out-
line their different forms of "relatedness" using a series of indicators
for the period 1990–2010. I thereby sketch the trajectories of *mondialisation* of these two cities to establish their similarities as well as their
differences.[2]

Regime Change in Hanoi and Ouagadougou

In Stone's (1989: 179) frequently quoted definition, an urban regime is an "informal arrangement by which public bodies and private interests function together to make and carry out governing decisions." Because such private–public arrangements are very recent in both Hanoi and Ouagadougou, we cannot talk about urban regimes in this specific sense. However, different important political changes have taken place in those cities since the 1980s. The most important regime change, as we will see, is in both cases a transition through different phases of economic and political reform from a revolutionary socialist system of state ownership of land, businesses, and housing to a neoliberal regime, in which since 2000, the private sector has come to play an increasingly important role.

Hanoi 1945–2012

On September 2 1945, after the capitulation of Japan, Ho Chi Minh declared the independence of the Democratic Republic of Vietnam in a region that had been invaded by the Japanese in 1940 and where France, the former colonial power, was proving unable to restore its political authority. From then on, Hanoi became a laboratory of socialist urban planning, importing housing and planning models from the socialist bloc. The following year, what the French call the "Indochina War" began. It lasted until 1954, when the French were defeated in Dien Bien Phu. Only two years later, in a country divided into North and South at the 17th parallel, the Vietnam War between the communist North and the US-supported South begins. The war ended with the withdrawal of the US in 1973 and the defeat of the South in 1975.

The following year, Hanoi became the capital of a unified country. Ten years later, in 1986, President Gorbachev decided, in the context of his *perestroika* (restructuration) policy, to cease Soviet economic support for other communist regimes. Having lost its main source of economic support and being therefore in a critical economic situation, in 1986 the Vietnamese government launched an economic reform program, the *Doi Moi* (meaning literally "renovation"), in order to develop a socialist-oriented market economy. Since the independence of Vietnam, Hanoi's development has thus been shaped by being situated in a socialist country at war for nearly 30 years and then in economic crisis. Thus, "for four decades Hanoi remained confined within [...] its four central administrative districts (1950–1990)" (Labbé, 2010: 33). Having briefly recalled these basic historical events, I now turn to a more detailed description of the transformations of urban governance in the Vietnamese capital since the beginning of the economic reforms.

There are two clearly distinct phases in Vietnam's economic transition: the first between 1986 and 1995; and the second from 1995 onward. In 1986, *Doi Moi* introduced market mechanisms into the hitherto centrally commanded economy, dismantling some components of the planned economy and increasing its integration into the global economic system (Leaf, 1999; Luan, 2002; Masima, 2006; Phe, 2002; Vu Tuan, 1994). Thus, in 1991 at the 7th General Meeting of the Vietnamese Communist Party, the government inaugurated a new era of "open-doors and friendly relations with the rest of the world" (Vu Tuan, 1994). However, for three main reasons, the reform was rather slow to take effect. First, the new policies were not actively implemented until the 1992 adoption of a new constitution introducing the possibility of private property of firms and long-term land leases (or land use rights). Second, until its removal in 1994, the US embargo had a strong impact on foreign investments. And, finally, after decades of colonialism and armed conflicts, Vietnamese authorities were diffident towards foreign interference and therefore reluctant to stimulate a quick pace of privatization. As a consequence, the early years of *Doi Moi* were characterized by rather slow economic development, based, unlike China, on national rather than foreign capital. Urban changes in Hanoi were thus first related to Vietnamese entrepreneurial capacities and took the form of small commercial businesses and self-built houses (Geertman, 2007: 41–60; McGee, 2009).

This was not simply a spontaneous process, however, as the State invited individuals to build their own houses in the context of a policy entitled "The State and People work together" (Labbé and Boudreau, 2011: 277). The "working together" meant that households invested time and money to build their houses – generally illegally – while the State legitimized self-building practices on one hand, and participated itself in larger redevelopment operations on the other, notably by converting agricultural land to residential use (ibid.). If many middle- and upper-class Hanoians improved their living conditions in the process, this policy also created sprawl and speculation without responding sufficiently to the question of housing shortage. In the 1990s, therefore, it was progressively "replaced by an approach to urban space production that gave a larger role to state planning authorities" (ibid.: 279). The "State and People" policy was eventually abandoned in 2000.

The second phase of post-*Doi Moi* urban policy consisted of the creation of new, planned urban areas equipped with public services and high-rise housing, à la Singapore, instead of the former unplanned low-rise developments. This policy was supposed to be implemented by private–public partnerships between State Owned Enterprises (SOEs) and foreign investors. However, as could have been anticipated, foreign

Figure 2.1 Trung Hoa Nhan Chinh, a SOE-driven development. Photo by Chu Giap.

investors were more interested in luxury housing and hotels than in affordable housing. This financial problem, combined with the 1997 Asian financial crisis, seriously hampered the implementation of the new policy in the late 1990s, and gave a central role to SOEs in the production of urban space as Labbé and Boudreau (2011: 281) explain: "Up until 2005, the vast majority of new urban areas built in the Vietnamese capital were indeed funded and carried out by the group of former state-owned enterprises selected by the state at the beginning of the 1990s" (Figure 2.1). The state and the SOEs collaborated in particular to coerce farmers on the urban peripheries to cede their land use rights in order to develop profitable new areas of urban development such as Trung Hoa Nhan Chinh (Figure 0.2). This was, and still is, a classic example of accumulation through dispossession (Labbé and Musil, 2011). Only after the revision of the Land Law in 1998 and the end of the obligation for foreign companies to partner with national companies in 2006, did foreign investors and development companies become central actors in the transformations of Hanoi, as we will see in the second part of this chapter. These two phases led to dramatic changes in the built environment, through enormous amounts of self-(re)construction in already built areas and through new developments at the rapidly growing margins of the city extending into former agricultural land.

The specificity of transition in Vietnam and Hanoi lies in the discrepancy between economic and political change: political change has not at all been of the same magnitude and pace as economic change. In fact, Vietnam's basic political structure has remained largely unchanged in Northern Vietnam since 1946 with the province (or city), district, and commune (or in a city, the ward) as the three official levels of government.[3] The organization of government is "shadowed" by the organization of the Communist Party: each administrative level has a People's Council, a People's Committee, a branch of the Communist Party, and a branch of the Fatherland Front (grouping the country's mass organizations).[4] Since the reunification of the country, these three levels and sets of institutions have been set firmly in place in most parts of the nation (Kerkvliet, 2004: 5). Nevertheless, prerogatives have been redistributed within this political structure through a process of decentralization initiated in the 1990s: responsibilities regarding land use management, public investment, and socio-economic planning have been transferred to local governments that have seen their share in total government expenditures grow from 26 percent in 1992 to 48 percent in 2002 (UN-Habitat, 2008: 9). But because Vietnam has remained a one-party regime, decentralization does not necessarily imply democratization: the power of the Communist Party remains absolute and, in most cases, central government continues to steer policies at the different levels of the state administration through a top-down process.

Within this political structure Hanoi is a "space of exception." First, like the four other major cities of the country (Ho Chi Minh City, Hai Phong, Da Nang, Can Tho), it is a Special Class city.[5] This means that it is under the authority of local *and* central government and that its development is oriented by a master plan designed by the Ministry of Construction. Second, and more importantly, the city is ruled by specific *Laws for the Capital*, a set of decrees issued since 1960 stating the ambition of the government for its capital. The 2000 decree states, for instance, that "Hanoi has to improve the material and mental life of its people to become a prestigious city in the region and deserve the title of *Heroic Capital*".[6]

Despite the inertia of political structure, the pluralization of actors involved in the production of urban space has been the major change in Hanoi's governance system. Apart from the powerful party-state, three other groups of actors have emerged since *Doi Moi*: the "popular sector" (individual Vietnamese entrepreneurs and civil society associations); private companies (including partially privatized SOEs); and foreign actors (multilateral or bilateral partners, private investors). As mentioned previously, individual entrepreneurs, stimulated by the new land use regulations, were crucial in the first post-reform phase: by the end of the 1990s they had produced 70 percent of the city's housing (Geertman, 2007). National companies, and especially the large SOEs involved in construction and planning such as VINACONEX (Vietnam Construction and Import, Export Corporation) are important actors in the extension and regeneration of the city. Since the mid-1990s, civil society has come to play an increasing role. Although many observers still consider that in Vietnam there is no real organized civil society because of its authoritarian regime, professional associations (such as the Vietnam Association of Architects), NGOs, and neighborhood associations increasingly intervene in issues of urban development, as recent controversies over projects and urban changes have shown (Wells-Dang, 2011). Finally, with the reform, foreign development agencies, multilateral organizations such as the UN or the World Bank, as well as smaller companies (such as architectural practices created by foreign architects or overseas Vietnamese having returned to Hanoi) and larger ones (such as transnational construction corporations) have also significantly increased their role in the city's urban development. Thus, while the political structure has largely remained unchanged, the influence of non-state actors, insignificant before *Doi Moi*, has markedly increased. Among non-state actors, private ones are largely predominant in Hanoi as we will see in the second part of this chapter. Unlike Ouagadougou, international organizations and foreign states play a minor role in a space of exception over which the Vietnamese government wants to maintain strong control.

This pluralization of governance has been accompanied by rising levels of illegality and corruption due to the fragmentation of the administration and opaque decision-making processes. Hanoi's structure of governance is both very centralized and very fragmented with over a hundred wards responsible for the control of building regulations (Koh, 2006). The inefficiency of urban policies, the low pay of members of the Party, and the proximity of ward officials to residents, encourage "arrangements" over illegal constructions in the city (Koh, 2004). State officials have also had priority access to state-planned housing and have often resold property bought at state-controlled prices at market value making important profit (Labbé and Boudreau, 2011: 288). Not surprisingly in this context, in 2012 Vietnam was ranked 123rd out of 176 countries in terms of perceptions of corruption.[7] Pressure from the international community has forced the government to take measures, leading to the adoption of an anti-corruption law issued in 2006. However, corruption levels are still very high and in the absence of a reform of the political structure of the country, change is unlikely to happen.

In sum then, in spite of political inertia, the privatization of land use (but not land property for the moment), the semi-privatization of firms active in urban development, as well as the liberalization of international economic flows, have radically changed the local political scene. Since 1990, a series of new actors mostly motivated by economic interests have become part of the largely opaque and corrupt governance of a city in very rapid transformation. Like Ouagadougou, to which I now turn, over two decades Hanoi has been through an accelerated urban transition.

Ouagadougou 1960–2012

On August 5 1960, what was then the République de Haute-Volta, a French colony since 1919, became an independent nation-state.[8] With no access to the sea, the country is situated between the Sahara Desert to the north and more forested regions to the south. The first years of independence were politically unstable, with a series of general strikes and military coups: six between 1966 and the latest coup in 1987 which brought to power the present president, Blaise Compaoré. In the early post-independence era, power in Ouagadougou was divided between a weak municipal administration and traditional chiefdoms present in the city's different neighborhoods. The governance deficit lead to an incapacity to meet the needs of a quickly growing population (less than 50,000 in 1960 to nearly 400,000 in 1983) and to practices of self-construction representing 60 percent of the city in 1983 (Sissao, 1989: 73–74). As a consequence, the city sprawled and speculation was rampant (Jaglin, 1995). Thus, for over 20 years until the Sankara regime in 1983, "the instability of administrative structures did not allow the development of a coherent urban policy" (Biehler, 2010: 120) in Ouagadougou.

Two successive regimes then characterized the governance of Ouagadougou: a revolutionary regime between 1983 and 1991; and a neoliberal one after 1991. The short-lived but influential revolutionary period was inaugurated by the military coup of Thomas Sankara and Blaise Compaoré on the night of August 3/4 1983. For four years the country was governed by the Comité National de la Révolution (CNR) with Sankara as president. The new regime's impact on the city is important in understanding its current conditions. The regime aimed to build a "modern capital" expressing the ideal of the revolution (Hilgers, 2009: 194), which translated primarily into a vast housing provision program, including the plotting of land (*lotissements*), to facilitate the poor's access to housing, and the construction of *cités*: areas of collective housing for the city's middle class. Like Hanoi, Ouagadougou was conceived as the crucible and the laboratory of a new society: housing, infrastructures, and services were improved, land was nationalized, and the city's administrative boundaries were redefined. The 66 old neighborhoods were transformed into 30 "sectors" in order to remove power from both the bourgeoisie and the traditional chiefdoms. Sankara's was also a postcolonial project: he wanted to free the country and its capital from dependence on foreign aid. Thus, between 1985 and 1987, and without foreign support, the regime created 42,000 land plots to provide housing for 220,000 economically deprived inhabitants – under the motto "one household, one land plot."

The CNR aimed also at turning Ouagadougou into a "real capital": new squares epitomizing an openness to the world – such as the Place des Cinéastes and the Place des Nations-Unies – monuments commemorating the revolution, and the commercial strip of the Kwamé N'Krumah Avenue were created to provide Ouagadougou with a sense of modernity and grandeur (Figure 2.2). However, the most important accomplishment of the Sankara regime was the creation of the *cités* in order to solve the problem of insalubrious housing in the center. Six *cités* were planned, four of them completed between 1985 and 1989.[9] The *cités* program was a turning point for the revolutionary regime as the government had difficulty securing funding for the project and had to outface the opposition of the World Bank, the UN, and donor countries (Cormier, 1993). The international community's opposition to the *cités* expressed more generally growing impatience with the socialist experiments of the Sankara regime and was a prelude to its fall.

Figure 2.2 The Avenue Kwamé N'Krumah. Photo by Blaise Dupuis.

On October 15 1987, the charismatic leader of the revolution and 12 of his collaborators were assassinated during a coup led by Sankara's ex-ally Blaise Compaoré.[10] Nevertheless, the CNR remained in power and the new president, Blaise Compaoré, did not change the orientation of the regime overnight. But in 1991, under pressure from the World Bank and countries like France, a Structural Adjustment Program (SAP) was signed. The SAP included the revision of the 1983 land reforms and the removal of subsidies for housing. The same year, the country adopted a new constitution reintroducing private property, multiparty elections and a semi-presidential regime. The four years between 1987 and 1991, labeled by the government as the period of "rectification" (of the revolution), marked the beginning of a new regime.

The consequence of these governmental changes for Ouagadougou was the introduction of a new system and a new agenda of governance. Through a process of decentralization initiated in 1993 with a law providing municipalities with legal status and financial autonomy, the city gained more political and economic power. The priorities of urban development were changed, with emphasis on the development of infrastructures instead of the production of housing (Jaglin, 1995: 67). In the context of the 1993 law, Simon Compaoré was elected as the first "new" mayor of Ouagadougou in 1995. Though the mayor, reelected three times since 1995, belonged to the same party as the head of state, political power in the city was now divided between the state (still intervening in "strategic" projects) and a very active municipality.[11]

Like Hanoi, Ouagadougou witnessed a pluralization of actors involved in urban development. The new urban regime favored the emergence of large Burkinabè construction groups, most of them closely related to the president's and his wife's families.[12] These groups have received a large proportion of state urban development contracts since 1991, notably for the creation of Ouaga 2000, a large area to the south of the city. Other smaller private firms, such as architectural practices and urban planning agencies, both local and foreign-based, have also appeared as actors in urban space production.[13] Common to both cities as well, in this context of private–public "coalitions," is the rise of corruption: in a 2010 report, the World Bank (2010: 15) estimated that during the year 2006, 87 percent of firms in Burkina Faso had bribed public officials to obtain public contracts. Moreover, the yearly reports published by Transparency International show year after year that the perception of corruption in the country is high.[14]

Finally, as in Hanoi, civil society in Ouagadougou has also come to the fore either through participatory planning processes promoted by foreign actors (UN-Habitat, the EU, City of Lyon),[15] or within more spontaneous social movements constituted to oppose large developments accompanied by massive evictions, such as the reconstruction of the city center or of the market area (Biehler and Le Bris, 2010). As I explain in more detail in the next chapter, tensions between the municipality and the state and between the state and civil society have characterized the past 20 years. However, since 2005 there have been signs of an emergent new order of urban governance aiming at a better integration of local and national government within a more coherent institutional framework. The approval in 2005 by the municipality and the government of a City Development Strategy (financed by UN-Habitat), and the adoption of a national housing and urban development strategy in 2008, are two illustrations of recent attempts to create a more efficient and consensual system of decision-making.[16] As in the Vietnamese capital, non-state actors have thus come to play a much more important role in urban governance, but in contrast with Hanoi where state-owned and foreign enterprises are predominant, political partnerships with donor countries and partner cities are central in Ouagadougou, as I show in Chapter 3.

In summary, then, we have seen so far in looking at changes in local governance systems that the trajectories of Hanoi and Ouagadougou display a series of parallels: economic liberalization, pluralization of actors involved in urban governance, and rising levels of perceived corruption (Figure 2.3). They differ, however, in the fact

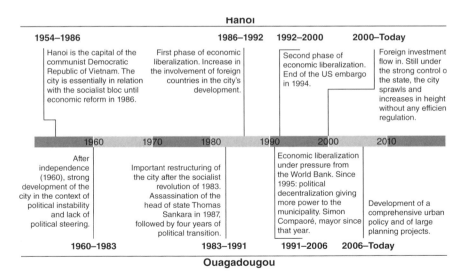

Figure 2.3 Timeline of urban changes in Hanoi and Ouagadougou. Created by Blaise Dupuis.

that decentralization and land privatization have gone further in Ouagadougou. We have seen that during the past 20 years local political history has in both cases been shaped by processes and actors (such as the World Bank) of globalization. This history has also in turn shaped the ways in which Hanoi and Ouagadougou have globalized. In the second part of this chapter I use a series of simple statistical indicators that allow me to better contrast the intensity, type, and orientation of globalization in both cities.

Forms of Relatedness

The geographies of *mondialisation* are uneven, not only because of the uneven development of capitalism, but also because of the resources and strategies of national, regional, and local governments. Connections to global flows are established and developed by transnational corporations, small or large firms, states, international organizations, local governments, NGOs, and the everyday practices of people (from tourism to video downloads). The differences between these actors and vectors of connections create different place-specific forms of relatedness.[17]

Although progress has been made since 2000 in the collection of data at city level, notably by the Globalization and World Cities (GaWC) network (Taylor, 2004)[18] and, although new dimensions of urban globalization are continuously being explored (Derudder et al., 2011), available information at city level is still characterized by a strong bias towards economic data. Municipal statistics also vary widely from place to place: Hanoi has a rich but not easily accessible[19] diachronic dataset, while there is little information specifically about Ouagadougou. Therefore, I use comparable *national* data, but show each time their relevance for understanding urban development at the scale of the two capital cities. I start with an aggregate index of globalization and then move to indicators regarding different types of global flows.

At an aggregate level, according to the KOF[20] globalization indexes calculated by the Swiss Institute of Technology in Zurich,[21] Vietnam is ranked 130th and Burkina Faso 140th out of 208 countries in the world in terms of their overall level of globalization. Thus, generally speaking, they both rank quite low, despite the sweeping structural changes described above. If we consider now KOF's more specific indicators, the cities' form of *mondialisation* appears as differentiated: economic globalization[22] is stronger in Vietnam (72nd out of 208 countries against 131st for Burkina Faso) while political globalization[23] is stronger in Burkina Faso (77th against 131st for Vietnam). There are no available comparable indexes at city level, but the rankings of world cities by GaWC to a large

Table 2.1   KOF and GaWC index. Created by Blaise Dupuis.

2012 KOF Globalization Rank (Countries)			
	Globalization	*Economic Globalization*	*Social Globalization*	*Political Globalization*
Vietnam	130	72	164	131
Burkina Faso	140	131	161	77

Note: 208 countries are listed. Rankings are based on data for the year 2009
Source: 2012 KOF index of Globalization, Definitions and Sources(http://globalization.kof.ethz.ch/static/pdf/definitions_2012.pdf)

2005 GaWC Political Connectivities Rank (Cities)			
	International organizations	*Non-Governmental Organizations*	*Diplomatic Activities*	*United Nations Institutions*
Hanoi	35	36	64	32
Ouagadougou	46	61	–	103

Note: International organizations, 178 cities are listed – Non-Governmental Organizations, 149 cities – Diplomatic Activities, 155 cities – United Nations Institutions, 404 cities. Rankings are based on data for the year 2004.

Source: the data were produced by P.J. Taylor and constitute Data Set 18, Data Set 20, Data Set 22, Data Set 24 of the Globalization and World Cities Research Network (http://www.lboro.ac.uk/gawc/) publication of inter-city data.

extent confirm this difference between economic and political globalization. Their 2010 "standard" ranking of world cities, based on indicators of economic connectivity, classifies Hanoi as a "Gamma+"[24] city, while Ouagadougou does not appear at all.[25] Research on political connectivity done by the same research group provides a picture that is somewhat different from the KOF national index (Table 2.1).

As shown in Table 2.1, in this index Hanoi scores higher than Ouagadougou on these three indicators of political globalization (International Organizations, NGOs, UN institutions). However, on the one hand, more specifically than KOF's, GaWC's set of indicators reflects a size-effect[26] as a larger population is likely to require larger and more connected offices. On the other hand, the methodology is different: instead of using indicators like KOF's showing the integration of the country within diplomatic networks and international agreements, GaWC uses the connectivity of different types of organizations' local offices. Although these two rankings do not allow us to assess which of the two cities is the more politically interconnected, we can conclude that, generally speaking and in relative terms, Hanoi is primarily connected to global economic flows and Ouagadougou to political networks. I now show this in more detail with indicators regarding flows of capital, people, and information.

Capital flows

As state capitals, Hanoi and Ouagadougou are primary destinations for different financial flows that have greatly transformed the physical and social landscapes of both cities. Economic reforms since the late 1980s have intensified FDIs, ODAs, and the transfer of private funds such as remittances. In addition, the origin of these financial flows has changed over time.

Before *Doi Moi* in Vietnam and during the socialist regime in Burkina Faso, foreign investments were scarce and primarily originated from communist countries. In both countries, FDIs fluctuated during the first period of economic reform, but grew then strongly after 2000 (Figure 2.4).

Figure 2.4 shows the take-off of Vietnam's economic globalization after its constitutional reform (1992) and the end of the US embargo (1994). The subsequent decrease is due to the 1997 Asian financial crisis, while the spectacular increase after 2002 is related to structural economic reforms in the early 2000s, including a bilateral trade agreement with the US in 2001; the integration of the country in the World Trade Organization (WTO) in 2006; and more importantly, a new law allowing foreign investors to operate alone without having to establish joint-ventures with local companies. Finally, despite the effects of the 2008 crisis, FDIs have remained at a much higher level than they were before 2006.

Although both countries had the same starting point in 1990, lower levels of resources and differences in investors' perception of business opportunities explain why Burkina Faso's economic globalization and development has been very different. FDIs had a first "peak" of US$10 m in 1994, after Burkina Faso's opening to foreign investments in 1991, and a second peak at US$20 m in 2000. In 2007, privatization of the country's telecommunications, and investments in the mining sector brought unprecedented FDIs (US$343 m) into the country. Since then they have remained at a higher level compared to the previous period (US$171 m in 2009; US$37 m in 2010). Thus, foreign investments in Burkina Faso since 1990 have mainly been related to cherry-picking in the context of the privatization of specific industries in what remains a predominantly rural economy, while they have played a major role in Vietnam's transition to an industrial economy.[27] These differences are

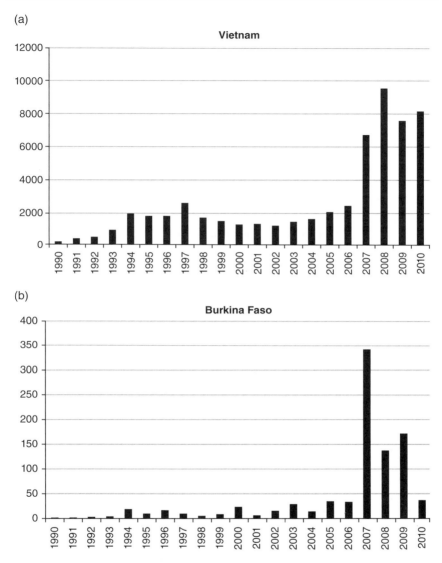

Figure 2.4 FDIs in (a) Vietnam and (b) Burkina Faso, 1990–2010 (millions of US$).
Created by Blaise Dupuis.

of course also explained by the regional context of the two countries:
Sub-Saharan Africa, for long considered a no-go region for foreign
investors, in contrast with Southeast Asia, which has emerged as one of
the major cores of the global economy.

Table 2.2 Evolution and origins of remittances in Vietnam and Burkina Faso, 2000–2010. Created by Blaise Dupuis.

Evolution of remittances in Burkina Faso and Vietnam										
Inward flows (millions of US dollars) 2000–2010										
2000	*2001*	*2002*	*2003*	*2004*	*2005*	*2006*	*2007*	*2008*	*2009*	*2010*
Vietnam 2000	2000	2714	2700	3200	4000	4800	5500	7200	6840	7215
Burkina Faso 67	50	50	50	50	50	50	50	50	49	43

Source: United Nations Conference on Trade and Development, 2012

Emigration: top destination countries, 2010	
Vietnam	United States, Australia, Canada, Cambodia, Germany, France, Republic of Korea, Japan, United Kingdom, Thailand
Burkina Faso	Ivory Coast, Niger, Mali, Italy, Benin, Nigeria, Gabon, Germany, United States

Source: The Migration and Remittances Factbook, World Bank, 2011

If the intensity of economic globalization is clearly different, the orientation is different as well. In Vietnam, investors are located primarily in Asian countries (South Korea, Singapore, Taiwan, and Japan), while in Burkina Faso they are located primarily in Europe (France especially), North Africa, and the Middle East.

At the level of individual economic exchanges, remittances – encouraged by governments and international organizations in both countries[28] – increased spectacularly in Vietnam (where they quadrupled during the 2000s from US$2 to US$8 billion per year), while they decreased in Burkina Faso after 2000 (Table 2.2). This is related to their origin: in Burkina Faso funds are mainly sent by migrants living in other African countries, especially from the Ivory Coast where the population suffered from the long civil war (2002–2011); while Vietnamese remittance senders live in North America, Europe, and in neighboring countries (South Korea, Japan, Thailand). Investments since 1990 by foreign companies and migrants have thus been significantly stronger in Vietnam than in Burkina Faso.

If private financial flows are proportionately more important in Vietnam, foreign states' public investment is higher in Burkina Faso, one of the world's poorest countries: in 2010 ODAs represented as much as 12 percent of Burkina Faso's but only 3 percent of Vietnam's Gross National Income (GNI).[29] Between 2005 and 2010, Japan was by

Table 2.3 Sources of ODAs in Vietnam and Burkina Faso, 2005–2010. Created by Blaise Dupuis.

Vietnam Top Ten Donors		*Burkina Faso Top Ten Donors*	
Country	*Disbursement (US$M)*	*Country*	*Disbursement (US$M)*
Japan	824.41	France	111.31
France	181.27	Netherlands	67.36
Germany	105.54	Germany	44.38
United Kingdom	87.72	Denmark	39.79
Denmark	77.47	United States	35.59
Australia	70.76	Japan	32.08
United States	64.66	Switzerland	24.11
Netherlands	45.32	Canada	23.57
Korea	43.44	Sweden	22.6
Sweden	31.88	Islamic Dev. Bank	18.17

Source: Organisation for Economic Cooperation and Development, Development Assistance Committee, 2012

far the most important donor country in Vietnam (US$824 m), ahead of France (US$181 m), Germany (US$105 m), and the UK (US$87 m). In contrast, France, the former metropole, remains by far Burkina Faso's most important donor (US$111 m), ahead of the Netherlands (US$67 m) and Germany (US$44 m).[30] In both cases, bilateral aid is still shaped by former colonial links, but the very important role played by Japan in Vietnam shows how this country's economic globalization – private and public – is increasingly oriented by East–East international relations (Table 2.3).[31]

ODAs also flow in through the activity of NGOs. Burkina Faso stands out in this respect as well, with a particularly dense presence of national and foreign NGOs. The country is often mockingly referred to as "NGO land." In the 1960s and 1970s, the NGOs were mainly faith-based organizations. With the decentralization policy of the 1990s, NGO orientation diversified and their numbers soared: there were 87 in 1988, 188 in 1996 and 570 in 2009. The total financial contribution of NGOs to development was nearly ten times higher in 2005 than a decade earlier in 1995.[32]

As we will see in Chapter 5, investments from abroad have had a significant impact on the physical and cultural landscapes of both cities. FDIs have been critical in the development of new middle- and upper-class residential areas, remittances have played an important role in the development of individual housing, and ODAs in the development of urban infrastructures. The type and origin of foreign investment have, however, produced different landscapes. To mention only two contrasting examples which will be examined in detail later: French ODAs have led to the development of public spaces in Ouagadougou, whereas Indonesian FDIs have created a large gated community in Hanoi.

Flows of people

The mobility of people is another factor affecting the changes in the forms of relatedness of the two cities. People's mobility is a multifaceted phenomenon but for reasons of availability of comparable data, I mainly focus here on migratory flows, visitor arrivals in the two countries, and the outward mobility of students. While absolute numbers are at a national scale, the tendencies described with these data permit an understanding of changes in the two capital cities which are, as transport hubs, major points of entry and exit.

As can be seen in Figure 2.5, demographic growth has followed the intensification of globalization and the economic growth of

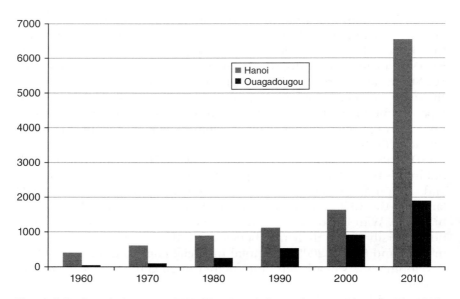

Figure 2.5 Population growth in Hanoi and Ouagadougou (thousands), 1960–2010. Created by Blaise Dupuis.

Ouagadougou and Hanoi since 1990. This demographic growth is explained by natural growth and intra- as well as inter-national migration.

With other West African countries such as Mali, Togo, and Ghana, Burkina Faso is a country of emigration with a diaspora abroad of 1.57 m (9.7 percent of national population) in 2010, but Ouagadougou has also been a destination for migrants. Between 1996 and 2006, 3 percent of its demographic growth (out of a total of 7.6 percent) was due to intra- and inter-national migrations (and 4.6 percent to natural growth). Difficult living conditions in rural areas, made worse by the SAP, have increased internal migrations towards urban areas in Burkina Faso and especially towards the capital. Since 2002, when civil war began in the Ivory Coast, "return migrations" of Burkinabè from there have constituted the major flow of international migrants (Boyer and Delaunay, 2009: 43). The impact of these international migrations on Ouagadougou since the 1990s is visible in the emergence of hotels, new types of night activities (bars, discos), and new built forms in the city's residential areas, such as styles imported from the Ivory Coast or the sloping roofs of European-style villas (Diasso-Yameogo and Ouedraogo, 2005: 27).

In Vietnam until *Doi Moi*, both intra and inter-national migrations were strictly controlled by the government. Only families receiving a *ho khau* (family registration) were allowed access to the city and its services (housing, education, etc.). The liberalization of people's mobility since the reform has generated substantial population movements within the country. Since 1997, 40,000 migrants per year migrate to Hanoi from other provinces. They are pushed from rural areas by economic difficulties related to the commercialization of agriculture, and pulled to the city by the employment opportunities in the sectors of industry and services. Return migrations are another important aspect of Hanoi's demographic growth: it is estimated that three-quarters of the 2.5 million Vietnamese outside the country live in the United States, Canada, or France, the vast majority being refugees who fled (mostly from Southern Vietnam) after 1975.[33] About 280,000 *Viet Kieu* returned for tourism or business in 1999, three times more than in 1992.[34] These return migrants have invested capital in large construction projects and brought their know-how with them, for instance, as architects, as we will see in Chapter 5. The pattern of outward flows has also radically changed after *Doi Moi*: the large emigration of foreign workers to countries of the socialist bloc (230,000 people in 1985) has been replaced by less important movements towards Malaysia, Taiwan, and South Korea (85,000 in total in 2008 according to the Ministry of Labor). This new diaspora is bringing new models of living, especially visible in Hanoi's youth culture, as we will see in Chapter 6.

Incoming visitors to each country constitute another aspect of the relatedness of the two cities in terms of people's mobility. In both cases, since 1990 there has been a constant growth of visitors (with the exception of two years in Vietnam – 1998, 2003 – and one in Burkina Faso – 1999) (Figure 2.6).[35] Since 2000, the government of Vietnam has developed promotion of the country as a tourist destination, while the government of Burkina Faso, where tourist infrastructures are rare,[36] as yet has no such policy. Rather, visits to Burkina Faso have mainly been business-motivated, with people coming from France, the Ivory Coast, and Mali. The increase has been close to exponential in Vietnam (4.24 m visitors in 2008, nearly three times more than in 1998). This spectacular increase is mainly due to the explosion of tourism: between 1995 and 2009, the number of holiday visits has been three times higher than the number of business visits. Here as well we observe relations oriented towards other Asian countries as, since 1990, the main countries of origin of visitors are, in decreasing order, China, Japan, Taiwan, and the US. The regional context plays again an important role here with the recent development of a tourist class in neighboring countries such as China.

Because of the increase of household revenues, outward tourist flows are more important in Vietnam than Burkina Faso. Before *Doi Moi*, there was very little holiday or leisure culture and it was impossible to obtain a passport, except for those having to travel for reasons of business or study in countries of the socialist bloc. Vietnamese are now increasingly traveling abroad to countries such as Thailand (first country of destination), Singapore, China, and Malaysia,[37] while airlines promote weekend shopping trips to Hong Kong and Singapore. In Burkina Faso, in contrast, only a very small proportion of the population travels abroad, mainly to other Western African countries, Europe, and North Africa.

Much like financial flows, the pace of change in the mobility of people has been very fast in both countries, but the intensity of globalization has been much stronger in Vietnam, a country which from being very isolated until the late 1980s has become an important destination for international tourists and entrepreneurs. The consequence of tourism on Hanoi's built environment has been dramatic, resulting in a hotel and restaurant boom in the historic center.[38] The orientation of flows reflects what we observed in the previous section: Ouagadougou is mainly related to countries of its region and Europe, while Hanoi is increasingly connected with China, Japan, and other Asian countries.

Finally, the outward flows of students are interesting as an indicator of potential knowledge transfer through the mobility of young people.

(a)

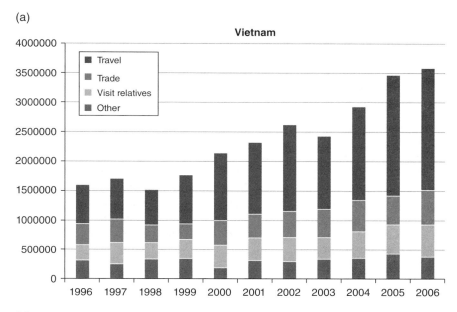

(b)

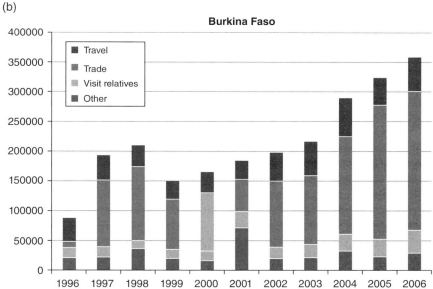

Figure 2.6 International arrivals in (a) Vietnam and (b) Burkina Faso, 1996–2006. Created by Blaise Dupuis.

This is not a new phenomenon: before *Doi Moi* in Vietnam and during the revolutionary period in Burkina Faso, students of both countries were trained abroad in the socialist bloc. But the number of students, as well as their destinations, have changed. English-speaking countries have now become major places of destination for increasing numbers of Vietnamese students, while a small number of Burkinabè students are trained in other African countries[39] or in French-speaking European universities. Knowledge transfer is also effectuated by the mobility of institutions of higher education. Since 2000, Hanoi has witnessed the development of branch campuses of large English-speaking universities[40] in the context of a governmental policy seeking to develop growth-oriented knowledge and technology transfers. In Ouagadougou, there are no branch campuses and foreign research institutions present in the city, like the Institut de Recherche pour le Développement, supported by France, or the School of Engineering, supported by Switzerland, are still mainly development-oriented.

Flows of information

Information flows are politically critical both in Hanoi and Ouagadougou, situated in two (semi-)authoritarian countries.[41] Until 1990, media both in Vietnam and Burkina Faso were owned by the state and were mainly tools for political propaganda. Since then the number of media – newspapers and magazines, radio and television networks – has considerably increased. In Vietnam, the state holds a firm grip on media[42] but authorizes paid access to foreign and international cable networks.[43] National TV channels today diffuse a large number of South Korean and Chinese series. A 2010 survey[44] shows that a large proportion of the population watches the Disney channel (38.82 percent), followed by two other US-owned channels: HBO (34.12 percent), and Star movie (21.18 percent); whereas Vietnam's television channels have a much smaller audience: 17.65 percent for VTV3 and 9.41 percent for VCTV3. In Hanoi, modes of consumption – music, clothing, leisure activities – have been influenced by this foreign media boom and their commercial advertisements (Drummond, 2003; Drummond and Thomas, 2003; Marr, 2003; McNally, 2003; Minh and Thuy, 2003). Thus, two fast-food chains, the Japanese Lotteria and US Kentucky Fried Chicken[45] opened their first outlets in 1997. More recently, since 2006, cinema multiplexes have opened in the Vietnamese capital.

According to Balima and Frère (2003: 13), after the end of the revolutionary period in Burkina Faso "there has been a flourishing of pluralism in the media, an important development of ICTs, movie and theater production." In 2008, there were 119 radio and 24 TV channels, as well as some hundred journals and magazines.[46] National networks and foreign networks, now available through cable, include programs from abroad (series from France, but also the ubiquitous Brazilian *telenovelas*). As in Hanoi, this diversification has brought new modes of consumption to Ouagadougou. But because of low income levels they are accessible only to a small sector of the population. It is noteworthy, considering Burkina Faso is a very poor country, that Ouagadougou is not only a recipient of information and cultural flows, but also an exporter: its movie scene, including the Pan-African Film Festival of Ouagadougou,[47] created in 1969, and its music scene, are especially dynamic, as we will see in Chapter 5.

Finally, Internet access and cell phone subscriptions are useful indicators of person-based connections to information flows.[48] The telecom market, and especially the sale of cell phones, has expanded quickly in both countries since the mid-2000s, but the spread of connections to global information flows is much stronger in Vietnam (Figure 2.7).

This is particularly the case with the Internet, to which 27.8 percent of the Vietnamese had access in 2010, in contrast with 1.4% in Burkina Faso. This is explained by Vietnam's higher standard of living, but also by the fact that 93.2 percent of its population is literate, against only 28.7 percent in Burkina Faso.[49] In Vietnam, this widespread access to the Internet does not mean unrestricted access to its contents or freedom to publish on the web, as the government tries to control access to oppositional websites and to blogs based in the country.[50] Bloggers and web journalists are regularly imprisoned and the country is therefore classified as an "enemy of the Internet" by Reporters without Borders.[51]

Such state control of ICTs does not exist in Burkina Faso. However, freedom of the press has been a very sensitive issue for the Compaoré regime because of the as-yet-unexplained murder in 1998 of Norbert Zongo, a journalist critical of the government.[52] Since then the situation has improved and a variety of independent media has emerged, some of them quite critical of the regime. Today, in spite of the crushing domination of one political party[53] and a strong personalization of political power, political freedom is more significant in Burkina Faso than in Vietnam.[54]

The spectacular change in access to global information flows and mass culture has had wide-ranging consequences on the development of Ouagadougou and Hanoi that I can only partially give an account of in this book, which focuses on particular aspects of urban policy, form, and production. However, in Chapter 5 I show how Internet access has contributed to the development of transnational forms of architectural design, and in Chapter 6 how cultural flows shape new forms of urban practices.

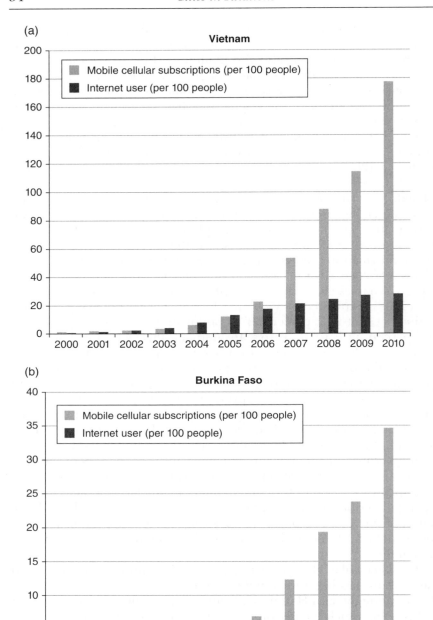

Figure 2.7 Mobile cellular subscriptions and Internet users in (a) Vietnam and (b) Burkina Faso, 2000–2010. Created by Blaise Dupuis.

Conclusion

In the 1980s, Hanoi and Ouagadougou were both capitals of revolutionary socialist states and conceived as crucibles for the creation of a new society. During this period the state was the only landowner, the only provider of housing, and the dominant actor in urban policies. During the past quarter of a century, Hanoi and Ouagadougo have followed similar trajectories in many ways: a transition from a socialist to a liberal economy starting in the late 1980s, coming into its own in the second half of the 1990s with new national constitutions; and the re-privatization of land, businesses, and housing as well as the liberalization of trade and foreign investments. In terms of urban governance, both cities are now governed by a system that involves public and private actors including foreign investors and – through acts of resistance rather than state initiatives – civil society. The rise of non-state actors has been paralleled by the rise of corruption and, particularly in Hanoi, of illegal constructions.[55]

If the chronology and milestones of both cities' transition are parallel, they differ in form. Whereas Ouagadougou has seen the rise of municipal power, through the implementation of decentralization, Hanoi's political structure has remained largely unchanged since independence with a complex, fragmented, and opaque territorial administration. Moreover, if private actors such as transnational developers and partially privatized SOEs are key players in Hanoi's system of governance, in contrast political partnerships, especially through the strategy of the municipality, play a major role in Ouagadougou.

Indicators of *mondialisation* – aggregate indexes and specific diachronic indicators of flows – have allowed me to further refine the tracing of both cities' trajectories of globalization. First, if Ouagadougou has mainly globalized by establishing political connections, Hanoi has done so by capturing global economic flows. The intensity and orientation of these connections clearly differ as well, reflected in incoming FDIs – nearly 45 times higher in Vietnam in 2009 – and in tourist expenditure – 14 times higher in Vietnam the same year. From being oriented towards the socialist bloc, Hanoi's transnational connections (FDIs, incoming visitors, migrant workers) are now clearly oriented towards the Asia Pacific region. In Ouagadougou, the old colonial route with France has remained an essential one, but since 1990 other relations – especially through decentralized cooperation with North Africa, West Africa, and with other European countries – have come to the fore, as I show in Chapter 3. When we consider different forms of flows, we can thus better see the emergence of new geopolitics of urban relations. These changes are naturally more spectacular in Hanoi with the dissolution of its links with the formerly socialist East European countries and the establishment of strong exchanges in all domains with the countries of the Association of Southeast Asian Nations (ASEAN),[56] than in Ouagadougou, still largely dependent on development aid. However, the trajectories followed by these two LDC cities are evidence of how the importance of traditional North–South relations is declining. Finally, the diverging trajectories of *mondialisation* of both cities during the past two decades has of course been largely determined by their inscription in different regional contexts. Hanoi has benefited from Southeast Asia's attractiveness for foreign investors and the economic emergence of many neighboring countries. Though the situation has improved in recent years, Ouagadougou, in contrast, is situated in an economically marginalized region – Sub-Saharan Africa – still generally perceived as a risky place for investments.

In the following chapters, I examine how the trajectories of globalization and also the forms and orientations of relatedness are shaping different aspects of urban development in Hanoi and Ouagadougou.

Notes

1 See also the research bulletins of the Globalization and World Cities network: www.lboro.ac.uk/gawc/publicat.html

2 For another author using the idea of "multiple trajectories" of socio-spatial change (in the South African context), see Hart (2002).

3 The province, district, and commune are the three local levels of administration stipulated in the 1946 Constitution. In Hanoi, the ward level did not come about until 1980. Between 1945 and 1980, however, there was a third level of administration, called "smaller area" (*tieu khu*), which the ward subsequently replaced (Kerkvliet, 2004: 19).

4 Districts, however, did not have People's Councils until 1959 (Kerkvliet, 2004: 19).

5 Vietnam's urbanization policy today is based on a hierarchy of places dating from 1972; a class system ranging from Class 1 to Class 5 (Geertman, 2007: 102). Class 1 cities correspond to "Special Class Cities."

6 "*Cac van ban cua Dang va Nha Nuoc ve Thu do Ha Noi.*" Documents of the Communist Party and the Government of Hanoi Capital, published by Hanoi's People's Committee in April 2004, p. 8 (document in Vietnamese).

7 See www.transparency.org.

8 The Haute-Volta was itself a colonial assemblage of different West African territories controlled by France since 1895. As a sign of epochal change, Haute Volta became Burkina Faso ("the country of righteous men") in 1984 under the revolutionary socialist regime of Thomas Sankara.

9 Their names, in the spirit of the French Revolution, are *Cité An* (year) II, III, IVa and IVb.

10 The circumstances of Sankara's death have never been clarified as no investigation was ever commissioned by the Burkinabè government. A wide variety of theses have circulated since 1987 designating alternatively France, Gaddafi, Compaoré, the CIA (or all of them together) as responsible for the assassination.

11 This double-headed system has led to a series of tensions and a lack of coordination, as I will show in more detail in Chapter 3.

12 The "Groupe Aliz," active in urban development and real estate for instance, is directed and owned by Alizéta Ouédraogo, the president's brother's mother-in-law.

13 I discuss this in more detail in Chapter 5.

14 However, in 2012, Burkina Faso was ranked 83rd out of 176 states in a measure of perceptions of corruption, compared to 100th the previous year. See www.transparency.org.

15 More on this in Chapter 3.

16 On the limits of these good governance schemes, see Pieterse (2008).

17 For analyses of these different geographies see, for instance, Barnett et al. (2008) and Lévy (2008).

18 See also the hundreds of research bulletins published by the GaWC network: www.lboro.ac.uk/gawc/publicat.html

19 Personal networks are indispensable for empirical research in Hanoi, even for accessing supposedly public information.

20 *Konjunkturforschungsstelle*, Business Cycle Research Institute.

21 Like all indexes, KOF's index is a simplification and depends on available comparable data. I use it here because it focuses on flows, and therefore on relatedness, and separates different forms of globalization. For the results and methods of calculation, see www.globalization.kof.ethz.ch/.

22 The KOF economic globalization index is composed of the following variables and their respective weight (in percentage of each variable): a) Actual Flows: trade 21 percent; foreign direct investment, stocks 28 percent; portfolio investment 24 percent; income payments to foreign nationals 27 percent; b) Restrictions: hidden import barriers 24 percent; mean tariff rate 27 percent; taxes on international trade (percent of current revenue) 26 percent, capital account restrictions 23 percent.

23 Embassies in country 25 percent; membership of international organizations 28 percent; participation in UN Security Council missions 22 percent; international treaties 25 percent. We can observe that the first indicator here regarding the number of embassies is directly related to Hanoi and Ouagadougou where they are located.

24 Gamma level cities are "world cities linking smaller regions or states into the world economy, or important world cities whose major global capacity is not in advanced producer services" (http://www.lboro.ac.uk/gawc/gawcworlds.html).

25 See www.lboro.ac.uk/gawc/world2010t.html.

26 Today Hanoi is three times larger than Ouagadougou, while Vietnam's population is five times larger than Burkina Faso's.

27   According to the data of the World Bank, industry represented roughly 20 percent of both countries' GDP in 1990. Its importance has doubled since then in Vietnam, while remaining stable in Burkina Faso (where no data are available since 2006, however).

28   For instance, in 2006, the government of Burkina Faso created a website in order to facilitate remittances and knowledge transfers: www.burkinadiaspora.bf. In Vietnam, since *Doi Moi* the government has allowed *Viet Kieu* (overseas Vietnamese) to send money to their relatives, which before was impossible.

29   However, both countries are two of the world's most important recipients of ODAs. For more data on ODAs, see www.aidflows.org, which is also the source of the other figures in this paragraph.

30   The aid from France is also channeled through multilateral institutions such as the European Union.

31   In terms of multilateral aid (provided by international organizations), which is quantitatively less important than bilateral aid (provided by a single donor country), the World Bank is the main donor in both cases.

32   Secrétariat permanent des ONG à Ouagadougou and Piveteau (2004: 202).

33   See *Asianweeks*, issue of May 4 2000.

34   Ibid.

35   Visitors include people in transit, not staying overnight, as well as longer term but temporary tourists. Persons paying regular visits to the country during the year are counted as one visitor each time.

36   However the number of hotels doubled in Ouagadougou between 1988 and 1999 (from 25 to 51).

37   In Hanoi, 20,000 people traveled abroad in 2000 and 49,000 in 2007 (Hanoi Statistic Office, 2008, p. 225).

38   There were 11 hotels and restaurants in 1980 and 748 in 2007 (510 of them catering for tourists).

39   As an example, architecture and planning is not taught at the University of Ouagadougou, and most Burkinabè architects and planners are trained at the University of Lomé, Togo.

40   Invited by the Vietnamese government in 1998, the Australian Royal Melbourne Institute of Technology established Vietnam's first international university campus in Hanoi in 2000. In 2006 the Ministry of Education and Training allowed nine universities from the US, UK, and Canada to open branch campuses in Vietnam.

41   In Burkina Faso, a country generally qualified as semi-authoritarian, human rights, in particular freedom of expression and freedom of the press, have been improving since the early years of the Compaoré regime. Vietnam's regime remains authoritarian, despite some progress in terms of freedom of expression: the press and Internet are strictly controlled and dissidents are regularly sentenced to years of imprisonment after unfair trials, according to Amnesty International. See their yearly report: www.amnesty.org.

42 There is no independent national media in Vietnam other than dissident publications and websites suffering state repression.
43 There were two national channels in 1960 and no foreign one accessible. In 2003, there were 45 national and 28 foreign and international channels.
44 See www.vn-zoom.com (accessed February 2 2010, in Vietnamese).
45 There were 14 KFCs in Hanoi in 2009.
46 *Rapport national sur le Burkina Faso du conseil des droits de l'homme des Nations Unies*, 2008.
47 See www.fespaco-bf.net
48 The first cell phone network in Vietnam was established in 1993 and in 1996 in Burkina Faso. In both countries, formerly national telecom infra-structures were privatized in the late 1990s.
49 Respectively, the years 2010 and 2007 (UNESCO Institute for Statistics, 2012).
50 According to Amnesty International's 2011 country report (www.amnesty. org), "Vietnamese language dissident blogs and websites suffered wide-spread hacking which internet companies Google and McAfee alleged may have been politically motivated."
51 See their Press Freedom Index (http://en.rsf.org/press-freedom-index-2010,1034.html), accessed September 10 2012.
52 Zongo was the director of the news magazine *L'Indépendent* and one of the founding members of the Burkinabè movement for human rights. He was assassinated while investigating the mysterious murder of the chauffeur of the president's brother: François Compaoré. Zongo's death triggered a strong emotional reaction in Burkina Faso and was followed by police repression of protests throughout the country.
53 In 2007, the opposition represented only 13.5 percent of the parliament.
54 In 2013, Burkina Faso ranked 46th out of 179 countries in terms of free-dom of the press by Reporters without Borders (www.en.rsf.org), while Vietnam was ranked 172nd.
55 These illegal constructions include both large-scale constructions built by investors and self-built housing of the poor and the middle class.
56 Vietnam joined ASEAN in 1995.

3

Transnational Policy Relations

One of the many consequences of global interconnectedness is the increasing importance of transnational relations in planning agendas. As this chapter demonstrates, even marginal cities such as Ouagadougou and Hanoi are no exception to the rule. I show here the growing importance of foreign expertise and inter-municipal networks[1] in the constitution of those agendas and how policy relations are strategically used by different and sometimes competing levels of the state apparatus. I also describe the rise since the 1990s of new (predominantly Asian) role models and consultancy firms indicating shifts in the geopolitics of policy relations. To do justice to the complexity and specificity of these processes, we need to consider them beyond the paradigm of neoliberalization.

In English-speaking academia, the analysis of transnational policy relations is often automatically couched in the terms of a study of neoliberalism. In other words, these relations are considered a priori as elements of state strategies aimed at increasing the scope of market- and growth-oriented urban policies. This is both understandable and problematic. It is understandable because for more than 30 years neoliberal policies have played a pervasive role as an international political *doxa* (Harvey, 2007). A focus on neoliberalism is therefore indispensable to critically assess the role of a dominant politico-economic discourse in patterns of urban development across the world. It is central, for instance, to the understanding of 1980s and 1990s urban

Cities in Relations: Trajectories of Urban Development in Hanoi and Ouagadougou, First Edition. Ola Söderström.
© 2014 John Wiley & Sons, Ltd. Published 2014 by John Wiley & Sons, Ltd.

policies in cities of the South, dictated or inspired by the World Bank. This focus is also understandable in a quite different sense: it manifests the role of context and power structures in academic research. By this I mean that the impact of neoliberalism as ideology and policy has been particularly strong in the countries of the Thatcher–Reagan axis, which are also dominant in terms of academic publications and thus have been the objects of sustained intellectual critique. However, as a scholar working on cities in the Global South in the French-speaking world, I find the extension of the concept and its role in contemporary urban studies doubly problematic. First, neoliberalism and neoliberalization are terms that, despite the increasing influence of Anglophone urban studies, are much less used as analytical categories in continental Europe. In France, for instance, where the state cannot be seen as a simple operator of neoliberal policies and where research tends to pay attention to the various institutional moorings of urban capitalism (Lorrain, 2002), it is barely used.[2] In Switzerland, where I live, most large cities have had over the past 20 years left-wing municipalities that have developed policies that can hardly be reduced to a process of neoliberalization. Second, and more importantly in the context of this book, the functioning of cities in the South is, in many respects, even more different from cities in the UK and the US than they are from each other. As we have seen in the previous chapters, chiefdoms and customary rights in Ouagadougou's socialist regime and the Communist Party's patronage system in Hanoi play important roles in urban development that do not easily fit in the paradigm of neoliberalization. This, again, does not mean that this paradigm is not relevant to the analysis of these cities or that it is not important to study its variegated and continuously mutating forms in different contexts (Brenner et al., 2010; Peck et al., 2013). But it does mean, however, that this is not all there is to analyze and criticize. In other words: "the range of urban processes shaping a diversity of urban contexts needs to be thought of as more than just contributing to the hybridization of urban neoliberalism" (Parnell and Robinson, 2012: 594).[3]

My way out of this – i.e. that neoliberalism is important, but not all there is – is to consider at the outset that transnational policy relations are "more than neoliberal." As Collier (2012: 189) puts it, there are two possible approaches to neoliberalism: "In one, neoliberalism is associated with a specified set of elements (thinkers, institutions, policy programs) that have to be teased out from a tangle of other things (local and trans-local policy conditions; countervailing visions of reform; structural transformations of the global economy that are not reducible to neoliberalism, and so on). In the other, the concept is expanded, and the entire ensemble of elements is identified with neoliberalism."

I believe the first perspective is heuristically more productive when we want to understand, as I want to do here, the various orientations in transnational urban policy relations. Therefore, in analyzing the role of foreign expertise in urban policies since the beginning of economic transition in Hanoi and Ouagadougou in this chapter and in the following one, I try to sort out the "tangle of relations" Collier refers to (in which clear neoliberal programs are to be found), rather than begin, a priori, with a study of processes of neoliberalization.

Policy connections are rarely of a single type. On the contrary, connections are often multiple in type and direction and they include both conservative and progressive types of policies. Thus, instead of searching a priori for processes of neoliberalization, I draw on the distinction between market-centered and social-centered policies elaborated by Savitch and Kantor (2002) in their classic comparative analysis of ten North American and European cities between 1970 and 2000. In their definition, "a social-centered development policy puts priority on strong public direction, activist planning, and preservationist policies. It also emphasizes collective benefits or public amenities [while market-centered] development emphasizes free development, minimalist planning, and strong economic growth" (Savitch and Kantor, 2002: 46).[4] This distinction is ideal typical: it should not be used to simply classify cities, but rather to situate them along a continuum between two poles. My aim here is not to reach the type of sophisticated categorization of urban policies produced in 2002 by Savitch and Kantor, but to use this simple but useful interpretive framework to look at how foreign expertise has transformed the planning of Ouagadougou and Hanoi since the beginning of their economic transition.

As in the previous chapter, the questions I ask here concern the intensity, form, and orientation of policy connections: what is their content? how do they develop in time? with which countries and cities are these relations established? In the following chapter, I look more precisely at the territorial aspect of these policies by focusing on how these relations generate the specific domain of policies for public space.

In this chapter, I show that transnational relations play an increasing role in forging both cities' policy and planning agendas, but that this role is largely dependent on local institutional strategies and on the divisions within state administrations. Social-centered policy relations are thus neglected in favor of market-centered ones in Hanoi, while in Ouagadougou the state and the municipality, both active in policy-making in relation to the national capital, tend to draw on differently oriented policy relations (market-centered for the state and social-oriented for the municipality). I first briefly explain my approach based on the distinction between market- and social-centered policies, and then show how Hanoi and Ouagadougou have developed their policy relations since 1990. In conclusion, I compare these two relational policy worlds and reflect on how Europe and North America are losing influence as providers of models of urban development.

Mobile Planners and City Networks

In 2010, an Italian urban planner I have known for many years told me of his visit a few days earlier to l'Elysée in Paris: as one of the invited participants in the design of the Great Paris project (*le Grand Paris*),[5] he had been personally received by President Sarkozy. The project for the metropolitan area of Paris, aiming to strengthen Paris' world-city status, was launched by Sarkozy in September 2007 and involved ten international and interdisciplinary teams in a consultancy round in 2008. The sophisticated and pompous process for *le Grand Paris* was suited to a long-established global city with ambitions to further climb up the few rungs to the very top of city rankings. It was clearly a process that went far beyond the nation-state since the French government had invited four teams led by foreign architects or planners. This demand for experts and expertise from abroad in a large city of the Northern hemisphere is symptomatic of the role of a global "consultocracy" in the domain of urban policy and planning.[6] These consultants are key elements in the making of transnational policy relations as they "are the type of actor creating connections across sites" (Prince, 2012: 10). But, as McCann and Ward (2010) point out, and as I show below, two other types of actors – local policy actors and informational infrastructures (individuals and institutions conveying interpretations of policies) – also play a role in establishing those relations.

In cities of the South such as Hanoi and Ouagadougou these policy relations are not new. During the colonial period, French architects and planners conceived master-plans for both cities. Then during the socialist period, Leningrad planners drew up master-plans for Hanoi, while foreign planners from donor countries contributed to master-planning in Ouagadougou. There is a long tradition of traveling experts and expertise in both cities; however, with time, foreign expertise has come to be more a matter of local choice and a search for innovative solutions, and less to do with (post)colonial domination or lack of local competencies in the domain. In the process, the role of experts has also changed: from being at the service of colonial administrations or embedded in the local administration, they tend now to be hired by local governments.

In narrating the story of transnational master-planning in Hanoi and Ouagadougou, I emphasize two points. The first is that connections with different political orientations and different effects often relate one city to many others. Thus, in the case of Hanoi, market-centered relations with other Asian countries have been much more effective in recent years than social-centered relations with European countries. The second point I make is that transnational relations are fields of tension and power struggle. The case of Ouagadougou shows that different institutional levels (national and local government) strategically use connections with different locales to foster policies with opposing aims. In comparative terms, the two cities have developed different kinds of policy relations: in parallel with what we saw in Chapter 2, the role of connections through private economy actors is stronger in Hanoi, while political connections are stronger in Ouagadougou, especially through the development of numerous inter-municipal collaborations.

Concrete and Paper in Hanoi's Urban Development

Plans and reality in urban development are often quite different things. In recent years, the gap between Hanoi's master-plans and the actual development of the city has been particularly notable. This might seem counter-intuitive in a country with an authoritarian state and a centralized government. But it is explicable when considering the collision between the great intensity of demographic and economic development and the incapacity of Vietnamese political institutions to deal with the consequences of rapid growth (see Chapter 2). Here I look at this discrepancy, focusing on policies supported by foreign consultants and analyzing which type of relations turns into concrete developments and which type remains on paper. In particular, I show that market-centered connections in today's Hanoi "get real" much more easily than social-centered ones.

Cosmetic master-planning[7]

Sharing with Ouagadougou a colonial past, Hanoi also shares a long history of foreign-conceived plans of urban development. The most significant colonial plan was made in 1924 by Ernest Hébrard for the French administration, one of the leading architects and urban planners in France at the time (Logan, 2000; Wright and Rabinow, 1982). Hébrard's plan, which remained a reference for some 20 years, was inspired both by the Haussmanian tradition – as developed in the metropole – and by the experience of French urban planning – developed in other colonies and particularly in Morocco.[8] The imprint of this plan is visible in the "French quarter," south of the historic city, characterized by its grid of 20–30 meter wide streets and its villas with surrounding gardens. With the establishment of the Democratic Republic of Vietnam in 1945 and the victory over the French nine years later, Hanoi did not shut itself out of foreign planning influences, but rather changed its orbit to revolve around the attraction of the Soviet Union.

In 1955, Vietnam became a full member of the Soviet bloc with access to institutions such as the Council for Mutual Economic Assistance, the International Bank for Economic Cooperation, and the (Soviet-sponsored) International Investment Bank. During that period, the Soviet Union was involved in implementing a large number of projects in Vietnam, notably in the industrial sector. It provided Vietnam with fuel, lubricants, iron, cotton, and 95 percent of its motor vehicles (Logan, 2000: 185). The big Soviet brother also provided consultants in urban planning. As a consequence, between independence and *Doi Moi*, Hanoi's master-plans were heavily influenced by Soviet planning if not directly designed by Soviet planners. In 1981, the fourth and last of the pre-*Doi Moi* master-plans, conceived to cover the period until 2000, was undertaken "with the assistance" of planners of the Institute of Urban Construction of Leningrad (Figure 3.1). These different plans focused on housing provision, industrial development, and the construction of public buildings.

The first post-*Doi Moi* master-plan in 1992 did not involve the active participation of any foreign consultants. However, this plan, focusing on heritage preservation and the development of new peripheral residential areas – with affordable housing and public services (parks, daycare, schools, etc.) – was heavily influenced by research conducted by the French between 1986 and 1988 (Genuit and Rijksen, 1994; Logan, 1995). Because this predominantly social-centered plan was not based on a sufficiently realist analysis of the resources available for its funding, it failed to meet its goals (Labbé and Boudreau, 2011). What happened instead in the 1990s was a boom in self-constructed housing, in which the new Hanoi middle class[9] invested its savings, and a similar boom in foreign invested commercial developments. Other national development agencies during the 1980s and 1990s (Australia in 1988, Sweden and New Zealand in 1999) like the French consultants, emphasized the need for heritage preservation, but these different efforts had minimal results.[10]

At the same time and progressively in the 1990s, the Municipality of Hanoi and the central national government were turning their gaze in other directions towards their Asian neighbors and the US for other types of development models. From the late 1990s onwards, we have

Figure 3.1 Hanoi Soviet master-plan.

a quick succession of foreign experts proposing great development visions with very little effect. Thus, the new 1998 master-plan, proposing a major expansion north of the Red River and the creation of satellite towns, was prepared by the San Francisco-based Bechtel engineering design consultants and was for the first time financed by a private corporation, the South Korean company Daewoo, which had already been active in the city with different completed projects. In parallel with this design process, a group of Vietnamese experts were sent abroad to learn from "advanced countries," for instance in the Office for Metropolitan Architecture (OMA) of Rotterdam.

The official version of the choice of consultants is that

> it was the chairman of [the City of] Hanoi who invited Daewoo, Bechtel, Koolhaas's OMA and Skidmore Owings and Merrill to work on this master-plan. They were chosen because they were the most famous companies at that time (Architect, interview November 19 2009).

This version indicates that the municipality took an active role in the selection of the foreign consultants. However, the unofficial version is different: "Daewoo and Bechtel had some relation with the People's Committee" (UN-Habitat Official, interview November 23 2009). Daewoo, for instance, had already built a hotel and a business center in Hanoi a few years earlier. The former Hanoi Chief Architect describes the relations this way:

> They did not ask for money. They did the consultancy totally for free [...] We paid the living cost for experts from Daewoo, Bechtel, and OMA. Later, we gave them some priorities in investment. For example, we gave Daewoo the chance to research [investment opportunities in] the West Lake Area (Architect, interview November 18 2009).

In other words, from the late 1990s onwards companies with direct interests in developments in Hanoi and therefore in the promotion of (massive) growth-centered plans became the main source of expertise in planning Vietnam's capital city. However, the 1997 Asian financial crisis seriously slowed down the regional economy for a couple of years and had important impacts on this development plan. In 1999, Daewoo, South Korea's second largest industrial conglomerate, went bankrupt and the projects north of the Red River did not materialize.

The early 2000s corresponded to a new round of economic liberalization in the country: through the new 2006 investment law and with the accession of Vietnam to a series of international organizations such as Asia-Europe Meeting, the Association of Southeast Asian Nations, and the WTO, foreign investment in Hanoi's urban development became very attractive. This context also created more opportunities for receiving support from international organizations such as the Japanese International Cooperation Agency (JICA), United Nations Development Programme (UNDP), and the World Bank. Within this new politico-economic framework, JICA, already active in the development of

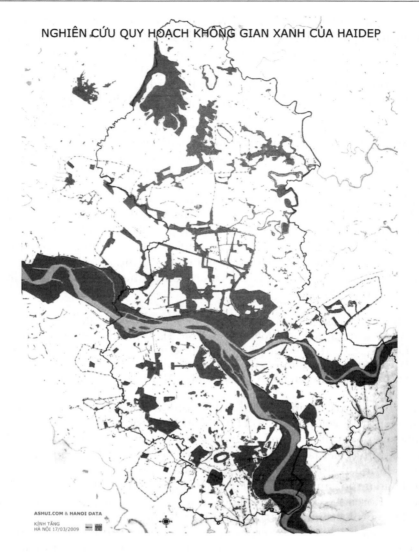

NGHIÊN CỨU QUY HOẠCH KHÔNG GIAN XANH CỦA HAIDEP

ASHUI.COM & HANOI DATA
KÍNH TẶNG
HÀ NỘI 17/03/2009

Figure 3.2   HAIDEP master-plan.

Hanoi's traffic infrastructure and one of the largest donors in Vietnam, approached the central government to give technical assistance to Hanoi's People's Committee in preparing a new master-plan for Hanoi. This new master-plan was developed between 2004 and 2007 under the name of HAIDEP (Hanoi Integrated Development and Environment Programme, Figure 3.2).

Again, there is an official and an unofficial version of this story. The official version serves to maintain the impression that the state is still in charge and continues some form of socialist development policy. According to the official version, the Japanese were approached by the Municipality of Hanoi. According to the unofficial one,

> the Japanese government wanted to extend business development in Vietnam [...] JICA suggested that HPC wrote a proposal to the Japanese government to ask for support [...]: they were the active ones (Urban Planner, interview November 19 2009).

So, here as well, the relations in terms of master-planning were, if we believe the unofficial version, established by interested foreign actors while the Municipality of Hanoi remained in a rather passive role. If the first (French) post-*Doi Moi* plan was poor in terms of economic and demographic projection, the "Japanese" plan relied on detailed 2010 and 2020 socio-economic projections. According to HAIDEP, urban development was meant to follow the creation of successive ring-roads while surrounding greenbelt was planned to contain sprawl and protect villages and agricultural land. In this 2007 plan, the achievement of rapid and large-scale development was conceived in quantitative terms rather than considering the qualitative or cultural aspects of development, such as environmental resources or architectural heritage. But, in comparison with previous and subsequent plans, it was probably the most feasible because it was based on a thorough analysis. Like the previous plan, HAIDEP's main target was to conquer the northern bank of the Red River. During the 1990s, the city had developed to the south where public investments had been targeted and road infrastructures had been improved, partly with the support of JICA. However, despite its positive qualities, the HAIDEP plan was never adopted because of a governmental *coup de théâtre*.

In August 2008, the government took specialists and the population by surprise: the prime minister announced a massive increase to the city's perimeter, to encompass large amounts of adjacent land, and in particular, the Ha Tay province to the west. This extended Hanoi had 6.23 m inhabitants on 3,344 km² in 2008 – in contrast with 3.4 m inhabitants on 1,000 km² in 2007, before the extension. The aim of this grand maneuver was to overtake the larger and more prosperous Ho Chi Minh City and make Hanoi a world city. For that purpose, a change of scale and an ambitious vision for the future, in the form of a master-plan for the metropolitan area, was needed. It is interesting to note that this decision was taken the year Beijing hosted the summer Olympics. Many government officials were impressed and inspired by Beijing's achievements for the Games.[11]

The new up-scaled master-plan was commissioned by the government in December 2008 with a contract of US$6.4 m awarded to a group of foreign consultants, PPJ, made up of POSCO Engineering & Construction (a South Korean company), Perkins Eastman (USA), and JINA (South Korea). It was the first time the Vietnamese government had invited and financed foreign consultants to design a master-plan. PPJ was personally selected by the prime minister from of a group of 12 invited contenders. Officially, the government chose the best project, but unofficially, observers[12] point to the personal ties between Perkins Eastman and the Vietnamese government. Moreover, the South Korean POSCO has been involved since 2006, together with the State Owned Enterprise VINACONEX, in the development of a huge residential area, An Khanh Splendora,[13] south of Hanoi. Considering the high level of corruption in the Vietnamese government (see Chapter 2), it would have been surprising if the choice of consultant had no connection with personal economic interests in the government.

The plan for the extended metropolitan area of Hanoi, presented to the government in April 2009, covers a timeframe to 2030 in detail, supplemented by a more general "vision" to 2050. It aims at creating a "top world sustainable metropolis" of 15 m inhabitants by 2030 with an average income per capita corresponding to South Korean levels.[14] A green belt and green corridors,[15] rapid mass transport infrastructures, and satellite cities in the new, enlarged city-region are a central feature of PPJ's plan for Hanoi (Figure 3.3). The plan is a promise of very important contracts for construction and infrastructure companies, as it supposes US$60 billion of investment to build technical infrastructure to 2030. It was heavily promoted during the festivities for the city's millennium anniversary, notably through a video showing Hanoi in 2030 as a mix of "Norman Foster-like" diamond-glass high-rises, science parks, and green spaces.[16]

The plan has been heavily criticized by Vietnamese planning professionals. They argue that it says very little about how it should be implemented: there is "no discussion of population density and population distribution, a necessary foundation for developing infrastructure" (Architect, interview November 23 2009); and "insufficient explanation concerning the nature of the green belt and corridors" (Municipal Official, interview November 23 2009). Others criticize the process: "the government invites foreign consultants and at the same time Vietnamese urban planners have no voice" (Architect, interview March 20 2010). The same influential architect suggested creating an opposing group of experts who would have designed an alternative plan to be submitted to the prime minister. In spite of these criticisms, the plan was approved in July 2011 by Vietnam's prime minister. However, it is

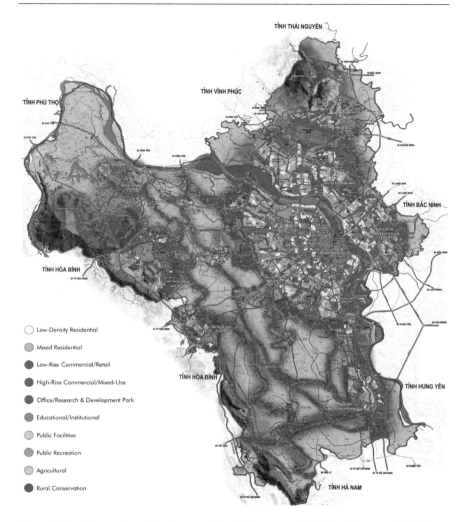

Figure 3.3　Master-planning Greater Hanoi. Courtesy of Perkins Eastman Architects PC.

more than likely that this master-plan, like the others since *Doi Moi*, will have very little effect on urban development. This is the case in many cities in developing countries (and elsewhere) and is often related to the difficulties foreign consultants have when engaging in the messiness of local political situations (Beall and Fox, 2009: 224). In this case, local observers point at the gap between the state's grand visions for the city's future and the "weak capacities to translate these political determinations into reality" (Sociologist, interview November 15 2009). They also consider that public administration "lacks the necessary skills [...] and does not know how to control urban development in Hanoi" (Architect, interview June 8 2009).

In addition, as long as the political structure and culture remain unchanged in Hanoi, elected government officials will have little interest in implementing long-term visions. They are elected for a non-renewable period of four years during which they seek to take advantage of their position and therefore encourage short-term projects in the area under their responsibility. Planners themselves mostly consider these plans as theoretical references, quite distant from actual planning realities. Master-planning in Hanoi can thus be seen as an aesthetic and political exercise, but it can also be seen as a useful smoke-screen behind which real development takes place with little consideration for the politically correct slogans (sustainability, heritage preservation, etc.) accompanying the master-plans. In other words, social-centered arguments have been mainly a gloss in official documents, while actually existing development has been very largely speculative and seeking short-term return on investment.

Master-planning of the type we see in post-*Doi Moi* Hanoi, with its insistence on a single image and development path for the entire city,[17] is an exercise that many planners across the world today would consider archaic as it supposes a strong public-steering capacity that generally does not exist.[18] The more collaborative and flexible strategic planning style, as developed in Ouagadougou and many other cities across the world, has not found effective support in Hanoi. A City Development Strategy (CDS), for instance, has been tested in seven Vietnamese cities, but not in Hanoi. Planners in Hanoi provide different explanations why this has not been the case, ranging from the size of the city (too big), insufficient funding, legal incompatibility (because of the special "laws for the capital"), lack of political support, and insufficiently competent municipal officials.[19] But also many officials lack specialized training and this is even more the case with the inclusion of officials from the rural areas that have been part of greater Hanoi since 2008: "they don't speak English and are not used to dealing with foreigners" (Former Municipal Official, interview November 23 2009).[20]

City networks, as we will see in the case of Ouagadougou, are another channel of policy relations, but they are rather weak in the case of Hanoi. There are exceptions, such as the renovation in 1999 of a "shophouse" – the traditional Southeast Asian building with a shop on the first floor – in the historic center (87, Ma May Street), with the support of the French city of Toulouse; the training of Vietnamese engineers by Lyon's Institut d'Urbanisme since 1997; and the cooperation between the Ile-de-France

Region and Hanoi, established in 2001.[21] But due to the government's desire to maintain strict control over the capital's development, such translocal relations have had a relatively limited impact on the recent transformations of the city. Therefore, on the whole, transnational relations are neither really generative of urban transformations through master-plans, which are essentially "cosmetic," nor through limited inter-municipal networks. They are rather to be found in thematic issues (such as public space policies, as I show in Chapter 4), in commercial developments, and in NGO interventions.

Performative transnational relations in Hanoi

While master-plans were suggesting their grand future visions on paper, SOEs and foreign investors were actively transforming Hanoi's built environment. Hotel multinationals like Hilton established themselves in the city center, fast-food giants like the US Kentucky Fried Chicken or the Japanese Lotteria opened outlets, large retailers such as the French group Casino established shopping malls, and transnational construction companies like the Indonesian Ciputra or the South Korean Posco were building high-rises or large peri-urban residential areas. Private companies have thus been much more effective than foreign planning consultants in reshaping the city's landscape.[22] This is a major difference from Ouagadougou, where planning through political partnerships is predominant.

The Pacific Place high-rises in the city center and Ciputra Hanoi International City in the northwest of Hanoi (Figure 0.2) are examples of "performative" transnational developments. Pacific Place, officially opened in May 2007, covers an area of 5,430 square meters and cost US$55 m (Figure 3.4). It was designed by the Hanoi-based, but French-owned, architectural studio Archetype. The project started as an investment by the Taiwanese Ever Fortune group and was initially named Forever Fortune, but was then sold to the French group Casino during the construction phase.

Pacific Place is a complex with pseudo-colonial architecture occupying the site of former industrial buildings demolished in the 1990s. Typical of developments in Hanoi since *Doi Moi*, it is a highly lucrative intervention in a prestige inner-city location (the French quarter) combining a commercial center, offices, restaurants, and a fitness club with luxury serviced apartments. It is promoted as a cosmopolitan haven for wealthy Hanoians and expats: "We offer you the ultimate in city living. Its unique location in the center of Hanoi will put you at the heart of the action; allowing you unrivalled access to all that the city has to offer," says its website.[23] It is one of many developments contributing

Figure 3.4   Pacific Place, Hanoi inner city gentrified. Photo by Bui Xuan Duong.

to the rapid and largely tourism-driven gentrification of Hanoi's center (see Chapter 5).

Ciputra Hanoi International City is on a much larger scale. Built on 323 hectares of former peach tree orchards, it is Hanoi's first master-planned neighborhood and also the city's first 100 percent foreign-invested urban development. The Indonesian company Ciputra was the initiator of the process and has been the investor, designer, and developer of this high-end gated community (Figure 3.5).[24] The total registered investment for the project was US$2.11 billion when it received building permission in 1996. The construction was halted by the Asian financial crisis and was subsequently undertaken in three successive phases between 2002 and 2010. For the Indonesian developer, Hanoi International City was a pilot project. Ciputra saw business opportunities in Vietnam at an early stage after the economic reforms of the early 1990s and approached Hanoi's People's Committee with their project in 1995. This US-style suburban development consists of a series of luxury housing high-rises and individual attached or detached villas strictly designed in uniform styles. Fifty percent of the residents are foreigners, somewhat below the developer's target of 60 percent. In 2010, villas were leased for between US$2,500 and US$4,500 a month, and apartments for between US$800

Figure 3.5   Ciputra Hanoi International City, entrance gate. Photo by Chu Giap.

and US$2,500 a month. The area has generated an exceptional source of income for the owners of property in the development: villas bought in 2004 for US$400,000 were worth US$2 m six years later. Noteworthy is the fact that the City of Hanoi let Ciputra plan the new town. They inaugurated thereby processes of private urban planning in the capital. Other similar developments have followed, such as the mixed-use development The Manor, and the South Korean-financed Splendora, both in the south of the city. Hanoi has thus become, like Phnom Penh, a new market opportunity for large Asian construction firms, notably South Korean companies seeking other opportunities when the national South Korean market became saturated.

Effective transnational planning relations in Hanoi are based on private master-planned developments, indifferent to official public comprehensive master-planning. Through such projects, the city, and especially its fringes, is witnessing the proliferation of very profitable middle- to upper-class enclaves inhabited by wealthy Vietnamese and expats.

However, transnational planning relations do also include other actors, in particular foreign development agencies and NGOs. Some development agencies, such as the Swedish International Development Agency in 1969, began their activity in Vietnam long before *Doi Moi*, but many others started their activities after 1986. In Hanoi, Scandinavian agencies have been involved in capacity building, while Japan, France, and the Asian Development Bank (ADB) have supported the construction of infrastructures. ADB, for instance, supports the development of metro systems in the country's two largest cities, Hanoi and HCMC, while the Agence Française de Développement (AFD) supports the development of Hanoi's public transport (bus and subway), and JICA the building of highways, flyovers, ring-roads, and the airport.[25] These are typical forms of development-based transnational relations which are progressively changing the city. However, infrastructures are still lagging behind urban development and many of these initiatives have not yet entered the phase of implementation. Critical observers consider that this is due to the fact that a significant amount of foreign aid "ends in the pockets of state officials" (Foreign planning expert established in Hanoi, interview September 20 2011).

Like Ouagadougou, Hanoi has a high density of foreign NGOs, some of them active in urban development and planning. The engagement of foreign and national NGOs in urban issues has been promoted by the World Bank in the framework of its "good governance" approach, emphasizing the role of civil society and public participation in urban development. The new national planning law (2009) requires authorities to "collect communities' comments" (art. 21) on plans. However, in practice, participation is still rare and experimental (Hoa, 2011). Rather, the involvement of civil society in urban development in Hanoi has taken place as resistance to speculative projects that threaten heritage and public space (Logan, 2000). The contribution of foreign NGOs in this context has been to support the voice of Hanoi citizens and associations resisting speculative projects, as well as trying to promote sustainable approaches to the city's urban development, as I show in more detail in the next chapter.

These alternative forms of transnational planning relations have limited impact compared to the activity of large foreign construction and planning companies. However, actors pleading for a more socially oriented form of urban development and who were quasi-invisible during the first years of economic transition, have slowly emerged and begun to be more visible in Hanoi's public sphere (Wells-Dang, 2011).

Policy relations through private enterprise have thus generally been more effective in Hanoi than state-to-state international relations. In Ouagadougou, the role of state-to-state relations has been more important, but they have been paralleled by – and in many ways contrasted with – the remarkable development of inter-municipal collaborations.

Ouagadougou's Competing Worlds of Policy Relations

When, in grasping power in 1983, Thomas Sankara conceived a revolutionary change in Burkina Faso, he gave a central role to a new urban policy for the country's capital. Ouagadougou was to reflect a national version of socialism and become the crucible of a new form of citizenship. It was a "laboratory to test and anchor the Revolution through the transformation of urban landscapes" (Fournet et al., 2009: 39). As we saw in Chapter 2, urban policy in that period was intended to crush the power of the old chiefdom system. Paradoxically when considering its anti-colonial aim, this revolutionary project was implemented using foreign models and consultancy. The new regime appropriated the methods of the French colonial authority, but gave them new symbolic aspirations: they created an orthogonal grid in the name of egalitarianism while the French had done it in the name of rationality and control. Moreover, while the government drastically reduced its reliance on foreign donors, it kept a close collaboration with the Dutch development agency. In 1984, a first master-plan was thus designed by the Dutch planning agency Haskoning following a concept (already proposed a few years earlier) of so-called "progressive settlement." The planning principle was to start with the allocation of land plots and then gradually to bring in infrastructures.[26]

In the late 1980s, Burkina Faso was put under strong pressure from the World Bank to neoliberalize its policy. Similarly, the City of Ouagadougou was pressured to implement the World Bank's urban development program. This program aimed at a reorganization of the administration, an increase in fiscal revenue, and the privatization of public services. Another World Bank program signed in 1994 and implemented in 1996 pursued the reform: it developed political decentralization, supported the training of city officials, and put emphasis on the development of infrastructures. Through these measures during the mid-1990s, Ouagadougou switched from a social-centered policy focusing on the production of housing accessible to the entire population to a more market-oriented policy focusing on infrastructures beneficial to economic development (Jaglin, 1995). New types of foreign experts, working for private companies instead of governmental development agencies, played a pivotal role in this policy change.

During these years, important ex-colonial linkages with France persisted. The Groupe Huit, a French agency founded in Tunisia in 1967, was active in the World Bank program and especially in the reorganization of the city administration. Since 1996, this agency, specialized in planning projects in cities of the South, has become the most important foreign consultant to the City of Ouagadougou, continuously present in its major phases of development and planning. Ex-colonial links also permeated the decentralization policy, heavily influenced by the French process led by François Mitterrand's socialist government after his election as president in 1981. This French model of decentralization, implemented under pressure from the World

Bank, has created a bicephalous form of urban governance, with each branch having different priorities and policy relations.

The state versus the municipality

Decentralization policy in Burkina Faso really came into its own with a legal framework of five new laws adopted in May 1993. This led to the first municipal elections, which took place in February 1995 in 33 communes of the country. In Ouagadougou, mayors for the city's five boroughs were elected and Simon Compaoré was elected mayor of the central municipality. This process of decentralization brought an important change in urban governance, since from the colonial period urban policy had been entirely under the purview of the central government. Ougadougou's development policy was decided by central government ministries and "all urban interventions were decided in function of governmental needs and without local participation whatsoever" (Zuppinger, 2005: 198).

Since the institution of municipal elections, urban governance has been bicephalous: the national government and the municipality develop their specific policies and development agendas. Despite decentralization, the national government strives to maintain its key role in urban development – through interventions in specific development projects of the Ministry of Housing and Urban Planning (Ministère de l'Habitat et de l'Urbanisme) or the head of state himself – and to leave issues of urban management to the municipality (Biehler, 2010: 533). However, the municipality is doing more than simple management: it is active in small and medium-sized developments, to a large extent thanks to its collaborations with other cities. Since 1995, the government has thus concentrated its efforts on major projects, deemed of national interest, while Mayor Simon Compaoré has elaborated a program based on more immediate needs, such as waste management, the creation of traffic infrastructures, and cultural facilities. To fulfill these programs, both "heads" have actively developed different forms of transnational collaborations. For the past 20 years, the state has favored two major development sites: the city center with the ZACA project; and the large area of Ouaga 2000, south of the city. These projects are two market-centered master-planned neighborhoods where foreign expertise has been mobilized in different ways by central government.

ZACA: building a capital   ZACA stands for Zone d'Activités Commerciales et Administratives (Commercial and Administrative Activity Zone) and corresponds to the business area in Ouagadougou's city center.[27] A first

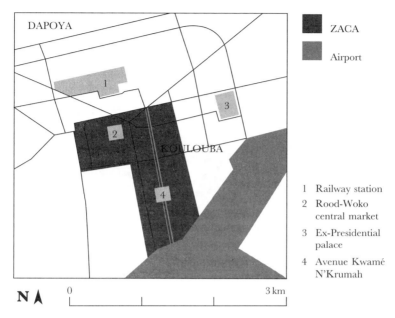

Figure 3.6 ZACA, in the center of Ouagadougou. Created by Blaise Dupuis.

phase of the ZACA development was planned in 1990, in the early years of the post-Sankara regime. It led to an intervention in the area of the central market, the Koulouba neighborhood, and the central Kwamé N'Krumah street axis (Figure 3.6). In November 2000, the council of ministers of the new regime decided to extend the area from 115 hectares to a total of 200 hectares with the aim of creating a business center worthy of a national capital. Improving the international profile of the city and providing investment opportunities are central aspects of the ongoing project.

It is significant that the municipality was completely left out of the picture as the national government provides itself with the means of total control over the operation. The government bought the land to gain control over property, set up an inter-ministerial organization to steer the project, and provided the financial means for its completion. Moreover, it used its legal right to expropriate landowners for reasons of public interest and provided evicted tenants or landowners with new housing in the periphery (Biehler and Le Bris, 2010: 419–420). This massive eviction of inhabitants did not go unchallenged: in 2001 it confronted a fierce opposition of inhabitants declaring "*on ne bouge pas.*"[28] The debate became national and for the first time urban planning was at the center of public attention. However, in contrast with the evictions

Figure 3.7   New cultural complex planned in ZACA. Courtesy of G2 Conception.

related to the projects of the revolutionary period, the government
decided to use persuasion and patience rather than force. This strategy
led to the hiring of a private communications agency and three years of
negotiation regarding the resettlement of, and compensation for, the
inhabitants (Biehler, 2010). Eventually, the large-scale demolition and
resettlement took place in 2003.

On this basis, in the same year the government launched the first
international planning competition in the country's history. With
this government-led master-plan competition for the city center,
Ouagadougou entered the circuit of publicly funded transnational
design.[29] The competition was won by a consortium of agencies from
Burkina Faso, Senegal, and France led by G2 Conception, one of the
country's largest agencies (Figure 3.7). The project consists of an
ambitious business and commercial area with activities in banking,
insurance, trading, and so on, complete with a five-star hotel
complex. A series of amenities – a park, an open-air theatre, public
spaces, and a square dedicated to "cultural promotion" – are planned
to make the area attractive for business. ZACA is considered by the
government as a "national priority" and is aimed at positioning the
city in the context of an international competition for economic
growth.[30] This typically market-centered project implies a radical
gentrification of the center for which it has been severely criticized.
Koulouba neighborhood's customary chief for instance declared: "I
have seen the model and for me the ZACA project is insulting for
a poor country such as ours. From what I see in the model, it's not
even Paris, it's New York: there are only high-rises and next to them
people starving to death."[31]

However, due to insufficient private investments and an over-ambitious project, the construction process has been very slow.[32] As a consequence, for many years the city has had at its center a huge no man's land.[33] In 2003, the same year the destruction of the area began, the large central market was destroyed by a fire. In the mid-2000s, the city center was thus "atomized" with both residents and merchants having to relocate in other parts of the city (Biehler and Le Bris, 2010: 476). But if the first of the government's two flagship projects is today still far from being completed, the second, Ouaga 2000, to which I now turn, has been completed at a faster pace.

Ouaga 2000: developing at the rhythm of international events Ouaga 2000 is more than a neighborhood. It is now the wealthy quasi-sister city of Ouagadougou, 10 km south of the city center. It was born out of the project to relocate the presidency and a series of governmental institutions, previously located in the center, for reasons of traffic congestion and security. It is also a new housing area planned for a total population of 90,000 inhabitants on 730 hectares of land. The project was first conceived in 1990 with a governmental decree creating a special planning zone of 1000 hectares, which then became "Ouaga 2000" in 1996. In 2003, the planning area was extended to 3116 hectares (Figure 3.8). But until 2007 there was no master-plan or functional zoning of the area to guide its development. A master-plan was eventually devised by the same agency working for ZACA: G2 Conception.

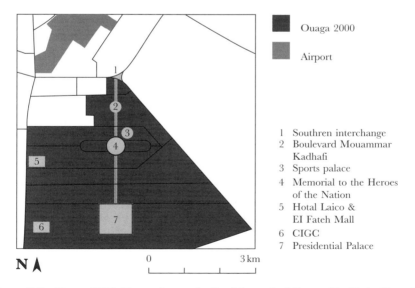

Figure 3.8   Ouaga 2000, Ouagadougou's elite "sister city." Created by Blaise Dupuis.

For the government, Ouaga 2000 should showcase the new Burkina Faso: modern, wealthy, ordered, and impressive. The area now hosts the presidential palace; ministerial villas; homes for the economic elite (bought mainly by Europeans and Burkinabè returning from abroad); embassies; and the five-star Laico Hotel and its adjacent shopping mall – all within a quasi-gated community.[34] The pace of its development has been set by the international agenda of the government and especially by large political or sports events, such as the France–African summit and the African Nations Football Cup in 1996, the African Union Organization meeting in 1998, and the 10th Sommet de la francophonie in 2004. Ouaga 2000's different phases of development have been completed just in time before each of these events.

Being a "presidential" special zone, Ouaga 2000 is the best place for partner countries to stage their "friendship." Therefore, ex-colonel Gaddafi's Libya[35] financed the first five-star hotel (Laico Hotel, formerly Hotel Libya) and the first shopping mall in Burkina Faso, inaugurated in 2005; while Taiwan provided more than half of the budget for the sports palace inaugurated in 2008.[36] In 2009, in order to enhance the area's profile and to develop the role of the city as a congress hub, the government launched Ouagadougou's second international architectural competition (after ZACA), this time for the building of the International Center for Large Conferences (CIGC). The competition was won by a French agency, Coldefy & Associés. In choosing this project, originally planned to be inaugurated by 2012, the jury chose a building with a strong iconic character, providing the city with a piece of global architectural capital (see Chapter 5).

Both in terms of process (with a quite flexible planning framework) and content (image-building, growth, and competition orientation), Burkina Faso's national government has thus been leading a strongly market-centered urban policy over the past 20 years. This policy consists of the creation of business and wealthy residential enclaves. In doing this, the government has carved out "spaces of sovereignty" where its vision of modernity is implemented within strictly defined borders. The pursuit of this particular vision of modernity has meant that connections to elsewhere have been more transnational than translocal, involving countries with which the government has intense diplomatic exchanges. In contrast, the municipality has been extensively and strategically developing translocal exchanges to sustain a different urban development agenda.

"Simonville" or the logics of translocal connections[37]

Since the beginning of the decentralization process in 1995, international relations have been important for the municipality. At first they were developed on the basis of personal contacts and targeted humanitarian interventions in the city. A second phase began with the second mandate of Mayor Simon Compaoré in 2001, with the creation of the Office for International Relations aiming at a more structured international activity around issues of economic and territorial development.[38] A third phase started in 2006, aiming at a reorganization of the municipality's administration and the reinforcement of its capacity to implement projects of urban development. Twelve conventions currently relate Ouagadougou to other cities in the North or the South.[39] In the framework of decentralized cooperation, funding for projects has also been provided by institutions such as the International Association of Francophone Mayors, the AFD, or the European Union (EU). In total, between 1995 and 2012, 25 billion CFA francs (US$47.3 m in 2012) have been invested by those different partners in the city of Ouagadougou.[40] In 2009, the budget of the city amounted to 16 billion CFA francs (US$30 m) of which 23 percent came from foreign funding.

A real globetrotter, Simon (as everybody in the city calls the mayor) travels a lot himself in search of new solutions and new inter-municipal collaborations. In some cases, he also travels to promote Ouagadougou's policies to other cities in the region. What is particularly interesting about the "foreign affairs" policy of the city is, on the one hand, the strategic use of international relations at city level, and on the other, the fact that South–South collaborations have clearly gained in importance in recent years. As the municipal official responsible for international relations put it:

> Future perspectives are primarily in South–South cooperation. Unfortunately, we were for too long concentrated on North–South relations and we only recently realized that cities in the South face similar challenges and issues. We need to mutualize successes but also failures to learn from our mistakes (Municipal Official, interview July 10 2012).

The municipality regularly receives African delegations – for instance from cities in Benin, Ghana, Djibouti, Madagascar, the Central African Republic, Congo-Brazzaville, Cameroon, or Chad.[41] There are cooperation projects with Douala, Dakar, Bamako, Cotonou, and Addis Ababa. The role of the city in such regional policy connections has been recognized and institutionalized with the creation of the Centre International de Formation des Acteurs Locaux in Ouagadougou in 2003. This center is supported by the United Nations and aims to reinforce decentralized cooperation in Francophone Africa.

The highlights of the visits by foreign delegations to Ouagadougou are the projects presented as the major successes of the city: the cleaning

Figure 3.9   The Green Squad, a translocal model. Photo by Pierrick Leu.

of streets, the waste management system, and green space policies. The "Green Squad" (Brigade Verte), for instance, a group of women working to clean the streets in the city center, has become a model, both in Burkina Faso and in neighboring countries: the cities of Koudougou in Burkina Faso and Cotonou in Benin created similar squads after visiting Ouagadougou (Figure 3.9). If Lyon provided technical tools and know-how in waste management, the Green Squad created in Ouagadougou is a solution that has been tailor-made to the economic means of the municipality and the social situation of its inhabitants. It is a telling example of how the municipality has not only imported "ready-made" urban policies from the North, but has also managed to "indigenize" them.

For the Green Squad initiative, Simon Compaoré drew inspiration from the "neighborhood departments," a social reinsertion policy in Lyon where socially marginalized people take care of public roads and collect garbage. The mayor established the Green Squad in 1995. It is made up of groups of (mostly) elderly and poor women (approximately 1700 in total), commonly called "Simon's women" in Ouagadougou, who sweep the asphalt roads and collect garbage.

This cleanliness policy with a social character focuses on embellishing the inner city: the political and touristic heart of the city. It has proved successful as the city center is generally considered to be much cleaner than those of other capitals in the sub-region. The municipality has been awarded various prizes for its Green Squad. It is also the reason for regular visits by delegations from cities in the region such as Niamey, Bamako, Abidjan, or Porto Novo. The Yaoundé prize ("Africités") was awarded to Ouagadougou as the cleanest city in Africa in 2003. Three years later it received the Dubai prize for Best Practices in Urban Management in the field of cleanliness. Finally, in 2008 the municipality received the Khalifa bin Salman Al Khalifa UN-Habitat Award of the prime minister of Bahrain. A delegation of "Simon's women" went to China to fetch it.

The Green Squad also has its downsides. It is a spatially selective cleanliness policy which tends to reinforce spatial segregation since peripheral areas, and even unpaved roads in the center, are poorly maintained or not cleaned at all.[42] As one of Biehler's interviewees from a peripheral neighborhood put it: "Simon's women only sweep where there's asphalt, where the rich live" (Biehler and Le Bris, 2010: 353).

The cooperation with the French city of Lyon is Ouagadougou's most important inter-municipal collaboration so far. In 1998, Ouagadougou first signed a convention of decentralized cooperation with the Grand Lyon (the metropolitan government), followed in 2002 by another with City of Lyon (the municipality). This collaboration was first concerned with the specific sector of waste and public space management and with a training program for the municipal administration.[43] More recently, between 2007 and 2010, Lyon contributed to the reorganization of municipal services through the work of an embedded adviser. This is a new approach for French cooperation activities as it is the first time a bilateral donor has directly supported a local authority. Together with multilateral organizations of collaboration, such as the EU and UN-Habitat, translocal exchanges with Lyon have also touched on the development of specific participatory procedures that I discuss in detail in Chapter 4.

The Lyon partnership is also pioneering in that since the 1990s it has put into practice the principle of decentralized cooperation. This form of policy relation focuses on concrete projects linking the technical services of municipalities, in contrast with the large-scale and often overly abstract urban policy programs of traditional state-to-state development aid. The role of Lyon has also been pivotal because of its involvement in the reorganization of Ouagadougou's administration.

However, a series of other inter-municipal cooperations with cities of the former metropole have also been established by the mayor in order to find resources for other aspects of the city's development program. Among them is a collaboration between the French city of Grenoble and Ouagadougou initiated in 1997 on four aspects of urban policy: cultural, civic, institutional, and academic. Within this framework, an innovative neighborhood-to-neighborhood partnership was established in 1999, which started with visits of groups of inhabitants from Grenoble's neighborhoods to Ouagadougou, as part of the civic cooperation program.[44] The aim of this form of cooperation is to establish long-lasting relations at the interpersonal level on the basis of neighborhood solidarity. Decentralized cooperation is thus downscaling policy relations from consultancy in master-planning to neighborhood partnerships.

Simon Compaoré has been the mayor of Ouagadougou since the beginning of political decentralization in Burkino Faso. According to Lyon's Project Manager for Foreign Relations, this guarantees the permanence of inter-urban cooperation (Pierre-Louis et al., 2007: 252). Moreover, since the beginning the mayor has emphasized foreign relations in a country that was progressively stepping out of a period of political and economic isolation. Financially, he has managed to find support for projects that promote social cohesion, cultural development, and community participation. Technically, his municipal services benefit from the knowledge of foreign experts. Politically, different prizes recently awarded to the management of Ouagadougou show that his promotion and style of local governance is well regarded by foreign partners. These results are the consequence of an efficient strategy aimed at finding the right partner to meet each of the main objectives of his program.

In contrast with the national government, the municipality has thus developed what is in many ways a social-centered urban policy. However, there are two important limitations to this translocal strategy: a social division of the city according to the services provided; and the personalization of political authority. First, projects undertaken through inter-urban cooperation respond to a series of important needs, but they are also part of an image-building process. The example of the Green Squad shows that the municipality places priority on cleaning the city center and the main roads in order to produce a favorable impression to the outside world. Secondly, Ouagadougou's urban policy is highly dependent on the charisma, initiative, and authority of its mayor. This personalization is efficient in the present but likely to be problematic in the long run. In the words of a French consultant who worked with the World Bank in the 1990s to improve the functioning of the administration:

> There are many actions that depend on the will of the mayor. My fear is based on the fact that many decisions are centralized – more than that, they are personalized. Obviously, the risk is that when the person is gone, things do not happen any longer (Consultant, interview May 19 2010).

To summarize then, there are clear tensions between two policy orientations in Ouagadougou led by different institutional levels and different forms of transnational relations. The transnational relations of the municipality are clearly more numerous and active. But, despite the existence of a municipal authority since 1995, the national government has acted forcefully from above to carve out two "zones of sovereignty" – ZACA and Ouaga 2000 – for its objectives and plans for the capital. These tensions between the government and the city are not only related to power games between parts of the same state apparatus that are controlled by members of the same party. As we saw in Chapter 2, they are also related to economic interests: all major entrepreneurs in the construction industry have relations with the president, Blaise Compaoré, his family, or his wife's family.

Most recently, these tensions have somewhat decreased with the institutional changes that have taken place aiming at a better coordination of territorial policies in the country. Urban planning is now considered to be a national priority within the framework of the national housing and urban development policy, adopted in 2008 and coordinated by the Ministry of Housing and Urbanism, which was created in 2006. The new national policy for the period 2009–2018 seeks to meet three targets: to increase the role of cities as poles of economic development within a balanced regional development process; to insure decent housing for the most disadvantaged sectors of the population; and to reduce urban poverty. Additionally, at the city level there are two initiatives with converging objectives: a CDS financed by UN-Habitat and a master-plan for the metropolitan area (*le Grand Ouaga*) were both made public in 2009. With these new tools and objectives seeking a balance between economic growth and poverty alleviation, Ouagadougou is today better equipped to develop a more coherent development strategy and overcome the tensions between the national government and the municipality.

As my analysis of Ouagadougou demonstrates, the world of policy relations in globalizing cities is often a battleground where different connections are used to support the competing strategies of different parts of the state apparatus. It also shows that two globalizing cities like Hanoi and Ouagadougou can develop very different policy relations generating very different forms of urban development.

Conclusion

I started this chapter by insisting on the fact that we need more than critiques of neoliberalism to make sense of newly established policy relations in globalizing cities of the South, and that we should, in particular, pay attention to local institutional strategies. In my analysis,

I observed how, since 1990, both Hanoi and Ouagadougou have witnessed the increasing importance of foreign expertise with a move from donor country assistance to locally funded private consultancy, and the emergence of master-planned neighborhoods catering for the economic and political elite – two quite neoliberal processes, in other words. But, using the distinction between market- and social-centered policies, I have also shown that there are substantial differences in the role of transnational policy relations between and within these cities, precisely because of institutional strategies.

In Vietnam's capital, a city with a booming economy, foreign experts, especially from the private sector, have eagerly tried to influence the planning and urban policy agenda. Large transnational companies have, for instance, "offered" their solutions through the design of long-term comprehensive master-plans. The discrepancy between predominantly symbolic and cosmetic collaborations and those with real effects on urban development is striking. I have shown how social-centered relations, in particular with European countries, are often of the first (cosmetic) type while market-centered connections – in particular with Asian partners – belong to the second. I have suggested that, in this context, large-scale master-planning in Hanoi since *Doi Moi* has acted as a sort of a smoke-screen hiding the predominance of speculative developments.

In Burkina Faso's capital city, transnational policy relations have been mobilized by the state and the municipality in a power struggle over the control of urban development. The national government has used them in the context of a strongly market-centered policy consisting of the creation of wealthy business and residential enclaves mobilizing transnational connections involving countries with which the government has intense diplomatic exchanges. In contrast, the municipality has extensively and strategically developed translocal exchanges to sustain a different, more social-centered urban development agenda. In Ouagadougou, therefore, the world of policy is a battleground where different connections are used to support competing strategies of different parts of the state apparatus.

What emerges from this longitudinal study of policy relations is also a new geopolitical urban development order. We saw in Chapter 2 how flows of capital, people, and information have changed in orientation since 1990. In this chapter, we have seen how this trend manifests itself in the domain of policy connections. In the early years of their economic transition, both cities were framing their urban policy in relation with their former metropole, France, and other predominantly European countries. In both cases, the scope of policy relations has widened over time. Ouagadougou maintains strong connections with

France; however, the very active role of its mayor in developing inter-municipal collaborations has opened the city to a much wider range of places – North Africa and the Middle East, in particular. The city has also become a regional model city and very self-consciously an exporter of "good practices" to other cities in the South. In contrast, Hanoi has witnessed a clear shift in geographical orientation, widening its policy relation horizon. The relations that count have clearly become those established with South Korea, Indonesia, and Japan, rather than with Europe. This geopolitical shift is accompanied by a transformation of priorities as these inter-Asian relations are much more market-centered than the waning European ones.

Here I have looked at policy relations to identify general changes in terms of their intensity, orientation, and content. As I argued in Chapter 1, in order to understand the generative power of the two cities' relational worlds, we need to look closely at how relations are territorialized in different domains of urban development (policies, forms, practices). This is what I do in the second part of this book (Chapters 4, 5, and 6), focusing first in the next chapter on a specific set of policies "in motion" – policies concerning public spaces – and their territorial effects.

Notes

1   For an analysis of these networks, see Clarke (2012a).
2   There are exceptions, of course. In his 1978–1979 teachings at the Collège de France, Foucault (2004) discussed neoliberalism at length. More recently, publications influenced by work in English-speaking scholarship debate the history of neoliberalism (Audier, 2012).
3   Inspired by urban research in the South and especially in South Africa, Parnell and Robinson (2012) take this discussion far beyond where I do here, identifying ways out of the "parochialism" of contemporary urban studies, of which critiques of neoliberalism, but also regime theory and gentrification studies, are part.
4   Savitch and Kantor (2002) also envisage a third hybrid form of urban policy in which public amenities can serve both social and market targets (such as attracting jobs).
5   The Grand Paris International Workshop aims at defining a long-term strategy for the development of the metropolitan area of Paris.
6   Washington's plan by the French engineer Pierre Charles L'Enfant in 1791, among others, shows that the phenomenon is not new.
7   I borrow the expression "cosmetic planning" from Crot (2006) and her work on Buenos Aires.
8   For an analysis of the circulation of French planning ideas and Morocco as a laboratory for social reform, see Rabinow (1989).

9   The fact that self-construction was a middle-class practice more than a practice of the poor in Hanoi during that period makes it a very specific case.

10   Heritage preservation only became effective in 2010 in relation to the city's millennium and the classification of part of the historic center as a UNESCO World Heritage Site.

11   See Chapter 5 on the impact of the Beijing Olympics on architectural design in Hanoi.

12   Interviews with Hanoi architects and planners in November 2009.

13   See www.splendora.vn.

14   According to the International Monetary Fund South Korea was ranked 34th in the world with a GDP per capita of US$22,778, while Vietnam was ranked 141st with a GDP per capita of US$1,374, http://www.imf.org/external/ns/cs.aspx?id=28 (accessed September 12 2012).

15   See Chapter 4 on the green belt policy.

16   See www.youtube.com/watch?v=nUqzlmYnQ-4&feature=player_embedded.

17   And therefore, not very different from pre-*Doi Moi* master-planning.

18   Vanessa Watson (2009: 2262) observes that "in much of the global South, master planning, zoning and visions of urban modernism are still the norm."

19   From interviews with Hanoi planners in November 2009.

20   For that reason, Vietnamese planners with experience across the country consider other cities like Da Nang, Vietnam's third city in size, to be more open to foreign expertise and contemporary planning methodologies.

21   The cooperation follows four axes: planning, public transport, environment, and tourism (www.imv-hanoi.com).

22   Examples of these projects are detailed in Chapters 5 and 6.

23   See www.pacificplace.vn.

24   The design process for Ciputra is developed in Chapter 5.

25   The Vietnam Urban Forum was created in 2001 to better coordinate the action of donors, both bilateral and multilateral, in the country's cities.

26   In 1990, three years after the end of the Sankara regime, a Dutch plan for the periphery projecting a series of centers at the margins of the city, was approved by the new government. Throughout a tumultuous political period, governmental policy for its capital was thus heavily influenced by the expertise of a foreign donor country.

27   It is also a reference to the courtyard (*zaka* in Mooré, the city's main language) in the traditional housing of the Moose, the largest ethnic group in Ouagadougou.

28   "We are not moving."

29   On the changing spaces of design, see Chapter 5.

30   This was made clear in Blaise Compaoré's presidential address at the beginning of his new (and theoretically last, according to the constitution) mandate in 2005.

31   Interview conducted in 2005 and quoted by Biehler (2010: 430).

32   Questioned about the near standstill of the project in a 2013 newspaper article, a French consultant with decades of experience in the city criticized the state's "megalomania" (*L'Economiste du Faso*, March 21 2013, p. 13).

33   It was still the case in July 2012, during my last visit to Ouagadougou.

34   "Quasi" because heavily controlled and cut off from the rest of the city, but without actual gates enclosing the whole area.

35   During the 1998 African Union Organization summit in Ouagadougou, Burkina Faso pleaded against the international embargo on Libya. The conception of the complex started the following year.

36   China was a partner of the Sankara regime, but Blaise Compaoré has turned to China's arch-enemy Taiwan in recent years, allowing Taiwan to gain some room for maneuver in a continent which has become a Chinese stronghold.

37   For a more developed analysis of translocal municipal policies in Ouagadougou, see Söderström et al. (2013).

38   Interview with a municipal official, July 10 2012.

39   After Loudun (France), Lyon (also France) was the first partner, followed by San Miniato (Italy), Kuwait City (Kuwait), Grenoble (France), Quebec (Canada), Turin (Italy), Kumasi (Ghana), Geneva (Switzerland), Bordeaux (France), Marrakech (Morocco), and Taipei (Taiwan).

40   This corresponds approximately to 32.8m euros (1,000 FCFA correspond to 1.52 euros). Source: *City of Ouagadougou, Report on Municipal Action, 1995–2008.*

41   Interview with the Head of International Relations, City of Ouagadougou, January 01 2010.

42   In this respect, there is a continuity between contemporary policies and the segregated planning of the colonial period which also neglected the fringes of the city (Quénot, 2007: 77).

43   Each year, 12–15 members of the municipal administration undertake two weeks of training in Lyon, while members of the Grand Lyon visit Ouagadougou each year to study specific themes.

44   This program has been developed by Grenoble's Service of International Relations. Currently it links three neighborhoods in Grenoble with three neighbourhoods in Ouagadougou: Berriat with Gounghin; Villeneuve with Tanghin; and Alliés with Dapoya.

4

Public Space Policies on the Move

In October 2011, the Vietnamese Ministry of Construction and a Canadian NGO jointly organized a workshop on public space in Hanoi that included Vietnamese professionals and officials and a group of international experts. I was one of the latter. The aim was to exchange experiences in public space policy. During the workshop, public space projects and institutional frameworks in Europe, Asia, Latin America, and North America were juxtaposed against the situation in Vietnam in a classic "best practice" perspective. This meeting is part of a web of connections that relate Hanoi to a series of other locales on issues of public space – a topic that takes on enhanced importance in a context of rapid urbanization and growing preoccupation with issues of urban livability. In a similar way, in Ouagadougou translocal relations – especially with Lyon, a city with an international reputation for its public spaces – are shaping public space policies.

In this chapter, I show that when we leave the general level of master-planning discussed in the previous chapter and focus on a specific domain of urban policy, the problems and contradictions of relationally produced policies become more visible. In other words, it is at this level that the differences in regulatory frameworks, spatial practices, and urban development histories across sites really come into play and that the tensions between the relational and territorial

Cities in Relations: Trajectories of Urban Development in Hanoi and Ouagadougou, First Edition. Ola Söderström.
© 2014 John Wiley & Sons, Ltd. Published 2014 by John Wiley & Sons, Ltd.

dimensions of urban policy-making come to the fore. This is particularly the case with public space policies, a domain especially sensitive to cultural diversity. Cities which are pioneers and best-practice exporters, like Copenhagen, Barcelona, or Lyon, all have ways of defining and regulating public space rooted in their specific contexts. These ways of thinking/doing public space cannot smoothly travel to cities like Hanoi and Ouagadougou, where ways of thinking/doing are different. Starting from the premise that policy mobilities are "dependent upon highly contingent translations and innovations" (Jacobs and Lees, 2013: 1560), my aim in this chapter is, therefore, to examine how these policies are fabricated through different and sometimes contradictory translocal relations, how different understandings and policies are sorted locally, and what happens when they are implemented.

As in the other chapters of this book, I compare the evolution and orientation of relational worlds in Hanoi and Ouagadougou. Here I also compare two different moments. In Hanoi I first look at a policy in the making because – if we consider the post-*Doi Moi* period – the issue of public space only recently appeared on the governmental agenda. Analyzing different and not-yet-assembled ingredients of a policy in the making allows me to pay critical attention to a series of potential and alternative policies (McFarlane, 2011). In Ouagadougou, a systematic public space policy came earlier than in Hanoi and was more directly influenced by European examples. Therefore I focus on problems generated by European-inspired public space designs, and especially on issues of public participation.

This chapter compares not only public spaces or public space policies, but the role of past and present transnational relations in their making. It shows how the type of relational comparison that this book promotes brings a critical postcolonial perspective to the analysis of cities in a world of cities. Arguing for the use of a repertoire of possible policy connections, it also advances methodological discussions in policy mobility studies. Hereafter, I first explain how this examination of public space policies speaks to recent work on translocal policy connections and define a typology of such connections useful for empirical analysis. Second, I clarify the specific meaning of public space in Hanoi and in Ouagadougou, showing the kinds of relations that have been critical in the making of their public space policies at different historical moments. Third, I analyze two specific processes: the emergence of public space as a policy problem in Hanoi; and the journey of participatory public space design from France to Ouagadougou. I conclude with reflections concerning the contrasts in the local reception of these policies, their acceptance or contestation.

A Repertoire of Translocal Connections

There is nothing new in the fact of urban policy connections. Policies "move" between cities for different reasons – emulation, learning, competition, and coercion (Peck 2011b: 786) – and have done so for a very long time. What has changed more recently, however, is the geographical pervasiveness, the intensity, and the velocity of the process. This process has been researched through various approaches in different disciplines. There is first a long tradition of work in political science and world polity theory on policy diffusion, policy transfers, or the globalization of norms and scripts in public administration (Dolowitz and Marsh, 1996; Meyer et al., 1997; Stone, 2004). Second, in planning history and theory there is a body of work that has moved from a diffusionist perspective looking at the power relations between sending places and receiving places (Ward, 1999) to perspectives that are more sensitive to the contingencies and complexities of these places (Healey, 2012; Healey and Upton, 2010; Nasr and Volait, 2003). Third, urban historians have looked at the constitution and evolution of transnational municipal networks in the 19th and 20th centuries (Saunier, 2001; Saunier, 2002; Saunier and Ewen, 2008). Fourth and finally, there is a growing body of work, mainly by geographers, on urban policy mobilities that pays specific attention to the spatialities of such processes (McCann and Ward, 2011a).

Authors in the field of geographies of policy mobilites have developed their perspectives mainly through a critique of the literature on unproblematized policy transfers, and have had little engagement with urban historians and planners.[1] They address three critiques to the literature in political science:

> it is limited in its definition of the agents involved in transfer […] it focuses solely on national territories without considering the possibility, or actuality, of intercity transfers […] Furthermore, it tends not to consider transfer as a socio-spatial process in which policies are changed as they travel (McCann and Ward, 2011a: xxii).

Drawing on Actor-Network Theory and Mobility Studies, McCann (2008) has proposed a research agenda paying attention to the unequal ways in which policies become mobile; the careful tracing of mobile policies; and an attention to the wider socio-historical contexts in which policies are developed and circulated (McCann, 2011).[2] Hence the term policy *mobility* instead of policy transfer, which pays less attention to the geographical trajectories of urban policies (McCann, 2008) and is less critical of policy content. Since 2006, there has been considerable discussion of the epistemological (Allen and Cochrane, 2007; Robinson, 2011c), methodological (Cochrane and Ward, 2012; McCann, 2011; McCann and Ward, 2010; Robinson, 2011a; Roy and Ong, 2011), and empirical (McFarlane, 2009; Prince, 2012; Ward, 2006) dimensions of policies in motion. What is at stake in this strand of research is an understanding of urban governance as going beyond both methodological nationalism, which limits policy-making to intra- or inter-national processes, and diffusionist approaches, which neglect what is contested and messy about the motion of policies. It leads us, in other words, to look carefully at *how* urban development is taking place within a global polity.

As I explain in what follows, looking at public space policies in the making, this chapter seeks to extend the empirical ground, the method-ological discussion, and the critical purchase of this field. In the broader context of this book, it allows for a better understanding of both cities' policy relations and a comparison of how they negotiate their positions as postcolonial cities.

Most empirical studies of policies in motion have been concerned with neoliberal policies, such as Business Improvements Districts (Ward, 2007), conditional cash-transfer (Peck and Theodore, 2010b), or creative city policies (Peck, 2011a; Wetzstein and Le Heron, 2010).[3] Public space policies are, in contrast, generally seen as progressive because the notion of public space, although differently understood by different actors, is generally associated with the development of meet-ing places, and sites of social interaction, democracy or contest (Staeheli and Mitchell, 2007). Moreover, material public spaces offer the possi-bility for non-violent dissent and therefore the struggle for their preser-vation, their free use, and development is central to emancipation and radical democracy (Springer, 2011).

However, neither the notion of public space nor actually existing public space policies can be considered as inherently progressive. First, because theoretical understandings of public space are not all partic-ularly progressive in their orientation: they vary widely from liberal-economistic to Marxist-feminist perspectives (Staeheli and Mitchell, 2007). Second, there is a gendered coding of the categories private/public, which makes the association between emancipation and (the often masculine) public space understandably problematic for fem-inist scholars (Bondi, 1998). Finally, historical (Harvey, 2006a) and contemporary (Staeheli and Mitchell, 2008) analyses of public space infrastructures show that they are often primarily profit-motivated and exclusionary rather than emancipatory. So, public space policies are only *potentially* progressive. Moreover, in postcolonial cities, there is, as we will see, a complex layering of forms and understandings of public space: 19th- and early 20th-century colonial urbanism inscribed bourgeois public spaces (squares, parks, promenades) in cities where private and public spheres were not clearly distinct. To put it in the words of the Indian political scientist Sudipta Kaviraj (1997: 86): "The idea of the public is a particular configuration of commonness that emerged in the capitalist-democratic West in the course of the eighteenth century." In recent years and in the context of entrepreneurial development strategies, such bourgeois public spaces make a comeback for the benefit of the middle classes and the elite but at the expense of the poors' access to urban open spaces (Arabindoo, 2011; Springer, 2009). This means that cities like Hanoi and Ouagadougou, with policy relations to multiple elsewheres are likely to be contentious fields for different understandings and types of public space policies.

This chapter also intends to advance a methodological contribution, arguing (as I show in the case of Hanoi) first, that translocal policy-making involves a whole repertoire of connections between various locales, and not simply the trajectory of a specific policy between two sites; and, second, that the critical purchase of urban mobility studies is enhanced by an analysis of policies "in the making." Until recently, there has been little methodological discussion in the field (Cochrane and Ward, 2012). However, since 2010, different contributions have defined specific ways of approaching policy circulations. McCann's (2011) research agenda proposes to trace the embodied and material means through which policies are put in motion. Building on work by Allen (2003; 2008), Robinson (2011c) suggests moving beyond a focus on the material trajectories of policies, not only to trace circulations and follow connections, but to look also at topological relations. Contrasting topographical relations in Euclidian space, topological relations refer to the reach of ideas, principles, or models through means that are not necessarily material and cannot always be easily followed across space. It refers to the "often messy and unmappable complexity" (Robinson, 2011c: 26) of policy circulation including "ephemeral spaces of interaction and communication, half-forgotten meetings, fleeting encounters, rumours, and long buried memories of policy terminology" (ibid.: 10). In her view the point is to study "how policies are arrived at, rather than tracing how they arrive from elsewhere" (ibid.: 9), which involves a detailed analysis of the places where policies are assembled (McCann and Ward, 2012).

In a similar vein, Roy and Ong (2011) consider what they call "inter-referencing" as one of the ways of imagining oneself in cities as part of the world. Ong (2011: 17) writes, "while urban modeling is a concrete instantiation of acknowledging another city's achievements, inter-referencing refers more broadly to practices of citation, allusion, aspiration, comparison and competition." In this case as well, the meth-odological implication is that policies are not to be followed across topo-graphical space, but studied through acts of imagination in discourse, texts, and visual representations.

This body of work invites us to examine policy exchanges by keeping in mind a repertoire that includes the actual travels of people, ideas, images, the role of meeting places (conferences for instance), and specific transfer agents, as well as more immaterial means of connection such as citations, visits, interventions, and policies present in the minds of actors such as planners, architects, or city officials. When we look at the making of public space policies, we have in fact a combination of these different elements – policy mobility, topological relations, and inter-referencing – of the policy circulation repertoire, as I show below for Hanoi.

Finally, by investigating the moment when a new type of urban policy is crafted, which is the case with public spaces in Hanoi, we can also observe the presence of "loose threads" – potential policies within these different translocal connections before the choice and black-boxing of a specific solution. As I show in the first part of this chapter, this gives us the possibility to critically examine the politics of policy connections.

To be interpreted properly, present efforts to develop a policy for public spaces in both cities need to be put into context. This is the aim of the following section that briefly describes how public space is generally understood and practiced in Hanoi and Ouagadougou, and shows that physical public spaces in both cities are the result of previous translocal connections.

Public Space: Understandings, Practices and Things

Cultures of public space in Ouagadougou and Hanoi differ for a number of reasons – climatic conditions, urban history, ethnicity, and so on – but they also display a number of similarities: the simultaneous multiple uses of streets; the presence of domestic and small commercial activities on the sidewalks; the French colonial legacy; the legacy of socialist conceptions of public spaces; and recent processes of privatiza-tion. These similarities and the contrasts between them, and also cities "elsewhere" that act as role models for contemporary public space pol-icies, are important in the context of this chapter on relational policies. Therefore, I briefly summarize these common features in what follows.

In a recent study, Drummond and Lien (2008: 185) show that public space is generally understood by both younger and older people in Hanoi as spaces for everyone's use. When interviewees were asked about what public space refers to, they generally mentioned streets, sidewalks, swimming pools, residential areas, squares, and parks. There was more disagreement on whether closed places such as hotels, game rooms, and Internet cafes qualified as public spaces (Drummond and Lien, 2008: 185). Our interviews with architects, planners, and governmental officials in Hanoi revealed that definitions among professionals are often just as imprecise as those of non-professionals. In other words, there is generally no clear consensus on what constitutes public spaces. In legal planning documents, the term has only appeared very recently. It is mentioned in the 2003 Law on Construction (art. 3), and in the 2008 Vietnam Construction Standard (art. 2.6.1). It also appears in an important governmental decree of 2009 (Decree No 42) as one of the criteria (art. 6) to be used to classify all Vietnamese cities according to six different grades. However, none of these legal documents defines the type of locations that are supposed to constitute public space, and the term is used in very different ways by architects, planners, and government officials. Therefore, the Urban Development Agency, the policy advising body under the Ministry of Construction, is presently (in 2013) working on a general and operational definition of the term as they revise Vietnam's public space policy.

The process of conceptual definition is thus still underway, which means that uncertainty and indeterminacy characterize debates over public space policy. This definitional phase is not anecdotal. It was important in the making of European public space policy in the 1980s and 1990s, as it allowed cities to reorganize their municipal services under a common "public space" office or service to manage domains of planning (parks, streets, plazas) that were previously considered separately within different technical services (Thomas, 2001: 81).

In Ouagadougou, understandings of public space vary according to ethnicity: Peulh nomads, Bobo from western Burkina Faso, or Lobi from the south of the country have different definitions and ways of using public space. However, beyond such differences, inhabitants of the city share a basic distinction between built and non-built space (Dévérin-Kouanda, 1990). The former corresponds to private properties and the latter to public space, understood negatively as "belonging to nobody" (Dévérin-Kouanda, 1990: 94). This understanding is related to the way in which streets are generated in Burkina Faso's urbanizing areas: streets emerge "negatively" from spaces that have not been built on, rather than from a priori public space planning. In the same spirit, Ouagalese tend to consider that no authority governs public space and to therefore use it to throw things away, to store building material and for unplanned social interaction – all the things they prefer not to do in their own courtyards (Dévérin-Kouanda, 1990: 97). This neglect of public space also pervades planning practice. As the state official responsible for urban planning at national level puts it:

> There is no strategy for public spaces, no structured approach [...] It is something we have forgotten. Our planning procedures are a colonial legacy: the relation people have to their spaces has been lost. If you go to villages, the relation to public space is crucial. But, when we first started creating residential areas after independence, we considered those spaces as empty spaces and built on them, forgetting they had a social function (State Official, interview July 12 2012).

However, this does not imply that there is no official definition of public space in Burkina Faso: in the "infrastructure grid" (*grille des équipements*) established by the Ministry of Housing and Urban Planning, public spaces fall into three categories: green spaces, squares, and gardens. Here again, we have a colonial legacy: these are French categories that do not correspond to a Burkinabè practice of urban space in which, as I show below, streets are privileged and there is no tradition of going to the park or the neighborhood square.

These understandings are, of course, inseparable from specific uses of public space. Lisa Drummond shows that sidewalks in Hanoi are used for domestic activities like cooking or washing and for commercial operations such as repairing motorbikes or selling food (Drummond, 2000). People also sweep the pavement in front of their homes and appropriate it with objects big and small, such as chairs, tables, or stalls (Figure 4.1). This is what Drummond (2000) calls the "inside-out" in the relations between private and public space. It is related to the high density of the city and the subsequent lack of domestic space, as well as to a long tradition in Hanoi's trade quarters, as well as many other Asian cities, of using the area in front of the shophouses as intermediate or mixed spaces.[4]

Additionally, to understand Hanoians' use of public space, one should look at it temporally. During the course of the day, spaces regularly change uses and users. In the morning sidewalks might be swept by the residents and used to cook and sell the popular Pho (noodle soup) for breakfast, while others might use the sidewalk in the morning as an outdoor quasi-private space to wash their hair, shave, or dry their clothes. In the afternoon, the same sidewalk might be used as a guarded parking space and in the evening plastic chairs and tables might turn it into a restaurant.

Similarly in Ouagadougou, streets and sidewalks are by far the most important public space. The type of activity varies according to the width of the streets and whether they are asphalted or not. In the center, the 20–30 meter wide streets are inherited from French colonial urban planning and are mostly asphalted. Spaces along these roads are the

Figure 4.1   "Inside-out" in Hanoi. Photo by Ola Söderström.

most attractive for informal commerce as they are the most densely used. They are therefore spaces where negotiations take place between street vendors, landowners, and the municipality around rights of use and taxes (Steck, 2006–2007). *Le goudron* – asphalt – is much more than a technical term in Ouagadoudou: it distinguishes formal wealthier parts of the city from others.[5] The non-asphalted six-meter streets that people simply call *les six mètres* host another type of public life. These are places where people have tea, have a nap on a mat, sell girdle-cakes, or play soccer. They are also nearly seamlessly related to the house court-yards, so that domestic activities, like washing dishes or laundry, take place in this continuous space between houses and streets.

Cultures of public space are also shaped by the specific physical struc-ture of the place. It is often claimed that Hanoi's particular structure was introduced by the French at the turn of the 20th century with the application of planning principles separating private and public activ-ities (Drummond, 2000: 2381). The infrastructure of public spaces would then be essentially a colonial legacy, raising the question of its meaning and appropriation by the Vietnamese. However, open spaces for public use predate the colonial period and, at the same time, are composed of different postcolonial layers. The ancient city of Thang Long (founded in the 11th century) had two main types of public space. The royal citadel had its open ceremonial space, while the public spaces outside the citadel were composed of trading streets, with public buildings – such as the communal house and the pagoda – and by other spaces of smaller sizes, such as the fountains and markets near neighborhood gates (Luan, 1997: 168; Thong, 2001: 17).

The French added a second layer of public space by importing the bourgeois concept of public space, recently developed by Haussmann in his transformation of Paris. Whereas in traditional Hanoi, public space was purely for people to meet in groups defined by their level of education, religious affiliation, or a common trade, this new form of public space was shaped for the leisure activities of the bourgeoisie, military control of the city, and the free circulation "of money, commodities and people" (Harvey, 2006a: 26).

A third layer is inherited from the "hard core" socialist period (1945–1986). It is composed of large squares used mainly for national parades and political propaganda, and collective playgrounds and athletic fields situated within the socialist housing estates (*khu tap the*), designed in partnership with North Korea, Cuba, and the former Eastern Europe. However, between 1954 (victory over the French) and 1975 (marking the end of the war with the US), public space policies were very limited and priorities were clearly elsewhere. The same is true for the subsequent phase between 1975 and the early 1990s.

Since then, Hanoi has been characterized by two contradictory movements. The first is a spectacular resurgence of public life driven by the development of commercial activities; and second, a radical change in the government's attitude towards urban areas – having been considered as places of depravity, with *Doi Moi* they became the pivots of the country's economic growth strategy. In research carried out in 2000, Mandy Thomas evokes the stark "contrast between the ascetic, carceral Hanoi of the 1980s and the sensuous, lively Hanoi of the present" (Thomas, 2002: 1616). Prior to the 1990s, there was indeed very little to buy in the shops and streets of the capital, due to the commercial embargo by many Western countries and to state control over the economy. With successive measures of economic liberalization and the end of US embargo in 1994, the streets now bustle with formal and informal commercial activities.

There has also been a second and much more negative development in the use of public space. With economic liberalization, Hanoi has experienced a process of destruction, privatization, and commercialization of public space.[6] The loss and transformation of public space in Hanoi has taken different forms: the disappearance of the lakes, victims of speculative developments; the invasion of motorbikes and cars; the introduction of entrance fees for public parks; the transformation of public markets into shopping malls and of socialist communal housing into commercial gated communities; and the construction of golf courses on village and rice-field land at the peripheries. This recent period has therefore seen the erasure of part of the pre-existing network of public spaces, but also its modest extension with some parks and plazas built within new public housing developments at the peripheries.

Public spaces in Ouagadougou include markets, gardens, squares, and streets (Biehler, 2010: 329–334).[7] The market is constitutive of the city's historical origin as I explained in Chapter 1. Open every day, it is a veritable structuring principle of public life, where people meet, work, and buy. Spaces around the market itself are multifunctional: they are often used for political gatherings and public discussions (ibid.: 329). Markets in Ouagadougou are located both in the center and distributed through the city's different neighborhoods. They are also historically "mobile," developing in squares and streets. This was specifically the case between 2003 and 2009, when the central market had burnt down and was not yet rebuilt. During that period, a series of small markets appeared and the city witnessed a proliferation of market spaces that diminished but did not disappear with the re-opening of the central market.

Municipal gardens – resembling small French "squares" – are recent additions to the city's infrastructure of public spaces that are closely related to inter-municipal networks. The first twinning, with the French city of Loudun in 1967, is at the origin of Ouagadougou's first municipal garden, situated in the center: le Jardin de l'Amitié. During the mayor's first mandate (1995–2000), which had the environment as its priority, some ten municipal gardens were created with the technical assistance of the city of Lyon. Since 2000, to reduce costs, gardens have been financed by the private sector: entrepreneurs pay for the construction, for which they have to follow municipal guidelines (Figure 4.2); and the management of the gardens is usually given to bar or restaurant-owners.

The municipality establishes the duties of the gardens managers but does not control the prices of what they sell – usually between one-and-a-half times and double the prices in other bars. Since the gardens can only be used by those buying beer or food, they are in effect the preserve of the city's elite, whom people in Ouagadougou call "those in charge" (*les responsables*). This is justified by the municipality in order to limit the number of users and their environmental impact:

> If beer was sold at the same price it is sold in the bars of the neighborhood, it would attract a lot of people and degrade the environment. By selling beer at a higher price, you can select your customers. It is true that logically these gardens should be managed by the municipality, but that's very costly: you have to pay for water, electricity, lamps, toilets, trimming and watering the plants, etc. (Municipal Official, interview July 9 2012).

Figure 4.2 A privately managed and densely built municipal garden in Tampouy, Ouagadougou. Photo by Jonas Haenggi.

The same process characterizes the management of the city's (rare) squares, leading inhabitants to criticize the disparities between the rich and the poor in access to public space (Biehler, 2010: 486). In the context of weak public finances, the municipality considers privatization the best solution, and equal access to those spaces is not a priority.

Both cities are thus grappling with the development of a postcolonial public space policy. From the colonial period they have inherited physical spaces as well as French ways of defining public space. In the present situation, characterized by intense urban growth, they are confronted both with the necessity to develop their public space infrastructure, and to make it relevant to local cultures of public space. To investigate the role of translocal connections in this context, in what follows I look first at the making of a public space policy in Hanoi and then at the problems related to the adoption of European participatory public space design procedures in Ouagadougou.

Translocal Connections and Public Space Policy in the Making

In Hanoi, public space came to the fore as a public problem with the urban development of the 1990s. In 1996, a vehement public protest, officially backed for the first time by professional organizations such as the Vietnamese Architects' Association, stopped the construction of the Golden Hanoi Hotel on the banks of Lake Hoan Kiem (Logan, 2000: 238; Thomas, 2002: 1619). The planned 11-storey building would have limited the views of the lake, the public space which constitutes the center of today's capital of Vietnam. A series of other generally low-intensity reactions followed other encroachments on public space in the years thereafter. In spring 2007, Hanoi's municipality approved the plan elaborated by private companies to turn Unification Park, the largest park in the city center situated south of Hoan Kiem (Figure 0.2), into a theme park. The reaction of local residents, of influential public figures, and of a Canadian NGO, eventually forced the city authorities to back down and freeze the plan (Wells-Dang, 2011).

Although Unification Park has continued to stimulate the appetite of developers – a project for a luxury hotel was announced and eventually halted after a new public outcry in 2009 – this event marks a turning point regarding public space policy in Hanoi because of the strong and massive indignation it provoked. Those who had opposed the project felt that it was time to move from informal to more formal types of action and organization.[8] Some government officials, on their side, interpreted the Unification Park controversy as a sign that more importance should be placed on the issue of public space and that institutional changes were therefore necessary.

I will now look at this process in more detail, putting special emphasis on the role of translocal connections, exchanges, and circulation and showing that the three different registers discussed in the introduction to this chapter are involved: policy mobilities, topological relations, and inter-referencing.

Policy mobility

When the present Hanoi master-plan was first officially presented in April 2009, the PPJ Consortium – author of the plan[9] – advised the government to address a series of important needs, among which were urban management, transport, and public space. In terms of public space, the most important contribution of the master-plan itself is the preservation and creation of different categories of green spaces. The master-plan includes a large green belt[10] that protects productive farmland, flood management areas, natural areas, craft and trade villages, and historic relics. In addition, there are green corridors that are intended to function as green buffer zones, and a series of east–west linear parks providing a link between the green corridors and the larger green belt. Whereas the main function of the green belt is to preserve agriculture and traditional villages, the aim of the green corridors and linear parks is to create leisure space for Hanoians.

Green corridors and belts are a classic feature of metropolitan-scale urban planning. Such functions gained prominence at the turn of the 20th century with the influential writings of Ebenezer Howard and Raymond Unwin. The policy was first adopted by London City Council in 1935 and was later taken up by Patrick Abercrombie as part of the Greater London Plan in 1944. Its main aim was to control London's urban sprawl, and it rapidly became a policy in motion: in the late 1940s, central figures of British urban planning such as Abercrombie and Frederick James Osborn traveled extensively to disseminate the green belt strategy abroad (Amati, 2008). It was adopted between the 1950s and 1970s in different contexts in Europe, North America, Asia, South Africa, and Latin America. Tokyo adopted it in 1956 and Seoul in 1970.

The importation of the green belt policy to Hanoi did not follow a straight route from the UK to Vietnam, but was filtered through the experience of such policies as they were implemented in Seoul, South Korea.[11] This is not surprising, given that Seoul has been a model city for Vietnamese authorities in recent years, and that Seoul's green belt was well known to the South Korean-led PPJ Consortium, author of the plan.[12] However, it is more surprising to see Hanoi emulating Seoul's green belt policy at a moment when that policy is being contested in the South Korean capital, for two reasons: first, it has failed to contain urban sprawl in Seoul; and second, such strict land-use regulation has been deemed "undemocratic" by some of South Korea's political parties (Kim and Kim, 2008). The apparent contradiction of Hanoi adopting a model that is in crisis elsewhere can be considered as either the result of a simple cut-and-paste policy-making process, or as a more subtle strategy. In the latter interpretation, it is the morphology of the city and political system of Hanoi that justifies going forward with the proposed master-plan. Despite recent sprawl, Hanoi remains, indeed, quite compact compared to many other cities with high growth rates. Moreover, its urban planning is still characterized by socialist-modernist planning principles, based on strict land-use regulation and standards of public service provision calculated on per capita bases.[13] In a country governed by a single party and a city ruled by special laws, authorities like to think they can still channel urban growth despite the fact that reality does not follow most of their plans.[14] This seemingly anachronistic mobility of a well-known, originally European urban policy would, in this case, proceed from Seoul's role as a regional model and an interpretation by PPJ of the Vietnamese authorities' ways of seeing their role in regulating urban development.

Not surprisingly, the authorities are already facing contradictions. Vietnamese planners are at pains to implement this imported policy, because it is already being undermined by part of the land within the green belts and corridors already being leased to developers.[15] As conceived, the possibility of seeing this metropolitan-scale public space policy realized would seem to be significantly compromised.

Topological policy relations

As noted earlier, the existence of a local public space policy became a criterion for the national ranking of urban centers in 2009. The 2009 decree was introduced at governmental level on the initiative of the director of the Urban Development Agency.[16] When asked about the motivations and origins of such an initiative, the director mentioned a summer course on Asian urban development she had attended at the East–west Center of the University of Hawaii. The course, organized by Michael Douglass, an internationally renowned specialist on the dynamics of public space in Southeast Asia (Douglass and Daniere, 2008; Douglass and Ho, 2008), had a strong focus on public space. Since 2000, over 100 Vietnamese planners have been sensitized to the importance of public space through this regularly organized training, by Douglass's frequent conferences in Hanoi, and through his numerous publications on public space in the region. Douglass is interested in what he calls "civic space," defined as "socially inclusive spaces with a high degree of autonomy from the state and commercial interests" (Douglass, 2008: 27): a definition that is very close to Habermas's definition of the public sphere (*Öffentlichkeit*) (Habermas, 1962). Douglass's influence does not take the form of a policy traveling from Hawaii to Hanoi in the way waterfront regeneration or business district programs, for example, can be seen to have traveled internationally. It is rather a discourse on the importance of a certain form of public space, which then "pops up" in particular work situations encountered by Vietnamese planners. The introduction of public space as a general criterion for the classification of Vietnamese cities in different tiers is one of those instances when a discourse becomes performative. If we refer to John Allen's definition of "topological policy spaces," we have here ideas which are not fully fledged policies but which, nonetheless, have a reach that makes them effective in policy-making (Allen, 2008).

Public space policies can be developed at governmental level by laws and decrees, such as the one issued by the Ministry of Construction in 2009. Even more important for a change to happen in this domain is a cultural shift both within professional circles and in the general public. "Inter-referencing" is an important tool of cultural change since it acts, as Ong (2011) points out, at the level of imagination: referring one city to another makes us imagine our city as it could be or become.

Inter-referencing

In 2007, when people in Hanoi reacted against the project to construct a sort of Disneyland in Unification Park, the Canadian NGO HealthBridge initiated a campaign to save the park by creating a platform to counter the plan. Its action was oriented towards directly communicating with government bodies, working with professional associations, and launching a public campaign involving traditional and electronic media (Wells-Dang, 2011). The impact of this campaign on public opinion, as well as the credibility attached to the sponsoring organization's international standing, played an important role in the decision of public authorities to stop the plan (ibid.).

Since then, HealthBridge has continued to work on urban planning issues, notably by promoting knowledge about urban policies in other countries or cities. Their *modus operandi* is, in other words, to promote translocal learning processes (McFarlane, 2011), organizing workshops and publishing reports on different aspects of public space policy, such as pedestrianization, fresh markets, or parks. Their reports effectively use before-and-after images to show how other cities have found successful solutions to questions of public space (Figure 4.3).

During the subsequent controversies over Unification Park in 2009 (this time involving the construction of a luxury hotel), 2010, and 2011, the NGO organized three further workshops on public space in Hanoi. Each workshop brought experts and examples from abroad

BOGOTA 'BEFORE'   BOGOTA 'AFTER'

Figure 4.3 Bogotà before and after. Courtesy 8-80 Cities, Gil Penalosa.

and discussed possibilities for how Hanoi could learn from this these examples.[17]

Finally, HealthBridge also played a strategic role in introducing Hanoi to the work of Danish architect Jan Gehl, a pioneer of public space design. Though he has been called in as a consultant in many cities throughout the world, Gehl (2010) is still strongly associated with the pedestrianization of the city of Copenhagen in the 1960s. In 2008, Gehl made his first visit to Hanoi to lecture at the Hanoi Architectural University. HealthBridge then decided to translate his book *Life Between Buildings*, initially published in 1971, into Vietnamese. Gehl returned to Hanoi for the launch of the Vietnamese version of the book in 2009, when he also gave his views on the master-plan to the public authorities. In this book, Gehl promotes a new perspective on urban design, which starts from the "void" of public space rather than from the buildings, as is usually the case: his take on public space focuses on material forms and the process of their design.

In the wake of examples introduced by the Canadian NGO, Hanoi professionals and city officials have been comparing their city with others and imagining it, or parts of it, morphing into Berlin, Bogotá, Toronto, or Copenhagen. These examples indicate different pathways for the future of Hanoi's public spaces, and support the imaginative projections of Vietnamese professionals, government officials and, through the media, of larger sectors of the population.

Through these different forms of connection to elsewhere – mobile policies, topological relations, and inter-referencing – Hanoi has been informed by different perspectives on what public space is, and could be, at different scales of intervention, from the metropolitan scale to that of the spaces between buildings.

The Politics of Translocal Connections

The structural conditions for the development of public space in Hanoi are clearly unfavorable. The city's population density is very high, the private sector puts great pressure on scarce available land for construction, and the government is reluctant to create spaces that could potentially foster political contestation. Nonetheless, some form of public space policy in Hanoi is today in the making, especially under the influence of non-state actors.[18] However, the contours of such a policy are still very uncertain. To put it in the terms of the sociology of social problems, we are in the phase of a construction of a new public problem (Gusfield, 1984).

In this situation of uncertainty, what is "on the table" is a series of different ideas, references, policies, and negotiations with different actors. There are as yet different translocal connections but no stabilized policy. The question now is what will be made of these different virtual policies: how might these connections generate changes in the city's public spaces? In what follows, I sort out different forms or "substances" of public space and address the question of the regulation of public space use.

Various ontologies of public space. Inescapably, with a polysemic term such as "public space," ways of understanding the question are bound to be very diverse. In the master-plan conceived by the US–South Korean consortium PPJ, the substance of public space is the green belt and corridors. Public space here is a physical attribute, as both specialists and the general public often understand it (Staeheli and Mitchell, 2007). Gehl's public space is clearly material as well (though he is interested in the vivid public life it may foster) and is approached as a matter of architectural and urban design (Gehl, 2010). Planners and city officials influenced by the courses and writings of Michael Douglass have a different understanding: for them, it corresponds to the spaces and places of civic life, where political matters can be discussed and opposed. Here we have public space as the space of polity which is so prominent in social science (Staeheli and Mitchell, 2007: 798). Finally in a more diffuse way, for instance in HealthBridge's approach to public space, it is also conceived as the spaces and places of everyday social interaction.

The policies derived from these understandings brought by different connections vary widely of course: green spaces for health and recreation, and spaces for political debate or social interaction are very different things. Looking at a policy in the making raises, therefore, the following questions: how will the sorting between these different understandings be undertaken? How will the voices of official discourse and the practices of regulation weight the balance between them? Will the present conception of public space as standard provisions of green space per capita simply be maintained and reinforced because it fits traditional forms of urban planning in Hanoi? This is the most likely outcome. It is less likely that freely accessible public/civic spaces will be developed, since this alternative may be incompatible with an authoritarian and neoliberalizing city such as contemporary Hanoi.

Regulating public space. Public space use in Hanoi is primarily regulated by informal norms and when conflicts arise between users they are generally settled by discussion and compromise. Such informal regulation is a central condition for the multifunctional and event-rich public life still found in Hanoi's traditional neighborhoods, including the activity of shop-owners, sidewalk eateries, and street vendors. These activities create a public space which is both lively and chaotic, forcing pedestrians to pay attention to how they navigate the encumbered sidewalk.

However, in the "best-practice cities" put forward by foreign or local experts in Hanoi, public space policies generally suppose tight control of commercial and other sorts of private activities in public space. If such regulations are applied "off the shelf" to Vietnamese public spaces – not distinguishing, for instance, between encroachments on public space of small-scale commercial activities (like barbers) and those of large shops (like electronic dealers) – they are very likely to destroy precisely what makes the streets vibrant and interesting public spaces. Strict regulations of the "benign privatization" performed by homeowners would have the same consequence.

Because the process was ongoing at the time of publishing this book, I cannot write an epilogue to this story on how these loose threads might eventually be woven together. However, in the second part of this chapter, I look at another moment of the process through which public spaces are relationally produced. I consider the reception of public spaces recently designed in partnership with French and other European experts in Ouagadougou. I then conclude by comparing the cities' different ways of developing a public space policy through different translocal connections.

Traveling Participation and Public Space Design

The interests of private actors, inadequate planning procedures, the weakness of public authorities, and corruption are the four main factors that hamper the development of an effective public space policy in Ouagadougou. "Empty spaces," as we saw earlier, are considered an anomaly, so that when the national government creates land reserves to be used as public space, they are rapidly used for other purposes. Entrepreneurs turn them into bars, they become spaces for brick production, or they are used for storage. Others try to build houses, or use vacant spaces as soccer grounds. When these "empty spaces" are officially reserved for open space, as government officials themselves admit,[19] there is generally no communication with the neighboring inhabitants to explain and promote the future function of the area. Similarly, and from lack of financial means, there is also rarely a material intervention – such as fences or a playground equipment – signifying this function and people using the area for private purposes are seldom prosecuted. Finally, offenders sometimes have connections with the political elite or belong to that elite, and bribes "solve" the problem in that case. One of the central questions for public authorities is their ability to secure the intended function of those land reserves planned as public spaces. The municipality believes that in the near future the land use plan will be the legal tool (missing for the moment) that will really empower the state's public space policy.[20]

However, it would be misleading to consider that the ministry and the municipality are simply fighting to convince a population uninterested in such issues. Like in Hanoi, the city has witnessed in recent years a growing mobilization against the privatization of public space. The struggle around a 2.8 hectare land reserve planned as a sports ground in the Patte d'Oie neighborhood, in southern Ouagadougou, is emblematic of this change (Biehler, 2010: 389–404). In 2002, inhabitants of the neighborhood discovered that a private school was going to be built and would occupy half of the reserve. The struggle against this illegal project ended in 2004 in favor of the inhabitants, who managed to close the building site. In 2012, this large public space was enclosed by a wall and exclusively used for sport activities (Figure 4.4). For Biehler (2010: 404), this popular mobilization marks a "real change in the way certain citizens in Ouagadougou see their life spaces in the city." Protests and resistance a few years earlier against the evictions caused by the ZACA project had only led to marginal adjustments by the state. This time a social movement had succeeded in maintaining a piece of open space for public use.

Figure 4.4 The sports ground in Patte d'Oie. Photo by Ola Söderström.

From such examples it can be seen that civil society is becoming an actor in the city's public space policy. Decentralized cooperation is another important vector in the making of this policy. Since 1994, public space planning has been promoted by the City of Lyon in particular, one of the European role models in the domain (Toussaint and Vareilles, 2009). I focus in what follows on one specific aspect of public space policy that has played a particularly important role in the city's international relations strategy: participatory planning.

During the past ten years "inclusive city" projects elaborated through public participation have become part of the mainstream in the policy of international organizations.[21] In Ouagadougou, the concept of community participation in its post-revolutionary form was first introduced during the third urban project of the World Bank (1996–2001).[22] In 2003, a program called the PRCCU,[23] which received technical support from the UNDP, was developed to generalize such procedures and make them durable. Since 2007, the EU has promoted a new development policy based on the direct support of local authorities and non-state actors. Attentive to this international context, the Municipality of Ouagadougou recently put these issues at the top of its agenda. Thus, the third mandate (2006–2011) of Simon Compaoré focused on the promotion of good governance and civic participation.

The "inclusive development project" in the neighborhood of Gounghin[24] in 2009–2010, supported notably by the EU and the Grand Lyon, has been one of the focal points of this policy.[25] Through a participatory process, the project principally aimed at improving the neighborhood's infrastructures (schools, health centers, green spaces, markets, lighting) and at helping women to raise their income. This is one of the instances where decentralized cooperation between Ouagadougou and Lyon has played a decisive role in the making of a neighborhood project and its approval by the EU. The process began when the head of Ouagadougou's Planning Department first traveled to Lyon to collect information concerning its neighborhood policies. Then, a technical adviser from Lyon worked with the Municipality of Ouagadougou to guide the completion of the project in terms of its content and communication. The process also involved a South–South dimension, as it involved a study trip by representatives of the neighborhood to look at community development in Cotonou, Benin.

The key element in the Gounghin project was the creation of a fruit and vegetable market (Figure 0.4). The market is a small but strategic part of the project because it was a prime motivation for the EU to fund the scheme.[26] The EU had noticed that many markets in Ouagadougou, like other African cities, had developed along main roads, putting vendors in risky situations because of the heavy traffic. In Gounghin, women selling their goods along the road were regularly injured and sometimes killed by cars or trucks. The EU considered that the creation of a market for the women in a secure side street off the main road was an important test-ground to solve the problem on a larger scale.[27] It was also seen as a strategic initiative, because the same type of participatory neighborhood improvement project could be replicated in the 12 neighborhoods of the city with the support of EU funds.[28] The success of the Gounghin project, and in particular of the new market, is therefore important in securing funds for a wider participatory urban improvement process.

Lyon contributed its expertise in technical aspects (such as lighting) and in the design of the participatory process.[29] Participation was organized in two phases corresponding to program and project definition. First, members of the associations present in the neighborhood formed as a neighborhood council *(Conseil unifié des quartiers Gounghin)* under the presidency of the area's customary chief – who was elected to that function by the participants – were involved in identifying the main needs and axes for the neighborhood's development. During the second phase, members of specific associations were then involved in the collaborative design of specific projects. In the case of the market, the municipality involved women members of the neighborhood's association of fruit and vegetable vendors. A series of meetings was thus organized involving the architects chosen for the design (ARDI Architectes), members of the district administration, members of the neighborhood council, and two women from the fruit and vegetable vendors' association in order to design the stalls of the new market. These meetings led to the approval of the project which was eventually built in 2010 (Figure 4.5).

However, a series of problems emerged after completion. First, though they had seen and approved the plans, the vendors were surprised by the size of the stalls (74 x 60 cm) which, in their opinion, was much too small. What the Lyon-inspired participatory design had not anticipated was the great difficulty the women involved in the process (who have little formal education) had in reading the plans. They had no precise idea of what they had formally approved. This was reinforced by the asymmetry of meetings during which, in the language of participants themselves, the "intellectuals" (i.e. architects) were explaining the design to the "analphabets."[30] A meeting organized to solve the problem only repeated the asymmetry, as a "mediator" was present to tell the participants when to applaud the district mayor and to conclude the meeting by stating that "great intellectuals and technicians have worked on the design and know what is good for us."[31] Thus, the knowledge of the vendors about how a market works was largely disregarded in

Figure 4.5 The new market of Gounghin under construction. Photo by Ola Söderström.

the design process. The issues raised by this process – related to power, hierarchy, cultural difference, and the importance of the participatory methods used – are well known in collaborative planning theory and methodology (Healey, 1997; Söderström, 2000), but their role is particularly important in contexts such as Ouagadougou and require locally relevant solutions.

The presence of customary Moose chiefs in the Gounghin participatory process is for instance a very strong bias as no Moose would publicly contradict her or his chief. If you want to access other opinions and inputs, it is therefore indispensable to create informal meetings with the participants.[32] Finally, in Ouagadougou the mere fact of proposing something for a specific group tends to be perceived as a priori positive and induces the approval of those involved. As an architect put it apropos of another participatory process (the design of the central market):

> Any new project would have been approved. Everybody was saying "yes, yes, yes" without looking at the details. They approved everything [...] without understanding really what they were approving. You know, Africans, they sign something and then they say "No." We were outside of oral culture here and they did not understand the significance of their signature (Architect, interview July 5 2012).

Figure 4.6   The market of Gounghin in 2012. Photo by Ola Söderström.

The result is that the market does not work. During my last visit in July 2012, there were not more than ten women working out of 154 stalls. To solve the design problem, each vendor was using the width of 4–5 stalls and had generally put a table in front of them for their goods (Figure 4.6). Further up the street and further away from the main road, the stalls were totally empty and the representative of the vendors' association told me:

> It doesn't work: nobody comes here. The problem is that we are too far away from the road. When the mayor came to put the first brick, it was very close to the road, but the technicians then decided to put the market much farther away [...] it's a good thing that the mayor did something for us, but it doesn't work. I don't have enough to pay my children's school or to buy food for them (Vendor, interview July 4 2012).

Those problems have incited some vendors to return to the main road, to which the municipality reacted first with dialogue and then with force, in order to get them back to the costly new stalls. The failure of the design has led the EU to ask the municipality for solutions. The stakes are high, because of the planned extension of the process to the whole city. Therefore, the municipality has taken the problem very seriously and tried to find resources for asphalting the street, creating parking places in front of the market, and helping the vendors to get microcredit loans. Municipal officials involved in the next phases of the participatory neighborhood improvement project also try to improve participatory methods and tools by, for example, exploring forms of visual representation of the project.[33] Interestingly, this new phase is led by the Municipality of Ouagadougou,[34] and does not involve Lyon. It is a collaboration with Cotonou, where a neighborhood with similar characteristics is also involved. The challenge for the municipality is thus to find the means to indigenize participation by mobilizing its increasingly active web of South–South translocal connections.

Conclusion

In this chapter, I have examined an aspect of urban planning which is particularly sensitive to cultural difference, in order to investigate the problems and contradictions of relationally produced policies. As cultures of public space widely differ across space and place, cut-and-paste policy transfers can be particularly problematic. I have shown how the development of public space policies in both Hanoi and Ouagadougou is composed of entangled elements: the material legacy of French colonialism; specific non-European ways of thinking/doing public spaces; and a set of policy connections with other locales in the North and in the South as well as their own histories, traditions, and practices. In this context, relational policy-making is far from being a smooth first-class trip of a ready-made solution from City A to City B. It is on the contrary made of different (and often contrasting) potential policies that are selectively territorialized. In the Hanoi case, I analyzed how different types of translocal relations are involved in the making of a potentially social-oriented urban policy. My study shows how a plurality of connections between different places are established, both by traceable routes – exemplified in the way British green belt policy arrived in Hanoi after being filtered through the Seoul green belt experience – and by immaterial and less traceable paths. Methodologically, the Hanoi case shows that a wide repertoire of ways of apprehending policy connections should be employed in order to understand the full range of relations at play.

In contrast with studies of more stabilized policies, the Hanoi case also shows that when analyzing policy in the making, we are in a better position to identify a series of "loose threads" – virtual policies suggested by a set of different connections to different elsewheres. When those threads are still visible, when the storytelling of planners and politicians has not yet "black-boxed" the making of an urban policy, we can emphasize alternatives and question the instrumental use of translocal connections.

In Ouagadougou, public space policy is more established, if not always efficient. Its recent development is related to the role of decentralized cooperation and the urban programs of multilateral institutions (World Bank, EU). I chose to focus on participatory design, one aspect of the collaboration with Lyon, because of potential problems in the transfer of French procedures to Burkina Faso. The uneasy circulation of participatory public space design in the case of the Gounghin neighborhood improvement project shows the importance of "policies on the move" developing a postcolonial sensitivity. Procedures developed in the Global North do not provide solutions for situations often characterized by radical (gender, class, knowledge, power) asymmetries and very different histories, traditions, and expectations. It is therefore important to develop a politics of relationality that puts cities in the South in a position to use both the expertise brought by North–South collaborations and to design solutions with regional partners corresponding to specific forms of urbanity in the Global South.

In this chapter and the previous one I have focused on how recent urban developments in two cities of the Global South are shaped by transnational and translocal policy connections. However, such connections constitute but one type of what I call "generative" relations (see Chapter 1). Urban forms are also increasingly "mobile" and generated by connections with different "elsewheres." To better understand this process I investigate in the following chapter questions of the mobilities of architectural design, analyzing both large-scale processes and individual built forms.

Notes

1 But see Roy (2011) on the relations between policy mobility and transnational planning, and Clarke (2012a; 2012b) on the relations with urban history.

2 See also McFarlane (2011) who, framing policy mobilities as processes of learning, has developed an analytical framework to look at and compare different policy learning processes. He proposes to look at the power (promoting the learning), the object (of the learning), its organisational form, and the imaginary involved (McFarlane, 2011: 145).

3 This is a difference with work in urban history which, as Clarke (2012b: 39) notes "sees more of this rich field than has been seen by those with views filtered through heavily theoretical lenses (e.g. neoliberalization) – which are heavily normative too in many cases." But see Darling (2010), Malpass et al. (2007), and Peck and Theodore (2012).

4 On Indian public space, for instance, and analogous "inside-out" situations, see Arabindoo (2011).

5 Mapping asphalt is therefore a useful exercise for social geographers of African cities.

6 The same is true for Phnom Penh in neighboring Cambodia (Springer, 2009).

7 My analysis in this section follows Alexandra Biehler's (2010) very detailed work on public space in Ouagadougou.

8 Interview with a US public space expert established in Vietnam, November 1 2011.

9 See Chapter 3.

10 See "Public Recreation," "Agricultural," and "Rural Conservation" zones in Figure 3.3.

11 Interview with an official of the Vietnamese Ministry of Construction, October 27 2011.

12 See Chapter 3.

13 The aim is, for instance, to reach $13\,\text{m}^2$ per capita of public space by 2030 (against $0.9\,\text{m}^2$ today in the city center). Interview, architect, August 26 2011.

14 In the 1998 master-plan, as we saw in Chapter 3, urban growth was for instance planned to happen in the north of the city, but it happened in the south.

15 Interview with a Vietnamese environmental expert, December 5 2011.

16 Interview, state official, August 25 2011.

17 For example, "3D Planning & Design," as implemented notably in Toronto, was presented in the 2010 workshop, and the arguments developed during the workshop were then used by the Committee on Social Affairs of the National Assembly to comment on the 2008 Hanoi master-plan.

18 Apart from those already mentioned, the Catholic Church has also recently been playing an important role: residents have challenged the government's attempts to use Church land for development, eventually leading to the conversion of some of these areas into public parks (Wells-Dang, 2010: 100).

19 Interview with state official at the Ministry of Housing and Urban Planning, July 12 2012.

20 Interview with municipal official, July 9 2012.

21 See Pieterse (2008) for a nuanced critical evaluation of such policies.

22 On community participation in urban planning during the Sankara regime, see Jaglin (1995).

23 *Projet de renforcement des capacités des communes urbaines.* Led by the UNDP, the government of Burkina Faso, and six municipalities, this project (2003–2006) aimed at promoting good governance and decentralization.

24 *Projet participatif d'aménagement des quartiers Gounghin.*

25 It lasted for 18 months (February 2009–August 2010) and had a budget of 842,000 euros.

26 Interview with municipal official, July 9 2012.

27 Ibid.

28 The city has recently reorganized its territorial boundaries with twelve districts instead of the formerly existing five districts.

29 Through its technical adviser present in Ouagadougou between 2007 and 2010.
30 Interview, architect March 15 2012.
31 Ibid.
32 Interview with municipal official July 10 2012.
33 Interview with municipal official July 5 2012.
34 *Projet participatif d'aménagement du secteur 20*, in the neighborhood of Signoghin, also funded by the EU between 2011 and 2013. After Gounghin and Signoghin, the next projected phase is a participatory project in each of the 12 neighborhoods of the city.

5

Connecting to Circuits of Architectural Design

Self-construction without the intervention of an architect is the most common way of producing the built environment in cities of the South. In Hanoi and Ouagadougou, the constitution of an association of local architects is only a few decades old. Economic transition and accelerated urban growth have increased the role of architects in urban transformation and has also led to the development of "stretched geographies of design" involving actors in different and sometimes quite distant places. In this chapter, I explore these new geographies of architectural design and show how, since 1990, both cities have become involved in different circuits of transnational architecture. My aim here is to understand how such relations are shaping the morphology of globalizing cities, and more specifically, to investigate the tensions in design between transnationalism and nationalism. More generally, by looking here at relations in design I seek to extend the purview of relational urban studies, which tend to overly emphasize the role of policy connections. Building on previous work (Guggenheim and Söderström, 2010b) I show that transnational design involves different actors and logics that should be distinguished from and articulated with those that have been identified by policy mobility studies. This chapter thus describes another facet of urban *mondialisation* governed by logics that are partly autonomous from the ones research on urban economic and political connections has highlighted so far. It also provides a broader vision of what

Cities in Relations: Trajectories of Urban Development in Hanoi and Ouagadougou,
First Edition. Ola Söderström.
© 2014 John Wiley & Sons, Ltd. Published 2014 by John Wiley & Sons, Ltd.

constitutes the contemporary geographies of architecture, especially in cities of the Global South.

The argument unfolds in four steps. The first discusses recent work on the geographies of architectural design and situates the present study within this body of literature. I argue that while most existing work predominantly focuses on global architecture firms and global cities, studies of "ordinary cities" like Hanoi and Ouagadougou give us a broader comprehension of present geographies of design. The second part of the chapter looks at the spatiality of the design of five built forms in both cities. I show here that transnational design does not simply connect a place of architectural production to a place of consumption, but takes place "in between" these places and involves processes of mutual learning and what I call "design in the wild" (involving non-experts). Design connections, more than policy connections, involve frequent exchanges and quick adjustments between individual actors in which communication technologies play a crucial role. The third looks at the promotion of nationalism in state-led projects as a means of controlling the cosmopolitanization of the built environment. In other words, I look here at the dialectics between relationality and territoriality in the world of architectural design. My concluding section summarizes these design biographies and argues that in the cities considered, but also more broadly, transnational design cannot be reduced to logics of branding and capital accumulation.

Stretched Geographies of Design

In a paper published some time ago now, Callon (1996) commented on the account of an architect's creative process by the French theoretician of architecture Boudon. Callon's argument was that Boudon left out of the picture a series of important elements active in the design process, albeit absent in the scene he described: the countless architectural "others" with whom the architect interacts in face-to-face situations as well as through drawings and texts. Callon contrasted his own pragmatist approach to architectural design with Boudon's cognitive stance, showing that when one moves from the theoretical discourse on architectural design to a study of its practice "the prominent role of the architect as designer is immediately complicated and dissipated" (Jacobs and Merriman, 2011: 215): the architecture as solitary artist is replaced by a (less heroic) collective of human and non-human operators of design. The renewed vision of design promoted by Callon is both an epistemic effect, related to the development of studies of architectural design practice, and the result of a more complex professional situation characterized, as Imrie and Street (2009: 2508) put it, by "the dispersal and decentering of the actions of the architect, in ways whereby architects are engaged, increasingly, in complex interdisciplinary teams of professionals in the negotiation of design outcomes." Thus, studies since the 1990s revising the heroic account of architectural practice coincide with a historical period in which architects have lost their role as indisputable central figures of the design process.[1]

In this situation of "dispersal and decentering" mentioned by Imrie and Street, the spatiality of design, which is the focus of studies in human geography, takes on more importance: it includes the rather confined and bounded place of the studio,[2] the broader ecology of neighborhoods or cities concentrating architectural practices[3] and the transnational networks created by large firms with branches in different cities connected by IT and the travels of their staff.[4] Geographers have also investigated the place/design relation, analyzing how the cultural, political, economic, or legal characteristics of a region or city give design specific local inflections. Studies of the relation between regulation and design have thus shown that "such standards do influence, in variable ways, aesthetic and design outcomes" (Imrie and Street, 2009: 2509) and that, for instance, regulations have the effect of territorializing design by global architects (Faulconbridge, 2009).

In this chapter's second part, I look at instances of territorialization of transnational design by analyzing the intervention of the state in public projects. However, my first and primary focus is on the *spaces* of architectural design practices rather than their *places*. These spaces are structured by the expanding and globalizing network of architectural offices organized, according to Knox and Taylor (2005), in four main arenas: the global city arena; the Austral-Asian Pacific arena; the Middle Eastern arena; and the US domestic arena. Within these spaces, there are places of architectural "production" – where projects are designed – and "consumption" – where they are realized. Two-thirds of the largest architectural firms, controlling a network of 516 branch offices in 198 cities across the world, are US or UK (read: London) based (Ren, 2011: 27). On the consumption side, if we take the number of branch offices as an indicator, we find at the top of the list: Shanghai, London, Dubai, Washington and Beijing (ibid.: 28).[5] This leads Ren (2011: 16) to argue that there is a "disjuncture between where the initial design is conceived," i.e. in Japan, the US or Europe, "and where it is consumed," i.e. in Asia or the Middle East. McNeill (2009) provides a telling example of this when describing how Renzo Piano, based in Genoa, designed a high-rise building in Sydney with minimal engagement with the site during the project phase, and letting a partner firm in Australia develop the project and manage the construction phase.

Another way of investigating the spaces of architectural design has been to study how, in global architecture firms, design stretches through their network of branch offices. On the basis of interviews with architects working in eight major firms, Faulconbridge (2010) shows that, mainly because of internal competition, design is rarely done in collaboration with architects located in different branches. However, what he calls "global communities of architectural practice" (Faulconbridge, 2010: 2849) are nonetheless created within these firms by professional journals, internal newsletters, websites, and by visiting works of fellow architects past and present. Non-human intermediaries are thus at least as important as human interaction in shaping spaces of architectural design.

My entry point into the geographies of design in this chapter is neither the global firm nor the global city, but instead, a sample of architectural forms designed and built between 2000 and 2010 in Hanoi and Ouagadougou. Generally speaking, studies of global cities and firms have highlighted how transnational design, driven by branding and entrepreneurialism, result in decontextualized projects (McNeill, 2009; Ren, 2011). In the capitals of Vietnam and Burkina Faso, we will see that these design spaces are driven by similar (global) interests, but also by other motivations – such as providing a house for a middle-class family in Hanoi, or creating a healthcare center for women in Ouagadougou (see below) – providing a more comprehensive understanding of contemporary geographies of design. My analysis draws on the existing literature by paying particular attention to the role of non-humans, and to the disjuncture between the sites of architectural production and consumption. I also use as a heuristic tool the distinction derived from Actor-Network Theory between "design in the lab" and "in the wild" (Callon and Rabeharisoa, 2003): if the traditional conception of design, with its focus on one figure (the architect), one place (the studio), and one time (the creative phase) paralleled the scientific laboratory, a renewed focus involving different actors dispersed in place and time parallels the principle of "research in the wild" where non-scientists (such as patients) and scientists are co-producers of knowledge. Of course, the latter has not simply replaced the former: depending on the type of project and client, on the fame and style of the architect, or on the size of studios, architectural design can be closer to one or other of these two models. Actual forms of architectural design can therefore be placed on a continuum between "design in the lab" and "design in the wild."

Circuits of Architectural Design in Hanoi and Ouagadougou

During the socialist period, architects in Ouagadougou and Hanoi were essentially state employees, while private practices emerged during the 1990s in the context of economic transition and urban growth. Beyond this process common to both contexts, there are important differences in size and activity, as Hanoi is a much larger market for privately established architects. I briefly compare below the local organization of architects in both cities, before I discuss the development of transnational design.

With *Doi Moi* in Vietnam, overseas architects of Vietnamese origin (*Viet Kieu*) returned to work in Hanoi. For example, Le Cuong, a well-known figure of Vietnamese architecture who left to study in France in 1951, came back to Hanoi in 1987: "After the start of *Doi Moi* I thought I should do something for Vietnam" (interview, November 4 2009). A number of other *Viet Kieu* architects came back in the 1990s, some of them having been contracted to build for the government. A second wave of foreign architects opened practices or branch offices in Hanoi in the wake of the 2003 law allowing foreign companies to establish their activity in Vietnam. For instance, two French companies, Site and Archetype, very active on Hanoi's architectural scene during the past decade, saw the market opportunities in Hanoi early on, and opened their practices in 2003.[6] Archetype now has 350 employees working in Vietnam and in other branch offices around the world (including France). Thus, the size of the Vietnamese architectural market has allowed the emergence of large practices. Since the 1990s it has also attracted, as I show in more detail below, large development and construction companies including the architects on their staff, especially from Southeast Asia. South Korean companies, in particular, such as Posco and Keangnam, are involved in large-scale projects in Hanoi: Posco has been involved in the new master-plan (see Chapter 3) and is currently building a large edge-city in the south of Hanoi. Keangnam completed the Keangnam Tower in 2011, which ranks fifth in the world for the floor area of a single building. Finally, foreign architects are also designing for the large equitized State Owned Enterprises, such as VINACONEX, that play a major role in the morphological changes of the city.

In Ouagadougou, there were close to 20 small or medium-sized architectural practices in 2008, and not many more at the time of writing. During the revolutionary period up to the end of the "rectification" in 1991, all Burkinabè architects worked for the government. The profession was recognized by the government in parallel with the liberalization of the sectors of real estate and construction in the early 1990s. The *Ordre des Architectes du Burkina* was thus created in 1991. Practices have then developed apace, with the large governmental projects of ZACA and Ouaga 2000, designing mainly office buildings and villas. Since the 1995 decentralization process, contracts from municipalities have also contributed to the development of architectural design. Because of a lack of legal obligation and insufficient income, individuals rarely employed architects for their private houses until very recently. Homeowners built what people call *des maisons de maçons* (mason's houses): houses that are either self-built or built by small local entrepreneurs. But since the adoption of the 2006 *Code de l'Urbanisme et de la Construction* (Urban Planning and Construction Code), building permits have been subject to the involvement of an architect in the project. However, this legal disposition is often not applied because of the additional costs created by the employment of architects. Therefore, although architects are no longer state-employed in Ouagadougou, the market is still very much state-driven.

In contrast with Hanoi, the national market is also too small to attract large non-African construction and development companies.[7] But economic liberalization and privatization have led to the emergence of large national construction companies such as AZIMMO, Kanazoé, or Fadoul. The State Owned Enterprise created in 1984 by the Sankara regime to implement the state's housing policy, the *Société de Construction et de Gestion Immobilière du Burkina*, was privatized and sold in 2001 to the AZIMMO group, a private company created in 1997 and belonging to a relative of the head of state.[8] Companies close to the president's family get the lion's share of public construction contracts, leading to frequent media reports on corruption and clientelism – what people in Burkina Faso call "*faire parler les feuilles*" ("let the banknotes speak")[9] – in the construction sector.

In Hanoi, the activity of large foreign architectural practices and development companies, as well as the importance of FDIs, are important factors explaining the differences between the transnational design processes in each city I explore below. It is clear that the urban design actors in the two cities do not belong to the same league or circuit. The original research project drew on interviews with urban experts to investigate these processes, identifying the main architectural programs related to urban landscape changes over the past 20 years in each city. Six of these programs are common to both cities: housing blocks, shopping malls, small commercial structures, hotels, office towers, and heritage preservation. For each program, we chose two interventions we knew had some transnational dimension (related to the building type, the origin or experience of the architect, the origin of the client or investors) to develop design biographies which I will draw on to compare how transnational design works in each city and the type of built environment it creates.

Hanoi: Design Spaces of an Emerging Economy

Hanoi's built environment is changing very rapidly due to foreign investment, the rise of a middle and upper class, and growing socio-economic inequalities. It is impossible to aim at a comprehensive study of the various and complex cross-border geographies of design involved in those changes. I have therefore chosen to examine three contrasting

forms of transnational design: iconic architecture, master-planned communities, and the single family house.

Becoming iconic

There are no Petronas Towers and no Sydney-like waterfront Opera
House in Hanoi. When media or the city authorities want to use built
form to symbolize the city, they use architectural heritage (usually the
gate of the Temple of Literature) or the Ho Chi Minh mausoleum.
Contemporary architecture is not as yet providing symbols of the city's
development and dynamism.

However, this is about to change as a series of actors are trying to move
the city into the glittering circuit of iconic architecture. It all started with
the Beijing Olympics in 2008: the Hanoi People's Committee (HPC)
was very impressed by the impact of Olympic architecture, such as the
"bird's nest stadium," and in 2009 asked one of Hanoi's most influential architects to invite a selection of "starchitects" to enter a competition for the design of a municipal building.[10] This architect contacted a
group of "usual suspects" – Renzo Piano, Rem Koolhaas, Norman Foster,
and Cesar Pelli – to submit design ideas. Piano won the competition
and will eventually be the architect building for the municipality. The
same year, the chairman of VietinBank, one of the largest Vietnamese
banks, visited Frankfurt where he was impressed by the Commerzbank,
a Frankfurt icon and the tallest building in the EU (259 meters), built
by Foster and Partners. Back in Hanoi, he contacted Foster and Partners
through the same influential Vietnamese architect asking them to build
a similar V-shaped (as in VietinBank) building in Hanoi (Figure 5.1).[11]
The construction of the VietinBank started in 2011 (Figure 0.2) and will
become Vietnam's tallest building (362 meters) and probably its first
contemporary architectural icon.[12]

This form of architecture and design is characteristic of an aspiring
world-city like Hanoi: there is today both the political will and the economic
capital necessary to access this exclusive circuit of architectural production. With its corresponding building in Frankfurt, the VietinBank is a
typical example of what Kaika (2011: 980) calls the serial "repetition of
successful design forms," where forms are parachuted in from elsewhere
and where architectural production is disconnected from consumption.
In a globalizing but, until recently, economically very marginal city, the
forms of access to this type of circuit are handled by very few and clearly
identifiable intermediaries. The Vietnamese architect contacted both
by the HPC and the Bank is thus the first (and at the time of writing
only) Hanoi broker in aspiring iconic architecture.[13] His international
professional networks have made him a key figure in the development of

Figure 5.1 VietinBank in Hanoi by Foster + Partners. Photo courtesy of Foster + Partners.

such elite cross-border spaces of design. Without him, the visits of Hanoi officials and businessmen to cities like Beijing and Frankfurt would not have led to the presently observable emergence of iconic buildings in the city with projects by Piano, Foster, Pelli, and others.

When considering the emergence of iconic buildings in Hanoi in isolation, one could see the city as becoming, like other Asian cities, a site for the fast-transfer of architecture: designed in the West and soon after cut-and-pasted into "the Rest."[14] However, the study of other types of interventions shows that these recently developed cross-border spaces of architectural design are often far more complex, and in particular are spaces of mutual learning.

"Ciputra Hanoi International City": conceiving large scale
in spaces in between

In the 1990s until the Asian crisis in 1997, Hanoi saw a rapid increase in foreign investments in real estate. In this context, the first master-planned edge-city development was planned in 1995. The Indonesian

Figure 5.2 A street in Ciputra Hanoi International City. Photo by Stephanie Geertman.

company Ciputra was the initiator of the process and has been the investor, designer, and developer of Ciputra Hanoi International City (hereafter Ciputra) located in the north of the city. Ciputra is a 300 hectares high-end gated community built by a company founded by an Indonesian architect who became the head of a very large firm with various activities (real estate, education, health, telecommunications, and media). It was the first overseas city for the company and the first master-planned neighborhood for the Municipality of Hanoi. Ciputra has therefore been a test-ground for urban globalization in Vietnam.

The general design of public spaces and housing, made of towers and mostly of semi-detached single-family houses, was produced by Ciputra's architects (Figure 5.2), but the final design of buildings was developed by two Vietnamese firms (UAC, a firm of real-estate consultants, and the largest Vietnamese construction company, VNCC). The role of those companies has been to insure that Ciputra was Hanoi-compatible. VNCC's architect describes the division of labor this way:

> Firstly, the foreign consultant would produce the concept; I mean they did the concept design. After they finished the concept design, they gave it to VNCC and we developed the design. By developing the design, we introduced more details, to comply with Vietnam standards and Vietnamese living costs (Architect, interview November 18 2009).

What was established between these companies was more than a division of labor, however: it was a two-way knowledge transfer. Ciputra learned to develop a housing typology integrating Vietnamese ways of living:

> Vietnamese cooking style smells quite strong, so I advised them to totally separate the kitchen from other rooms in the apartment. We also advised them to design more fresh air circulation for the wet areas like the bathroom. That area needs to have air directly from the outside (Vietnamese Architect, interview November 18 2009).

On the other hand, Vietnamese authorities and architects learned how to plan and realize a new large "piece" of the city. Surprisingly, at this scale, the foreign architects are not the ones considered to be producing a decontextualized design: quite the opposite:

> I learned from them the way they work, the way they develop the concept. Before designing, they do careful research. And when they produce the concept, it is very reasonable and freethinking. They don't think the same way, the same track, as Vietnamese architects do (Vietnamese Architect, interview November 18 2009).

At a larger national scale, Ciputra has been conceived by the Vietnamese government as a laboratory for learning from foreign architects how to design and manage large-scale developments. In parallel with Ciputra, the state sold land in the south of Saigon to a Taiwanese development firm to develop an even larger edge-city in Ho Chi Minh City, Phu My Hung. Drawing on the experience of Ciputra, other similar kinds of edge cities have since then been designed and built in Vietnam's two major cities.[15] Cross-border spaces of design in an emerging economy like Vietnam's are thus quite consciously conceived as spaces of learning, so that firms and cities can become more competitive, but also in order to better meet the demand of future inhabitants.[16] I now turn to a shorter vignette on a self-built house, in order to explore quite different small-scale forms of transnational knowledge transfer.

Fusion architecture designed at a distance

Self-built houses are ubiquitous in Vietnamese cities. However, these houses are rarely shacks in Vietnam but informally built attached houses, generally of a fairly good standard. They reflect both rising standards of living and the illegal character of a large part of the built environment, as they are often constructed without a permit or do not respect regulation. Their architecture is generally a testimony to the owner's dreams of different types of elsewhere (Geertman, 2001) and

Figure 5.3   Self-built house in Dinh Cong district, Hanoi. Photo by Nguyen Quang Ninh.

increasingly of their experience abroad. This is the case for a self-built house we studied, designed for a middle-class family (Figure 0.2). In 1999, when the parents in the family bought a piece of land in the new area of Dinh Cong and planned to build a house there, their two daughters were both studying architecture abroad, the first in Russia and the second in Japan. In 2001, they both produced designs for the house from where they were studying, getting the necessary information from Hanoi and then sending their designs back by email. Eventually, the daughter studying in Japan convinced the rest of the family to use her design (Figure 5.3). This "design at a distance" was largely influenced by Japanese architecture and by the designer's collaboration with one of her fellow Vietnamese students in Japan, Vo Trong Nghia.[17]

> Actually, my house is the combination of spatial ideology from Japan and the whole detailing and technology is from Vietnam [...] In Japanese architecture, they tend to use natural materials; for example, they use a lot of wood for flooring or making the windows and doors. They use much more wood than people do in Vietnam. That's why I also wanted to use wood in my house. Also, the glass roof is an idea from Japan. No one had a glass roof at that time in individual houses like my house. And also the idea of the entrance came from Japan (Architect, interview November 19 2009).

The elements of Vietnamese architecture in the design include the use of traditional *Phong Thuy* rules for the location of the kitchen and of the parents' altar and the choice of having the living room, dining room, and kitchen on the second floor (and not on the first floor, according to Japanese habits).

This project exemplifies the role of Information and Communication Technologies in spatially stretched processes of design, including the case of small projects. On a more specific level, it shows how different forms of "diasporic design" are developing in an emergent country like Vietnam. Another aspect of this process is constituted by the older generation of *Viet Kieu* who, as mentioned above, have worked as designers in Hanoi, some of them eventually returning permanently and establishing their practice in the city.

My choice of three design biographies in Hanoi aims at showing that this is a multifaceted process, certainly including fast-transfer, but also mutual learning and diasporic design. In Ouagadougou, architects are involved in other spaces of design including more radical forms of co-produced design, or what I have suggested calling "design in the wild."

Ouagadougou: Architectures of Development

Ouagadougou has not entered the circuit of iconic architecture yet and is not likely to do so in the near future, because it lacks economic resources and is generally thought to be unattractive for international business. However, the political will is there as shown by the project for a large conference center: the *Centre International des Grandes Conférences* (CIGC) launched by the government in 2009 (Figure 0.4). The 17 m euros project planned for 3,000 conference delegates was won by a French practice from Lille, Coldefy et associés, with a design inspired by the calabash, a central utensil in the daily life of local people (Figure 5.4).

This is the first project in the city which, through its size and symbolic language, aims at "becoming iconic," but the budget does not allow the state to attract "starchitects," and it is uncertain whether the center will be built or not.[18] Similarly, despite ZACA and Ouaga 2000, and for the same reasons, there is as yet no "Ciputra-like" master-planned community in Ouagadougou. If Hanoi is progressively entering the league of cities present in the global arenas of architecture described by Knox and Taylor (2005), Ouagadougou is not yet a dot on the radar-screen. This does not mean that design is not globalized, as I will now show, describing the role of city networks, NGOs, and ICTs in the recent transformations of the city's built environment.

Figure 5.4 Project for the CIGC, Ouagadougou, by Coldefy & Associés. Photo courtesy of Coldefy & Associés.

Reemdoogo: a co-produced city-network design

As we saw in Chapter 3, since the election of the city's first mayor in 1995, the municipality has developed an intensive network of foreign relations resulting in numerous inter-municipal cooperations, and for instance, cultural policies and infrastructures have thus been developed in collaboration with the French city of Grenoble. At the end of the 1990s, both cities were looking for ways to professionalize and valorize their musical scenes. On the basis of the experience of having organized, between 1998 and 2001, a program of "cross-residences" for musicians in African and French cities, the French NGO Culture et Développement suggested creating places of musical production in Ouagadougou and Grenoble. Quite innovatively both cities then worked together to develop those infrastructures in parallel – La Chaufferie in Grenoble and Reemdoogo in Ouagadougou.

The Reemdoogo (the "play-house" in Mooré) is a cultural facility set in a garden which aims at sustaining and promoting the production of Burkinabè music (Figure 0.4). Inaugurated in 2004, it has rooms for rehearsal, administrative offices, a terrace with a bar, and a semi-open stage for performances (Figure 5.5). It was designed by an architect from Ouagadougou, Dieudonnée Wango, but the process was collective and highly transnational. Between 2002 and 2004, the architect and the manager of the project for the City of Ouagadougou traveled several times to Grenoble, while members of the NGO *Culture et Développement* and French music specialists traveled to Ouagadougou.

Figure 5.5   Reemdoogo music-garden, Ouagadougou. Photo by Jonas Haenggi.

The choice of the site resulted from this co-produced design. Describing discussions with *Culture et Développement*, the director of Reemdoogo told us:

> There was this idea of an infrastructure of proximity [...] not bringing people to consume culture in the city center but bringing it to them. This idea of proximity made us choose Gounghin, a popular neighborhood with a lot of artists. It is a very dynamic neighborhood and somewhat at the periphery at the same time (Director, interview October 22 2009).

The architect then worked on the morphological and social integration of the facility with its chosen neighborhood.

> We started from the idea that it had to be totally immersed in the neighborhood. It should not be dominant, not frightening. Because in Africa there is a generational conflict: places like this, with music, are seen as places of depravity [...] So I chose to bury it, to make it as discrete as possible [...] and to put the stage four meters underground to keep the human scale of the infrastructure (Architect, interview October 22 2009).

The same principle applied to the limits of the garden: Wango struggled against the traditional Ouagadougou principle of an encircling wall, wanting to avoid "an introverted, opaque facility." To take into consideration questions of security, he eventually created a low wall with a small metal grid "that lets the gaze go through and maintains the fluidity of urban space" (ibid.).

Both the design process and the architecture of Reemdoogo are characteristic of the recent development of city networks beyond the North–South divide, where actors collaborate closely on quite specific projects. The exchanges within this transnational design collective has led to a very successful design, sensitive to different aspects of the site and local conditions.[19] I turn now to a similar but more contested design process.

The Centre pour le bien-être des femmes: a contested NGO design

Although political stability and relative good governance has made Burkina Faso a favorite spot for development aid, the rural bias of development agencies and NGOs (Beall and Fox, 2009) has long hampered projects in urban areas. The *Centre pour le bien-être des femmes* (Center for the Well-being of Women, hereafter CBF) is thus a rare example in Ouagadougou of a space specially designed by and for an NGO.

The Center focuses on the prevention of genital mutilation and aims at providing women in Ouagadougou with a holistic healthcare center integrating medical, psychological, and legal consultancy. It originates in the meeting of the presidents of two NGOs, one based in Ouagadougou (*Voix des Femmes*, presided over by a then minister of the Burkinabè government); the other in Rome (*Associazione Italiana Donne per lo Sviluppo*). In 2005, they decided to develop the CBF and involved two architectural practices in the design process: FAREstudio in Rome and Answer Architectes[20] in Ouagadougou. The CBF is located on the periphery of the city, away from the main roads in a low density area without water or electricity infrastructure (Figure 0.4).

The design of the CBF, which is the result of a bioclimatic approach based on low energy consumption, natural ventilation, and autonomous water supply, was also determined to a large extent by its location. The buildings are made with local material (compressed mud) elevated on piles and covered by detached roofs (Figure 5.6). The design draws its inspiration from two vernacular elements – the covered marketplace and the *arbre à palabres* (palaver tree), the political core of West African villages. During the design process, the Italian architect Riccardo Vannucci traveled several times to Ouagadougou, sometimes with members of his practice. Sketches, ideas, and plans also frequently traveled between Rome and Ouagadougou through email exchanges during the design process. The design has received four international awards, including the 2008 prize of the World Architecture Festival in

Figure 5.6   CBF, Ouagadougou by FAREstudio and Answer Architectes. Photo by Jonas Haenggi.

Barcelona in the category "health architecture." Both architects (Wango and Vannucci) recognize the influence of the most famous contemporary Burkinabè architect, Francis Kéré, particularly the school he built in Gando, his home village and for which he received the 2004 Aga Khan Award.[21] Kéré is trained and established in Berlin but regularly works in Burkina Faso.[22]

Thus, the design followed quite complex transnational routes between Ouagadougou and Rome, but also, and more virtually, Berlin and Gando. Like Reemdoogo, the resulting design is context-sensitive and subtly integrates knowledge from those different design "sites." However, the life of the building after its completion has led to some tension within the design collective, as the architects disagree when it comes to authorship. The Italian studio does not mention Wango as one of the designers in their online publications: he is described as a "precious collaborator in the first phases of the project," but the project is described as being "entirely conceived" by Vannucci.[23] Wango, on the other hand, describes a long process of design across borders. He recognizes that his Italian colleague "brought a lot" to the project, but considers that his "partner" then took the project "to make an advertisement out of it":

> You know architects always look for a project that they can turn into a cult object, the reason for their work and the creation of their practice (Architect, interview October 26 2009).

I mention this small controversy because it shows that collective design in extended spaces is fraught with a series of potential problems. Local architects can be turned into the equivalent of mere informants in anthropological research. The positioning of architects within their respective national professional fields can also complicate collaborations: what brings symbolic capital in Italy or Germany, like the reinvention of vernacular building techniques, may bring very little or none in Burkina Faso.[24] And, finally, ways of understanding authorship and its ethics can vary widely.[25]

In the designs analyzed so far, I have emphasized the functioning of stretched spaces of design. As the previous cases show, such designs involving actors established and trained in different places, are often aesthetically hybrid. Assembling different styles, the resulting buildings contribute to the cosmopolitanization of cities. If we want to understand how these design relations are territorialized, it is important to look at how states curb these processes in their own interests or how nationalism responds to cosmopolitanism. In what follows, I therefore focus on how the state tries to ground such designs by encouraging nationalist or regionalist architectural styles.

Grounding Design

Transnational design is becoming increasingly common, even in cities that are not major world cities. This leads to the import of new urban types (as I show in Chapter 6) but also, as we have seen above, to the import of new architectural technologies and styles. This evolution is often welcomed by local or national governments as it can be taken to signal a process of modernization, of "world-city-becoming." In certain cities of the Global South, such as Delhi, we thus witness the use of "world-class aesthetics" to justify the destruction of slums (Ghertner, 2011). However, states can also perceive such aesthetic normalization as unsettling because it weakens the role of architecture in supporting nationalist or regionalist narratives. Architecture is indeed one of the means of a "banal nationalism" (McNeill and Tewdwr-Jones, 2003). In other words, through its presence in the urban environment, architecture, together with sports teams or champions, flags, statues, or anthems, reproduce an idea of the nation in everyday life. In this section, I want to show that state control over public building design is a means of maintaining this role of architecture in an age of increasingly transnational design. By doing this I also want to look at a specific aspect of the dialectics between relational and territorial logics in contemporary urban development.

In the sample of 32 artifacts we analyzed, national or regional styles are more present in Ouagadougou than Hanoi. In Ouagadougou, public and office buildings completed since 1990 all display some regional character rather than an international modernism. In contrast, regional character is rare in Hanoi's recent architectural designs. There appear to be two causes for this difference and for the role of regionalism in Burkina Faso's capital: the training of local architects, and aesthetic intervention by the state.

There is no school of architecture in Burkina Faso, and all local architects are educated abroad: some in Morocco, Algeria, or France, but most receive their diploma from the *Ecole Africaine des Métiers de l'Architecture et de l'Urbanisme* (EAMAU) in Lomé, Togo. The School, created in 1975, is financed by 18 states of Western and Central Africa and trains architects, urban planners, and managers. Originally, lecturers were European and strove to promote an "African" architecture valorizing regional architecture and developing a style called the "Sudan–Sahelian style." This style – to be found in Burkina Faso, Mali, Senegal, and the Ivory Coast – is characterized by the use of conic forms with buttresses and wood elements projecting from buildings. According to the President of the Order of Architects in Burkina, and a former student of the School:

> In general, the vision of the studies in Europe and here is not exactly the same. In Europe, the accent is on economic and functional aspects of design. At the EAMAU, there is this imprint of African architecture, it is much more symbolic. We have more symbolism in it, which does not exclude work on function, of course (Architect, interview July 2 2009).

In Ouagadougou, the Sudan–Sahelian style alternates with modernist buildings, but the former is especially used in public buildings. As another Burkinabè architect explains:

> In the urban landscape, the Sudan–Sahelian style is predominant. But, this is a question of taste, because that style was not really born here, it was also imported. It originates from Arab influence, in fact, and the mosques. So, it's not our style. What is peculiar to us, and that we should draw inspiration from and promote, is for instance Gourounsi architecture (Architect, interview May 4 2009).

Figure 5.7 BCEAO building, an example of Gourounsi-inspired architecture, Ouagadougou. Photo by Pierrick Leu.

In a multi-ethnic country like Burkina Faso, vernacular architecture has very different shapes (Drabo, 1993). Being quite distinct, with flat roofs and an orthogonal plan, Gourounsi architecture is a good marker of territorial mooring. The state, especially during the revolutionary period, therefore promoted Gourounsi-inspired architecture, and it was used, for instance, for Ouagadougou's first real high-rise, the fortress-like BCEAO[26] building, completed in 1991 (Figure 5.7).

This aesthetic intervention by the state has continued with the recent development of national and international architecture or planning competitions. The instrument of this intervention is the Ministry of Culture, with a delegate in the competition juries to ensure that sensitivity to vernacular architecture is one of the evaluation criteria. As a consequence, participants in architectural competitions are encouraged to use local or "African" styles in their projects:

> Each time you participate in a competition, they will tell you to valorize local architecture [...] There is something they call "architectural and aesthetic research" in their notation criteria and you get better marks if

you interpret a local style than if you do what you want (Architect, interview May 28 2009).

In the recent international competition for a large conference center, launched by the government in 2009 and designed by Coldefy (discussed above), the winner used symbols (the calabash) and a visual rendering referencing the region. In smaller interventions, such as the Reemdoogo and the CBF, we saw how an EAMAU-trained local architect, Dieudonné Wango, was inspired by vernacular architecture. In Ouagadougou therefore, both the cultural project of the Lomé School and the aesthetic intervention of the state in public buildings regulate transnational design and "moor" it regionally.

In Hanoi, national narratives are not present to the same extent in recent architectural design. State Owned Enterprises like VINACONEX, playing an important role in Hanoi's housing production, could be an important vector of architectural nationalism, but it is not the case: VINACONEX projects very rarely reference regional styles and the overseas-trained head of the company's Research and Development (R&D) is more eager to attract "starchitects" and import Western building technologies than to develop neo-vernacular architecture. However, the state does not totally disregard the question, as the design of Hanoi's conference center shows.

The National Convention Center (NCC) in Hanoi, set in a landscaped park, was completed in 2006 in time for the 14th Asia-Pacific Economic Cooperation Summit (Figure 0.2). The client was the Vietnamese state, through its Ministry of Construction, and the process directly involved the prime minister. The German architect of the building, Meinhard von Gerkan of the Hamburg-based GMP International – active worldwide[27] – won the international competition for the design of the NCC. The design process was typically transnational, involving the German GMP for the design, and the Vietnamese VNCC[28] as a local partner for the development of the design, while the Chinese SFECO GROUP supervised the project management and construction process. Nevertheless, the design was territorialized in two different ways. First, *Phong Thuy* principles were required by the Vietnamese leaders and used in the design. The orientation of the building was thus adjusted in order to follow the principle of "lakes in front and mountains behind": the artificial lakes created in the park were placed at the front and the conference center has the Ba Vi mountains as a backdrop. For the same reason, the two doors of the initial plan's main entrance, a solution in opposition with *Phong Thuy* principles, were replaced by a large single door.[29] Like other recent buildings in Hanoi with a foreign design, the NCC was thus "domesticated" by *Phong Thuy*.

Figure 5.8   NCC's undulating roof, Hanoi. Photo by Chu Giap.

Second, the initial design by von Gerkan included a clear reference to Vietnamese national mythology. The undulating roof of the NCC with its different levels of height recalls both the waves of the East Sea and the Vietnamese dragon with its wavy tail (Figure 5.8). This was one of the reasons for the choice of von Gerkan's design by the competition jury,[30] who immediately perceived the symbolism of the roof.[31] It is interesting to note that the same designer won another international competition in 2005 for the Hanoi museum (completed in 2010) with a similar strategy. In this other state-commissioned building, GMP used an inverted pyramid accessible from all four cardinal points and Vietnamese ornaments as a recurrent motif.

Although nationalist narratives do not figure prominently in recent Hanoian architecture, they do surface in the public programs in which the state is directly involved. In this way, a national symbolism becomes, in the context of the city's rapid architectural cosmopolitanization, a visible marker of state presence.

Conclusion: Transnational Learning Processes and "Banal" Nationalism

In this chapter I have looked at design processes from the standpoint of recently built forms in two ordinary cities, rather than from within global architectural firms or global cities. This methodological stance has allowed me to describe more diverse and layered transnational spaces of architectural design than those generally described in the existing literature.

First, I have shown that even ordinary cities like Hanoi and Ouagadougou increasingly participate in spatially stretched processes of design. But, although they share many characteristics, they are clearly not involved in the same circuits of architectural conception: Hanoi, like other cities in emerging countries, is "becoming iconic" and is a target for privately driven master-planning, whereas Ouagadougou is not. I have argued that this is related to their distinct trajectories of globalization: if, as I show in Chapter 2, Hanoi is increasingly connected to global economic flows, Ouagadougou is primarily connected to global political flows.

Second, we have seen that these transnational spaces of design are held together by a series of more-than-human elements. Internet, telephone networks, journals, airplanes, drawings, etc. are crucial for these processes. It is striking, however, that physical travels to the site of construction, and also to other sites involved in the design, remain central to connecting and coordinating actors across space.

Third, whereas previous research focusing on the location and networks of global firms has highlighted the divide between the sites of architectural production and consumption (Knox and Taylor, 2005; Ren, 2011), this chapter has shown how different sites are also related in these spaces of design. In Hanoi, the divide between sites is manifest in the emergent demand addressed to "starchitects" to repeat successful forms built elsewhere, like the Frankfurt Commerzbank by Foster. But when we switch to other types of design, more complex processes of mutual learning come to the fore. In the design of master-planned communities, for instance, Indonesian architects contribute their experience of large-scale developments, while their Vietnamese partners develop the detailed design on the basis of their knowledge of local regulation and lifestyles. As a consequence, if Ciputra Hanoi International New City seems copy-pasted from other Ciputra cities because of its use of the ubiquitous neo-classical repertoire, it appears much less so as soon as we look at its design in more detail.

Moreover, the biography of a single-family home in Hanoi shows that, in a period of increasing mobility, knowledge transfer is not limited to large-scale interventions. The Japanese–Vietnamese design of this house was created at a distance and prefigures the subsequent development of an Asian–Vietnamese fusion architecture by young contemporary Vietnamese architects. It also expresses one aspect of what I call "diasporic design," related to the role of longer- or shorter-term migrants and exemplified by a figure like Francis Kéré working between Berlin and Burkina Faso, or by *Viet Kieu* architects who have returned to work in Hanoi after years of exile.

Architectural production in Ouagadougou since 1990 points to interesting and unexplored forms of transnational design related to development aid and, more specifically, to the role of city networks and NGOs. I have argued that actors, connected here by concrete small-scale projects, are developing progressive forms of "design in the wild" highly sensitive to social and morphological contexts. However, as one of my cases shows, such collective transnational design is facing the problems of authorship and symbolic capital that have been present in the profession for centuries.

This chapter shows that transnational architectural design is multifaceted. It cannot be reduced to the search by investors for new sites for capital accumulation, the attractiveness of weakly regulated cities for architects interested in new sites of experimentation, or the demand by local governments and entrepreneurs for the branding power of architects with big names. It is also a space of mutual learning, where design is co-produced among actors with quite different backgrounds.

Finally, I looked at how these stretched processes of design get moored in specific places. This local inscription can be studied from different viewpoints, and here I chose to look at how and why transnational design is combined with national and regional narratives. Each city differs in that respect: these narratives are more present in recent architectural design in Burkina Faso's capital than in Vietnam's. This can be explained, on the one hand, by the role of foreign architects and large foreign construction companies in Hanoi, and on the other, by the influence of the regionalist ethos of the Lomé school on Ouagadougou's architects. However, in both cases, these narratives appear in the architecture of state-led projects as a form of "banal" nationalism, such that in Ouagadougou, for example, such national or regional symbolism is an explicit criterion in international design competitions.

This chapter shows at a more general level that, although sometimes related, design and policy connections should not be conflated. In certain cases, such as Ciputra International City in Hanoi, the distinction between policy and design is difficult to establish. In other cases, designers follow routes established by municipal policy-makers. However, in general, design connections are established from person to person or company to company independently from the state and follow quite independent routes and logics. Issues of reputation, aesthetics, costs, and technical competence are here crucial factors. Such design relations play an important role in the material production of cities. Therefore, in order to extend our understanding of how places mutually constitute each other, policy mobility studies and studies of the geographies of architecture – two fields that speak little to each other – should be better articulated.[32] The present chapter has looked at how transnational design connections shape the landscape of globalizing cities. However, this is not the only generative dimension of these connections: they also influence the way those cities are used and how users position themselves in the world. How this happens – to what extent built forms can be said to reconfigure urban cultures – is the subject of the final chapter focusing on what new imported urban types actually "do."

Notes

1 Opening up the collective of actors involved in forms of architectural design (or redesign), beyond the professionals of construction and planning, geographers have, for instance, looked at the role of users, such as squatters (Vasudevan, 2011) or maintenance workers (Jacobs and Cairns, 2011; Strebel, 2011).

2 Yaneva's work on OMA (Yaneva, 2009), though she is not a geographer, is a case in point.

3 Kloosterman (2008) has studied Amsterdam and Rotterdam showing how interactions between architectural practices is more limited than expected but how they are connected by the mobility of their employees and the creation of spin-offs.

4 See for example Faulconbridge (2010) and McNeill (2009).

5 If we look at another set of architectural firms – the most reputed boutique firms (such as the Japan-based SANAA or Switzerland-based Herzog & de Meuron) – we have a slightly different geography where European and Japanese firms, with projects worldwide and especially in Asia, figure more prominently (Ren, 2011: 34).

6 The founder of Site Vietnam, Claude Cuvelier, first came to Hanoi in 1997 as a consultant for the construction of the Hilton Hotel, then stayed in the city before he opened Site Vietnam six years later.

7 Some large construction companies are not originally from Burkina Faso. The BTM group for instance was founded in the Ivory Coast in 1979 and established itself in Ouagadougou in 1995.

8 This does not mean that all state-owned companies active in architectural design have disappeared: the SONATUR *(Société Nationale d'Aménagement des Terrains Urbains)* is a significant actor in the sector of construction, notably responsible for the residential area in Ouaga 2000 hosting the inhabitants evicted from the center by the ZACA project.

9 See Chapter 2 on corruption in the country.

10 Interview, architect, October 27 2011.

11 Ibid.

12 How a building becomes iconic has traditionally been unpredictable because the process has been dependent on its acceptance by the public after construction. However, contemporary iconic buildings tend to be marketed and mediatized as such before they are even built (Kaika, 2011).

13 Holding a PhD from a UK university and a former lecturer at another UK university, he was encouraged by members of the HPC and Hanoi colleagues to return to Vietnam when economic growth in Hanoi really took off in 1999.

14 On "fast-transfer" in the domain of public policies, see Peck and Theodore (2010a).

15 The largest one south of Hanoi is Splendora; see Chapters 3 and 4.

16 On cross-border forms of learning about cities, see McFarlane (2011).

17 Nghia has since then become one of Vietnam's most famous young architects. He has received a number of international awards and is especially known for his bamboo architecture (www.votrongnghia.com).

18 It was planned to be completed in 2012, but at the time of writing (October 2013) the construction had not yet begun. A more detailed design by Coldefy raised the estimated costs to 30m euros and made it, for the moment at least, an unaffordable project.

19 Reemdoogo has become a very popular place in Ouagadougou. Its extension is now planned, a larger "Reemdoogo 2" is also planned on the other side of the city, and other African cities are emulating the concept.

20 The practice directed by Dieudonné Wango, also the designer of Reemdoogo.

21 Email exchanges with FAREstudio, February 2010; interview with D. Wango, October 26 2009.

22 See www.kerearchitecture.com.

23 Email exchanges with FAREstudio, February 2010.

24 The CBF has drawn very little attention in the country: "the project is perceived as banal, nobody is interested in it" (interview, architect, September 26 2009).

25 In Vietnam, for instance, the principle of copyright is still very vague.

26 The *Banque Centrale des Etats de l'Afrique de l'Ouest* is a large regional bank.

27 See www.gmp-architekten.de

28 VNCC has over 400 employees and is specialized in state-led projects.

29 Interview with project leader at VNCC, August 12 2009

30 Interview with state official, November 2 2009

31 According to Vietnam's myth of origins, all Vietnamese descend from a sea dragon and a fairy of the mountains. This reference made by the roof was spontaneously mentioned in the user interviews we did at the NCC in November 2009.

32 It is the aim of a forthcoming publication building on the case of the mobility of US penal policies and high security prison models to Colombia (Söderström and de Dardel, forthcoming).

6

On Road Interchanges and Shopping Malls
What Traveling Types Do

Urban forms have politics. Norms are, as we know, inscribed in forms (Rabinow, 1989). However, urban forms not only reflect, but also enact power relations. They do so through their capacity to shape and modify social practices. Urban forms can function as urban pedagogies: they "teach" their users forms of living. This was particularly obvious in the case of colonial cities when "traveling urban forms" were imported from elsewhere, with the intention of leading city users "from tradition to modernity" – a process which has been well-documented (Guggenheim and Söderström, 2010b; Harris, 2008; Hosagrahar, 2005; Myers, 2003). In this chapter, I would like to push this line of argument further in two ways: first, by looking at modernization in contemporary postcolonial cities such as Ouagadougou and Hanoi; and, second, by looking at traveling urban forms beyond pedagogy. I demonstrate how traveling forms act as "long-distance government tools" to create business-friendly urban milieus and how, at the same time, they can be used as occasions for self-government and learning. I thus turn in this book to a third and often neglected dimension of relational urban studies: how transnational investments, policies, and architectural forms shape new urban practices and imaginaries.

Drawing on science studies and governmentality literature, I examine the discipline these traveling types impose and the resistance, domestication, or subversion strategies developed by their users. However – and this

Cities in Relations: Trajectories of Urban Development in Hanoi and Ouagadougou, First Edition. Ola Söderström.

is rarely studied in the literature – the power of urban forms resides not only in their capacity to discipline their users, but also in the fact that they enable them to practice the city differently and to position themselves in society by experiencing and expressing in words or deeds new senses of themselves. Therefore, a critical understanding of the mobility of urban types should consider, on the one hand, how they enact and convey pedagogies and, on the other, how they provide new "affordances," i.e. new possibilities of action. I define "urban types" as a category larger than "building types." Building types, such as the bank or the railway station, are generic spatial patterns of buildings elaborated to host specific activities (such as taking the train). Urban types encompass not only buildings but also generic spatial patterns of infrastructures (like the road interchange) or developments of specific urban areas (like waterfronts). Urban forms, specific actualizations of urban types (like the shopping mall around your corner), very rarely literally "travel" or can be said to be "mobile," but urban types do. For instance, we can see how shopping malls as a type of building have been introduced in certain areas where they did not exist before.[1]

There is an important literature on how homes (Blunt, 2005; Tolia-Kelly, 2004) and housing (Flint, 2003; Jacobs and Cairns, 2008) participate in shaping identities and communities. Jacobs and Cairns, in particular, have convincingly shown how "modernist highrise housing came to be one of the key sites through which the post-independence Singapore subject was made and made themselves" (Jacobs and Cairns, 2008: 591). However, little work has been done on how other non-residential urban forms, such as those I consider here, play similar (or different) roles (Farías and Bender, 2010; Rentetzi, 2008). Even less frequent are urban studies that have looked at urban forms as "affordances," i.e. as providing possibilities to perform an action. Drawing on and extending the literature regarding the educative function of built forms and their affordances, in the first and conceptual part of this chapter, I propose ways of analyzing the relations between urban forms and subjects in everyday situations. Subjects and urban forms are always embedded in structured contexts. The process and discourse on modernity and modernization is one central aspect of this context, especially in the cities of the South. In the narrative of their promoters (developers, state officials, designers), modernization is the "promise" accompanying the introduction of new urban types. This narrative is also often present in users' discourse regarding urban change in those cities. Thus, I first clarify what I mean by modernity and modernization, maintaining that modernization is a form of morality and power that manifests itself in discourse, practices, and material forms. I also reflect on the shifting geographies of modernity – how the reference of what it is to be modern is related to different regions and places. I then try to specify the role of traveling urban types in everyday use as both pedagogical and enabling. On this basis, I look at the importation of traffic infrastructures and shopping malls in Hanoi and Ouagadougou. As in other chapters, I investigate here how relations with elsewhere are territorialized or how these forms are not only imported but locally "translated." I conclude with a discussion of the necessity to further develop a critical cultural analysis of the everyday consequences of the mobility of urban types.

Modernization as Morality and Power

Modernity is "a normative attitude constructed in the extreme inequities of colonialism" (Hosagrahar, 2005: 1). In other words, historically speaking, the very idea of modernity and modernization has been an instrument of power, legitimizing change and domination.[2] However, Euro-American thought was long blind to the moral content of European modernity, developing the idea that social change all over the world converges towards a similar rationality, and projecting Western cognitive categories on other societies and other periods in history (Taylor, 1995). Taylor (1995: 28) argues that we need to escape from this "ethnocentric prison" in order to understand "the full gamut of alternative modernities in the making in different parts of the world." This call has been heard.

In recent years, a series of important contributions have deconstructed classic theories of modernity, unpacked the moral power of the idea of the modern, and explored a series of alternative processes of modernization.[3] Chakrabarty (2000), in particular, has been influential in insisting on the temporal imagination underlying the European idea of modernity. Historicism – seeing phenomena as entities maintaining their unity and gaining their complete identity through time – is, he argues, central to European modernity. But such historicism should be superseded because it suggests that non-European societies lag behind, hampered by a series of archaisms, and does not allow us to see non-European societies as varieties of multiple modernities.

However, the idea of modernity is also shaped by a geographical imagination. If, following Chakrabarty's invitation, we need to step out of a teleological vision of social change through time, we also need to recognize the spatial variety and complexity of modernity. Doing this implies not only looking at how modernity is conceived differently in different regions or locales, but also investigating shifts in modernity's reference points, which leads us to see how the Euro-American world should not only be provincialized intellectually speaking, but *is* actually being provincialized in a very concrete geographical sense. In many parts of Asia and Africa, modernity is no longer associated with Europe or North America but with Asia or the Middle East. In recent years, postcolonial urban studies have, as we will now see, contributed towards the further re-conceptualization of modernity precisely in that direction.

Postcolonial urban modernization

Different contributions to postcolonial urban studies have shown that a simple diffusionist conception of the history of urban modernity is historically inconsistent. First, because a series of features generally considered as characteristic of European modernity, like multiculturalism, first appeared in cities of the Global South like Calcutta or Jakarta and not in the North (King, 2004: 74). Second, because features of urban modernity theorized in the North, such as the modern movement in architecture, did not simply follow a North–South route (Robinson, 2006: 74). Third, because certain colonial cities have been laboratories for European modernity and in that sense "ahead" of cities in Europe instead of "behind" (Bishop et al., 2003; Rabinow, 1989; Wright, 1991). Fourth and finally, because when modernity was not "home-grown" in cities of the South, it was more than simply imported and copied: it was adapted and indigenized (Hosagrahar, 2005; Nasr and Volait, 2003).

So in brief, urban modernity from the 19th century onwards was not simply rolled out from cities in the North to cities in the South. It was multipolar and relationally constructed. Today, urban modernity has become even more multipolar because of the diversification of geographical references to what modernity is. Emergent economies, especially in Asia, have not only transformed global geopolitics and geo-economics, they have also imposed new coordinates for the location of avant-garde modernity. In cities of the South, modernity is increasingly seen as being located in non-Euro-American cities. If, as Robinson (2006) argues, modernity has long been another word for "the West" (and still is for most people in the West), it is increasingly less so in cities of the South. This is true, for instance, of lifestyles in a city like Hanoi, where young people tend to be primarily influenced by trends from South Korea (Geertman, 2007). It is also true for urban policies: Kuala Lumpur's development strategy, for instance, has become a model for other Asian cities, such as Hyderabad in the 1990s (Bunnell and Das, 2010).[4]

The concepts of urban modernity and modernization have thus been thoroughly revisited by recent postcolonial approaches. It is beyond the scope of this chapter to discuss whether this has deprived modernization theory of its value as a general theory of social change altogether. I am more interested here in the persistent performative effects of these concepts outside academic debates: how they work as emic categories in the discourses and actions of developers, state officials, or city users. Classical ideas of modernity and modernization continue to shape their narratives and justify their actions, and these ideas continue to frame urban change, especially in globalizing cities. Tools such as the City Development Strategies promoted by UN-Habitat and the World Bank since 1998 are, for instance, accompanied by a narrative assuming that "modern, gleaming skyscraper-filled cities, with adequate networked infrastructures in place to support them is the only and ineluctable way into the urban future" (Pieterse, 2008: 108). In order to understand how modernization narratives are articulated with urban forms, it is useful to turn to governmentality studies.

Pedagogies and affordances in modernized urban forms

Foucauldian-inspired governmentality approaches have informed a range of studies of the relations between built forms and society (Osborne and Rose, 1999; Osborne and Rose, 2004; Rabinow, 1989). Geographers, in particular, have examined asylums (Philo, 1989), the workhouse system (Driver, 1993), or the city as a whole (Legg, 2006)[5] as tools for governing conduct. In these historical studies, built form is seen as regulating behavior mainly within punitive and disciplining forms of government. Drawing on the work of Rose, some recent analyses have also begun to look at contemporary (Flint, 2003) and postcolonial urban situations (Jacobs and Cairns, 2008) showing how housing consumption is framed by moral state discourses, or "ethopower" (Osborne and Rose, 1999), which translates into interiorized "grammars of living" (Flint, 2003: 614). State institutions and officials teach city dwellers how to behave like virtuous and responsible citizens through an involvement of tenants in the management of their housing. In other words, urban forms are endowed with a pedagogic (rather than a disciplining) role in a process of social modernization.[6] In Hanoi and Ouagadougou this pedagogy acquires, as we will see, a specific meaning as the shopping malls and road interchanges are new types of built form and correspond to norms of conduct unknown to most of their inhabitants.

As a response to such ethopower, users are generally considered to be capable of developing a counter-power defined as resistance or subversion. While I do not wish to deny the importance of actions opposing the changes brought by new urban forms, or "action against," I think we should pay more attention to "action with," in other words to actions that use new built forms as opportunities. "Affordance" is the concept that captures best this role of built forms. For the psychologist James Gibson (1979), who theorized the term, ecological reality, as opposed to physical reality, is made of meaningful things providing humans (and other animals) with affordances or possibilities to perform an action. An obstacle on a path affords a possible action of collision, for instance (Gibson, 1979: 36). This simple idea opens up fruitful ways of looking into the materiality/society nexus, encouraging, with its focus on *possibilities*, a non-deterministic analysis. However, few authors in urban studies have looked at this aspect of the power of built form.[7]

A whole series of urban types introduced since the beginning of economic transition in Hanoi and Ouagadougou can be analyzed in this double light: housing and office high-rises, pedestrian streets, shopping malls, discos, road infrastructures, etc. They have introduced or "taught" (more or less successfully) new ways of living, working, using public space, shopping, having fun, or circulating in cities. They also provide people with new means of being city dwellers and creating "arts of being global" (Roy and Ong, 2011). Actor-Network Theory and especially "script analysis" as developed in the study of innovations in industrial design (Akrich, 1992) is methodologically useful in order to grasp how artifacts "act." In script analysis, technology is considered as the materialization of a program of action that prescribes certain types of uses. The principle of following a script from its conception, to its inscription in artifacts, and finally to its adoption or rejection by its users is potentially useful for urban studies (Söderström, 1997). These perspectives on the technology–society nexus can be extended to understand how buildings and other categories of urban forms (public spaces, for instance) are attempts to shape human action. Here I will not systematically follow how these scripts have been elaborated, turned into material form, and received by users, but rather more loosely conceive of traveling urban types as programs of action.

In this chapter, I consider a series of built forms in each city, which in each case is representative of the important recent physical and social changes in these cities. I describe how they bring both new norms and new opportunities to urban life. In the case of Ouagadougou, I focus on traffic pedagogies, while in the Hanoi case I focus on the affordances and pedagogies related to shopping malls. I occasionally also refer to other new urban types and to what they "do." My aim is to investigate how built forms that are the product of transnational connections generate new discourses and practices. I begin by showing how building types have been part and parcel of previous phases of urban modernization.

Modernization Through Ouagadougou's Built Environment

There is a long genealogy of precolonial, colonial, and postcolonial modernization in Ouagadougou. The farming land territory of present Burkina Faso was first colonized by the Moose, an ethnic group originating from the region of contemporary Ghana, during the second half of the 15th century. From the 18th century onward (see Chapters 1 and 2), Ouagadougou (then Waogdogo) was the court city of the Moaga kingdom structured around two foci, the royal palace and the market (Fourchard, 2001).[8] The rational principles on which the city was founded can be read as a first modernization of a rural settlement as the city is organized "through a functional specialization of neighborhoods, a thoughtful spatial organization of squares and places of representation and through a comprehensive strategic ordering of the city" (ibid.: 41). A second phase corresponding to colonial modernization was inaugurated by the installation of a French military camp, flanked by a prison and a military training field, in place of the Moaga royal palace which had been razed to the ground by the troops of Captain Voulet in 1896. This modernization process came into its own in the 1920s, when the lieutenant-governor of the Haute-Volta colony, Charles-Edouard Hesling, developed a functionalist and hygienist urban development scheme strictly segregating local and European populations. According to Hesling, importing a new building type was the means to civilize the locals: "the construction of European-type houses is," he wrote, "our best intermediary with primitive populations in order to tame them and make them adopt the new ways of life."[9] He thus very clearly attached a pedagogical task to the introduction of new built forms.

Independence in 1960 did not correspond to a new project of urban modernization, but opened a phase during which the city sprawled and developed through informal settlements. As we saw in Chapter 2, the first substantial act of urban postcolonial modernization was introduced by the revolutionary regime of Thomas Sankara in 1983. The transformation of former neighborhoods into "sectors," the allocation of a land plot to each household, and the development of a collective housing typology are the central features of this project. The different *Cités*, with their modernist African stylistic language and three-storey structure (a novelty in Ouagadougou), were thus conceived as crucibles for the emergence of new citizens (Figure 6.1). The aim and support of pedagogy had changed, but its principle remained.

Finally, the city entered a fourth phase of entrepreneurial neoliberal modernization in 1991 in which urban transformations were geared towards attracting foreign capital and establishing the city's regional role. Here again urban types are meant to exercise their "ethopower." We saw in Chapter 3 that this political power is not monolithic but characterized by a tension between the national government and the municipality. However, it has been the state-led projects which have had the major impact on urban practices and identities. ZACA and Ouaga 2000 have fractured the city along class lines (Figure 0.4). ZACA, promoted as a new urban way of life and the means to transform the city into the

Figure 6.1   Cité An IV A, Ouagadougou. Photo by Pierrick Leu.

Figure 6.2   ZACA, promoting a new lifestyle. Photo by Ola Söderström.

"Geneva of Western Africa,"[10] has led, on the one hand, to the eviction of inhabitants of popular neighborhoods, and will imply, on the other, an eventual gentrification of the city's core (Figure 6.2).

The wealthy Ouaga 2000 development, on the other hand, has created a social and class divide between the political and economic elite to the south and the rest to the north. Such processes of social fragmentation and segregation are, unfortunately, very common: a real urban signature of neoliberal times. But here I want to investigate other less researched forms of modernization in entrepreneurial Ouagadougou, focusing in what follows on a state-led intervention that I have not yet touched upon: the development of traffic infrastructures.

Economic development means access to new forms of mobility: cities like Ouagadougou and Hanoi have seen a spectacular increase in motorized transport since 1990.[11] In Ouagadougou, the arrival of cheap Chinese motorcycles in the early 2000s has led to a significant increase in motorcycle traffic. In both cities, the obvious correlates of increased mobility are air pollution and traffic congestion. Other less obvious changes appear when one looks at the "scripts" embedded in traffic infrastructures, and at the ways in which they are domesticated by their users. This is particularly visible in the case of road interchanges in Ouagadougou.

In June 2008, the southern road interchange was inaugurated with great solemnity (Figure 0.4). It was the first of a series of interchanges planned by the state. Two other interchanges in the east and west were finished in 2010. The state's aim with this important and costly infrastructure is to improve traffic conditions, to anticipate future developments of the city, and to improve its image.[12] The system of interchanges was conceived by the Ministry of Infrastructures[13] on the basis of a study carried out by a Canadian agency.[14] However, the president himself has been involved in the conception of the interchanges, which are classified as "presidential infrastructures."[15] The development of the interchanges is also part of a regional competition between national capitals.[16] Bamako, for instance, started constructing road interchanges in the early 2000s, and has been ahead of Ouagadougou in that respect, whereas Niamey lags behind. Funding for the interchanges in Ouagadougou comes from a series of donor countries: Taiwan for the eastern interchange, Japan for the western one, and Libya for the southern one.[17] The southern interchange is of particular interest, as it is used by the state as an instrument of functional and symbolic change of the city (Figure 6.3).

Symbolically, it is part of a governmental narrative of modernization. The president himself intervened to make sure that the southern interchange would be the first to be completed. This interchange connects the new presidential palace to the south, located in Ouaga 2000, to the circular boulevard around the city. The Memorial to the Heroes of the Nation is situated halfway along that axis, between the palace and the interchange (Figure 6.4). The monument was erected after three years of political unrest following the murder of the journalist Norbert

Figure 6.3   Southern interchange, Ouagadougou. Photo by Jonas Haenggi.

Figure 6.4   The Memorial to the Heroes of the Nation, Ouagadougou. Photo by
Jonas Haenggi.

Zongo in 1998 (see Chapter 2). In an effort to improve his image,
in 2001 Blaise Compaoré decided to erect two monuments as acts of
contrition – one for the Martyrs and the other for the Heroes of the
Nation. The monument for the Heroes of the Nation was built in two

phases: the first between 2007 and 2009, and the second between 2010 and 2012. It is 47 meters high and supported by four pillars representing the four periods of the country's history since the precolonial period.

The axis leading from the presidential palace through the monument to the city, of which the interchange is an important part, can therefore be interpreted as symbolizing an attempt to establish a new type of relation between the head of state and the country's population in a context of political turmoil.[18] This segment of road infrastructure represents the first (and for the moment, only) monumental piece of urban planning in the city since independence. Connecting different places and symbols of power it is related to a planning tradition which finds its origins in Rome during the Baroque period when avenues where created to valorize its main churches. Its homologies with the Champs Elysées in Paris are striking. Like its "counterpart" in the former colonial metropole, it has at one end the Presidential Palace (the Palais de l'Elysée in Paris), a monument for national heroes in the middle (the Arc de Triomphe in Paris), and continues to a major circular boulevard (the Boulevard Périphérique in Paris). This piece of urban planning can therefore be seen as a fragment of European modernity. But a fragment that has been "indigenized," since the monument for the heroes in Ouagadougou is (of course) dedicated to figures of Burkinabè history and its architectural language uses emblematic local forms such as the calabash.[19]

In Burkina Faso, this axis, inspired by prestigious European capitals, is used as a manifesto of a nationalist modernization process. The interchange, in particular, has become one of the main icons of Ouagadougou, standing as a synecdoche of the city. It is represented on numerous official documents: governmental publications and websites; touristic brochures; and in the opening images of the news program of the national television network.[20] These urban forms are more than symbolic devices, though: they are also attempts to change the ways in which cities are practiced.

Functionally, the southern interchange facilitates the access of people and goods to the city center. With the interchange, the route for trucks from Ghana to the city's main road station has become easier. It is also part of a road belt around the city allowing for faster traffic and transport because the bumpy and narrow streets of Ouagadougou's internal road network can thereby be avoided. For the central government, the interchange is also a pedagogical tool: through such new infrastructures users should learn how to take part in a more fluid and high-speed form of urban modernity. To ensure fluidity, only certain types of users are permitted on the interchange system. The plan was initially to ban bicycles and motorcycles from using the interchange, but ultimately only pedestrians and animal-powered carts were forbidden. Former roadside users such as fruit vendors, cigarette vendors, and *colleurs* (literally "gluers": mechanics mainly repairing motorcycle tires) have also been evicted from the area, officially for security reasons. Users are thus filtered and selected. After (rather unsuccessful) attempts to exclude them from the city center, informal activities are now being excluded at its margins.

In contrast, those allowed to access the interchange are actively taught how to use it: police officers are posted along the road to ensure that the infrastructure is "correctly used" and that no unwelcome activity is taking place. This was necessary since drivers are often illiterate. In addition, a two-minute instructional video was shown on the national TV channels to explain how to use this complex new infrastructure.[21] Interviews with users showed that accepting the new rules was not easy. Some tried avoiding the interchange by using alternative routes, some avoided using the bridge, some used it in the wrong direction, while others did not manage to go where they wanted – at least not during the first months after inauguration.[22]

Ouagadougou's new southern interchange is thus an operator of the city's modernization as much as it is one of its symbols. It helps to inscribe a form of modernity in daily urban practices as much as in the city's visual landscape. By importing an urban type that previously did not exist in the local urban environment, the state introduced a monumental grandeur that the city did not possess. It also contributed to speeding up the pace of the city and to educating its inhabitants by separating slow and rapid users and by teaching them how to smoothly move through a "modern" city. The state is thus using urban infrastructures to rationalize the city and configure its users (Woolgar, 1991) into citizens of an economically dynamic regional center.

Despite occasional accidents, people in Ouagadougou are progressively getting used to these new infrastructures and the forms of mobility they imply. Another transformation regarding street-use during the same years (2008–2011) has been less successful. It shows, as we will now see, that different scripts and different conceptions of urban modernization contained in built forms often compete and sometimes clash.

In 2003, the city's central market (Figure 0.4), Rood Woko, was destroyed by fire. Financed by the *Agence Française de Développement* conceived under the guidance of the French planning agency, the Groupe Huit, a new central market was built and opened in April 2009. In July of that year, barriers ensuring that the surrounding streets remained for pedestrian use only were destroyed and police surveillance sheds were set on fire by users of the area opposing the new

Figure 6.5 The pedestrian area around the central market (2010), Ouagadougou. Photo by Jonas Haenggi.

design of the market (Figure 6.5). They were protesting against the lack of motorized access to the market and the interdiction against using the streets for commercial purposes. Controversies around the introduction of pedestrian areas are common throughout the world, but usually take place before or shortly after the inauguration. However, in Ouagadougou the controversy has endured, with continuous acts of resistance against the new regulation and continuous negotiations between vendors and the municipality. In 2011, the merchants seized the opportunity presented by a more general contestation of the government by the population in Burkina Faso[23] to reintroduce traffic and parking in the area. As a result, negotiations now revolve around the introduction of one-way streets and speed bumps. In other words, the municipality has given up the fight for a pedestrian area.

The pedestrian area was initially planned to be much larger, in order, as one of the architects of the project put it, "to get people used to walking, even though it is not a city where it is easy to walk" (Architect, interview July 5 2012). The idea was introduced by Groupe Huit and embraced by their local partner, who firmly believed it was a good idea:

> I am shocked that there is not yet an area in Ouagadougou where one can shop, walk with one's wife and kids holding hands, and where there are no obstacles. There are so many obstacles everywhere. I thought, if people taste this pleasure once, other streets would be contaminated by this approach. But I was totally wrong (ibid.).

Figure 6.6 The victory of motorized traffic (2012). Photo by Ola Söderström.

This controversy indicates that there was a serious gap between the project's embedded "program of action" and many of its actual users' expectations. In this case, the importation from France of a design for a commercial space – the market surrounded by a pedestrian belt – was heavily contested. This type of design is representative of a contemporary French conception of urban modernity characterized by a concern for public space and "walkability."[24] What happened around the central market of Ouagadougou can therefore be read as a clash between this version of urban modernity and another, related to functionalist planning and characterized by priority given to access, consumption, and motorized traffic (Figure 6.6). The latter version has been embraced by users of the city of Ouagadougou who make a living from informal commerce in the streets of the center and don't see themselves, at least for the time being, behaving like French bourgeois *flâneurs*. As a result, the script contained in the new market area, where non-humans (barriers) and humans (policemen) were supposed to ensure that motorized traffic was banned and the surroundings of the market turned into a calm and walkable area, became the target of contestation.

Globalizing cities in the South are cities where different planning cultures meet, where different scripts and injunctions related to different traveling urban forms clash with each other, or – to put it in other words – where different versions of urban modernization are entangled and played against each other.[25] However, traveling urban forms also provide users with new types of resources, as we will now see in the case of the importation of another urban type – the shopping mall – to the city of Hanoi.

Staging New Social Identities in Hanoi's Shopping Malls

Like Ouagadougou, Hanoi has been through different phases of modernization. Founded in 1010, when the Emperor Ly Thai To defeated the Chinese, who had dominated the region for a thousand years, the original city was organized around the citadel (*thanh*) and the market place (*thi*). Modeled after the Chinese city of the time, this spatial divide corresponded to a social one distinguishing the two castes of the mandarins and the commoners. During the long feudal period, the city remained the economic center of the region even when the political capital was moved to Hue by the Nguyen dynasty (1802–1883) (Logan, 2000). Its economic role led to the development of the 36 trade streets of the present historic center, each specialized in a specific trade (Figure 0.2). The shophouse building type, with its mix of production, retailing, and storage space on the first floor and residential space on the top floors, plays a central role in this context (Ros, 2001).

Between 1883 and 1945, the French colonial presence brought about modernization in Hanoi, which accelerated after 1900, when Hanoi became the capital of French Indochina. Modernization was much more ambitious than in Ouagadougou, whose economic and political role was much less significant. During this period, Hanoi was remodeled as a French city with the introduction of large administrative buildings, 80–90 meter long building blocks, a large number of villas, the railway, a tram, a grid of wide (20–30 meters) streets, and an industrial zone on the northern bank of the Red River (Koperdraat and Schenk, 2000) (Figure 6.7). This new urban design for the entire city was part of what the French called their *mission civilisatrice*: bringing a feudal backward society to a bright republican future (Wright, 1991).

The third phase of urban modernization corresponds to the socialist period until *Doi Moi* (1945–1986). As we have seen in previous chapters, Russian planners played an important role in the reshaping of the city, even though urban transformation was hampered by 30 years of war. The socialist housing estates, the *Khu Tap The*, scattered in the second ring around the city center, are emblematic of that period. These rational collective housing units, in which kitchens and bathrooms were shared, were, like the *Cités* in Ouagadougou, meant to be operators of a cultural conversion to socialist values.

Figure 6.7 Hanoi 1929 with the French quarter south of the Petit Lac (Hoan Kiem Lake) from Sion (1929) *Asie des Moussons* in Paul Vidal de la Blache, *Géographie Universelle*, vol. IX, p. 432 © Armand Colin.

Such operators of change are not confined to socialist cities, however, and are numerous in the present entrepreneurial phase. Through the introduction of new urban types – from office towers to shopping malls – ways of life in the city have dramatically changed during the past 20 years. Extended families living in shophouses, for instance, now live in European housing typologies as nuclear families in high-rises on one floor. I focus hereafter on one of these elements of change: shopping spaces and shopping practices.

In pre-*Doi Moi* Hanoi, shophouses and wet markets[26] were the traditional spaces for residence and shopping. Shopping practices have

Figure 6.8   Big C, Hanoi. Photo by Chu Giap.

been transformed by increased standards of living and the investments of retail firms eager to extend their markets to new, unexploited areas. As a result, supermarkets and shopping malls are built where they formerly did not exist, changing former ways of selling and buying. Like the interchanges in Ouagadougou, these urban types accompanying narratives of urban modernization have a deep impact on everyday life.

In Hanoi, supermarkets began to appear in the 1990s and shopping malls in the early 2000s.[27] Their development is not only due to the initiatives of the retail industry but also to governmental policy as, in 2007, the municipality launched a large project aimed at the replacement of wet markets by shopping centers and malls (Geertman, 2010). Predating this policy, Big C and Vincom were among the first shopping malls in the city: the former is a lower-end mall, while the latter caters for more affluent consumers. Located at an important crossroad in the rapidly growing southwestern part of the city and facing the recently built National Convention Centre (Figure 0.2), Big C was built between 2004 and 2005.[28] It belongs to Casino, a leading European retailer with more than 9,500 stores worldwide. Casino began its activity in Vietnam in 1998 and this particular Big C – designed by a Hanoi-based French architectural firm – was the first to be built in Hanoi (Figure 6.8).

Vincom (Figure 6.9) is a complex of three high-rise towers. The first two towers were completed in 2005 with investments from a Ukrainian company owned by a Vietnamese-born entrepreneur and a large Vietnamese real-estate company. The third tower opened in 2009 and

Figure 6.9   Vincom, Hanoi. Photo by Chu Giap.

was developed by Vietnamese companies. Centrally located south of the French quarter (Figure 0.2), this shopping mall offers a large variety of shops and brands as well as cinemas, restaurants, and game halls. Big C and Vincom not only represent new forms in the landscape of Vietnam's capital, but are also important mediators in the transformation of Hanoi's urban culture.

In functional terms, going to the mall implies the development of new spatial practices, especially for women. Traditionally, Hanoian women went every day to a wet market to buy fresh food (and many still do). Women shopping at Big C or Vincom buy food once or twice a week. They also tend to mix different activities in one visit to the mall: buying food and clothes, eating out, etc., and make shopping more of a family event by going with their husbands and children instead of on their own, as they did previously. In other words, changes in shopping practices imply more general changes in the spatial and social patterns of urban practices in Hanoi. Malls also change the meaning of "doing shopping" both for the shop-users and the shop-workers.

For the users we interviewed,[29] the idea of modernity was prominent in how they described the malls and what they do there. Our respondents used qualifications belonging to a common semantic field: the malls are described as "clean," "cool," and especially "modern." It makes Hanoi, they told us, "more modern," "more beautiful," "more professional," and "more civilized." As in other emerging Asian countries, "being modern and civilized" is a common trope of state rhetoric in Vietnam. It is endlessly repeated in the political posters found in the streets of the capital. This rhetoric is also recurrent in ordinary citizens' ways of talking about urban and social change. In the case of the malls, this modernity discourse frames users' experience of them: "it makes me feel more civilized," "it makes me feel more modern," "more stylish" were the most frequent replies when we asked why people were going to these two malls. They also told us that they come to "learn" what is modern and "new." Seeing lavish shops, new brands (or just "brands"), observing how others – more accustomed to such places or pretending to be so – go around doing shopping is described as part of a learning process. Shopping malls are, in other words, portrayed by the users as operators of the modernization of selves.

The emergence of this new urban type also has important implications for the other side of the commercial transaction: the shop-workers. Traditionally, shop-workers in Hanoi lived and worked in the same space (and many of them still do). In the shophouses of the historic center, the boundaries between public and private spaces are very fuzzy: shopkeepers often eat or take a nap in the front, or "shop area," and not in the back, or "house area" (Figure 6.10). In these traditional shops, spatial – but also temporal – distinctions between work and non-work are difficult to establish.

In the malls, the situation is quite different. Spaces and times of work and family life are clearly distinct: workers commute to the malls at fixed hours during the day. Malls also modify the interaction between customers and shop-workers: fixed prices are the rule and bargaining, increasingly seen as an archaic practice, disappears. Users of Big C for instance, express distrust of traditional shops: the mall offers "more comfort," they say, products have fixed prices and can be returned in case of problems. The shop-workers we interviewed said that in the malls they "learned how to behave," mentioning that they are not allowed to sleep and eat in the shop or to talk to other shop-workers. They also said they learned to "manage money," "to know the price of good quality," and to interact with a wider spectrum of customers, including wealthy foreigners.[30] In the characteristic language of Hanoians, they told us that acquiring these new skills make them "feel more confident as individuals."

Hanoi malls, like Ouagadougou's interchanges, are therefore pedagogical tools. They are places where new shopping practices are learnt. However, the malls are also places of experimentation. Users come even

Figure 6.10 Shop and shopkeeper in Hanoi's historic center. Photo by Ola Söderström.

if they cannot afford to buy, in order to get an experience of a world which is still unknown to them. This is especially true for Vincom, which offers not only shops, but a variety of different activities (cinemas, game halls, etc.). For people from rural areas "a trip to Hanoi includes a visit to Vincom. These people come for all the services, eating, drinking, shopping, going to the movies".[31] They tend to come once a month and stay for much longer than other users: 5–6 hours.[32] These users explain that such regular visits enable them to meet a diversity of people and ways of being that they otherwise are not exposed to. For instance, a 22-year-old student who moved to Hanoi from a rural area told us that "Coming here helps me to see how people behave, how people think, how people act, and then realize how people here live." Another respondent said that this confrontation with diversity made his life "more interesting." When respondents say that they "feel more modern and civilized" when they come to the shopping mall, it is therefore not only the result of interiorized propaganda; it can also be understood

Figure 6.11   Doing-looking cool in a Hanoi mall. Photo by Chu Giap.

literally as a sensorial experience of social change: they encounter new colors, odors, and sounds compared with those of more traditional areas in Hanoi and its surroundings. Malls are, in other words, perceived as places where new cultural capital can be gained.

Experimentation also includes trying out new social identities. In a paper on the uses of shopping malls in another globalizing city, Cairo, where this urban type appeared in the 1990s, Abaza (2001) shows how malls afford users spaces where new gender roles and relations are tried out. What makes Cairo malls interesting, she writes, "is not shopping but rather that they are a locus and meeting place for groups of young girls" (Abaza, 2001: 117), who use them for flirting or conquering the right to use public spaces without a male presence. For the groups of young people we observed and interviewed in Hanoi, Vincom and Big C provide similar affordances.[33] Playing videogames, wearing a branded T-shirt, and "doing-looking cool" (Figure 6.11) are ways of staging themselves as urbanites and as radically different from members of their family who often work in the suburban or rural paddy fields.

These affordances have both a very material and "atmospheric" character. Figure 6.11 shows a place in Vincom with undefined and flexible possibilities of use. It offers space for hanging out or flirting that traditional markets rarely provide. Moreover, a large number of our respondents, regardless of age, told us that air-con, clean air, as well as tranquility and silence (compared to Hanoi's very busy and noisy streets) were some of the reasons they went to the malls. Thus, the

ambience or "atmospheric" quality of malls is not only appreciated but
supports specific (and sometimes new) social practices.[34] These young
users of Hanoi shopping malls are therefore certainly interiorizing a
new "grammar of living the city" and are, more specifically, learning
how to be consumers of mass-produced goods. But they are also accessing a wider range of urban practices and identities. Put differently,
if shopping malls have scripts teaching their users to act in ways that
are beneficial to their owners and promoters, they are also spaces of
learning, open to "interpretive flexibility" (Gieryn, 2002) that thereby
do more than just shaping neoliberal subjects.

Conclusion

In order to better understand the role of traveling urban types in the
social transformations of globalizing cities, in this chapter I have looked
at the introduction of road interchanges and shopping malls in the cities of Ouagadougou and Hanoi. In the first part of my text, I argued
that *governmentality, modernization,* and *script* are useful heuristic concepts for such an analysis. Together they enable the unpacking of the
relation between discourse and artifacts in the practices of different
types of urban actors.

   In general terms, a *governmentality* perspective means looking at
the organization of conduct through rationalities and technologies
(Miller and Rose, 2008: 15). Compared to the more narrow concepts
of government or governance, governmentality ("the conduct of conduct") leads us to see that urban types and forms are technologies used
by the state and private enterprise to govern society and its transformations, but also used by ordinary citizens to govern themselves. For the
state and private enterprise, built forms are tools that allow configura-
tions of new uses of the city and new subjectivities adapted to aims such
as commodity consumption and the political steering of social change.
The road interchanges in Ouagadougou categorize users according
to the function of their transport mode and induce a speeding up of
the city's everyday rhythms. Users learn how to change their practices
by engaging with the infrastructure and through state-sponsored pedagogical videos and policing. Supported by the state and developed
by foreign investors and companies, shopping malls train consumers
and shop-workers in new forms of commercial exchange. In these new
urban spaces, users get accustomed to the triggers of mass consumption: the seduction of brands and the delights of social distinction.
But, as we saw with the troubles generated by the new central market
of Ouagadougou, such processes of social transformation mediated by

urban forms can also be resisted when they are perceived as too disruptive of former spatial practices.

However, to put it in the words of Osborne and Rose (1999: 740), the liberal city cannot be reduced to discipline and tactics of resistance: it is "the milieu for the regulation of a carefully modulated freedom." Modulated freedom, or what I referred to previously as "acting with,' is manifest in how many users self-consciously use shopping malls as spaces in which to encounter and experiment with ways of life or to try out new social identities. In other words, in these new urban spaces, users are shaped and governed by exterior forces, but they also use them as occasions of self-government and learning.

Although heavily criticized in recent social theory, the concept of *modernization* has helped me here to understand both the rationalities behind urban change and how this change is experienced by city users. Outside academic debates, the rhetoric of modernization, justifying change in the name of progress, remains a powerful narrative. Not surprisingly, therefore, in Ouagadougou and Hanoi, modernity and modernization are ubiquitous in governmental discourses accompanying the construction of malls or road infrastructures. However, in neither city do ordinary citizens buy into that rhetoric in the way the state assumes they will. Respondents in Hanoi tend to celebrate the introduction of new building types and systematically associate urban change with positive values: beauty, civilization, modernity; whereas respondents in Ouagadougou are generally much more critical.[35] In Ouagadougou, several urban development projects have thus been contested during the past 20 years (Biehler and Le Bris, 2010). The ambitious modernization of the city center, in particular, has been the target of different oppositional actions led by civil society since 1995.

Moreover, as postcolonial critiques of modernization theory have insisted, we should consider the different "geographies of modernization." These differences between the two cities also illustrate, as Africanist Ferguson (2006) has argued, that Asian and African popular attitudes towards modernization tend to be quite divergent. In Asian examples where economic growth has been much stronger, attitudes are associated much more strongly with hopes for a better future than are African attitudes, where modernization often appears as a "broken promise" (Ferguson, 2006: 187).

Finally, the notion of *script* has been used to understand the relations between "rationalities" and "technologies" (in this case, new urban types). In this perspective, interchanges and shopping malls are seen as materialized programs of action, and their physical shape as tools for channeling their uses and users. The power of such scripts becomes particularly visible when developments are contested, as in the example of the barriers and police sheds built to make sure that users acted according to plan in Ouagadougou's new market area, which became the main target of protesters. In this case, protesters were contesting scripts that had traveled (from France) to Ouagadougou with a new urban type for that city, the pedestrian area. So, one of the important things traveling types do is to transport social norms from one place to another, and this may create tensions since the conditions of production and acceptance of such norms vary from place to place. French assumptions about uses of public space embodied in French public space design are not easily transferred to other parts of the world, as we saw in Chapter 4. More generally, a focus on scripts leads us to consider that globalizing cities are cities where different planning cultures meet, and where different injunctions related to different traveling urban forms clash with each other. The scripts embedded in traveling types are, therefore, not perfect predictors of how urban forms are used. They are resisted, as in the case of the Ouagadougou market, and open to interpretive flexibility, as we saw with the ways in which groups of young people use shopping malls in Hanoi.

Built forms can be considered as means of governing populations at a distance. Forms, analyzed here, that are the product of transnational connections can be defined as long-distance governing tools. This does not mean that there is somewhere a *Deus ex machina* pulling the threads of urban practice from afar, but that contemporary urban relations are also the vehicles of new norms of conduct. Traveling types in particular shape new uses of the city and new forms of subjectivity. In Hanoi and Ouagadougou, they are technologies which make everyday urbanism more amenable to business and economic growth. Most of the new forms related to imported types – malls and interchanges, but also high-rise office towers or the creation of heritage streets – can be seen as enacting a progressive micro-scale and business-friendly process of cultural change. However, I have insisted in this chapter on the fact that such an analysis is too limited. Transnational connections also provide urbanites with new affordances and possibilities for autonomous action and self-reflection.

Notes

1 For more elaborate discussions on these different points, see Guggenheim and Söderström (2010b).

2 The first uses of the term "modern" as referring to a feature of the current period appear with the constitution of the colonial world system in the 16th century (King, 2004: 66).

3 The idea of multiple modernities has been suggested to contest two central tenets of classical theories of modernization: the equation between modernity and the West; and the assumption that modernization leads to the

convergence of societies undergoing it (Eisenstadt, 2000) (for a critique of the concept of multiple modernities, see Schmidt (2006)). Appadurai (1996) has also proposed a broader conception of modernity considering the complexities of contemporary globalization. Similarly, Randeria (2006; 2007) has investigated the "entangled modernities" in the postcolonial situations encountered in a country like India. See also Therborn (2003).

4   These transformations in the geography of urban modernity have been encouraged by a series of political initiatives. In recent years, international organizations such as the World Bank, or networks of local governments such as UCLG, have stimulated increasing levels of South–South exchange regarding urban development strategies.

5   See Huxley (2007) for a general assessment of governmentality studies in geography.

6   Two recent papers have explicitly looked at urbanism as pedagogy: Simpson (2011) interprets Macao as a space where mainland Chinese learn to become neoliberal subjects and Berney (2011) looks at the role of public space policy in Bogotà in attempts of the state to reform civil society.

7   Among them, Borden shows how skateboarders use affordances of the urban environment, like sidewalks for sliding, that are not taken advantage of by other city users, in a way that "makes us rethink architecture's manifold possibilities" (Borden, 2001: 1). In another context, McFarlane (2011: 40) shows how Mumbai slum dwellers use what they have at hand to improvise sanitation facilities. See also Edensor (2002; 2005) on the affordances of cars and ruins.

8   "Moaga" is the singular form of "Moose." The adjectival form is "moose."

9   "Circulaire du 14/4/1926 au sujet des instructions pour la concession des permis d'occupation urbaine," quoted by Fourchard (2001: 69).

10 From an article in the newspaper *L'Observateur* in 2006, quoted by Biehler (2010: 415).

11 During the past 15 years alone, Hanoi has gone through two transitions in traffic. The first transition was from bicycles to motorcycles; the second is from motorcycles to cars. In 1990, over 80 percent of trips were made by bicycle. Fifteen years later, in 2005, nearly 65 percent of daily journeys were made on motorbikes. The constant increase in motorcycle ownership is now paralleled by a growing number of cars. In 2005, only 2 percent of households in Hanoi owned cars, but between 2004 and 2007 new vehicle registrations in Hanoi increased at a two-digit rate, reaching 20 percent over the last two years. Only ten years ago, the city still had no traffic lights (Söderström et al., 2010).

12 Interview with the person responsible for the presidential infrastructures in Burkina Faso, February 9 2010.

13 *Ministère des Infrastructures et du Désenclavement.*

14 Interview, municipal official, December 1 2009.

15 Interview, state official, February 9 2010.

16 In particular, with neighboring Mali.

17 Eventually, Libya covered only part of the costs (7.5 percent of the total). Still, the southbound avenue has been baptised "Boulevard Mouammar Kadhafi" as an acknowledgement of Libya's contribution to the infrastructure.

18   Interestingly, the Boulevard is a dead end: it terminates at the portal of the president's palace, which no ordinary inhabitant of the city dares to approach.
19   On the concept of indigenized modernity, see Hosagrahar (2005).
20   The news program begins with images of the globe and then zooms in to the country and to the interchange (www.rtb.bf).
21   See www.dailymotion.com/video/x5r6im_spot-echangeur_shortfilms (last accessed July 22 2011). The video-clip, financed by the Ministry of Infrastructures, aims at facilitating the acceptance of the interchange and raising money for the other interchanges (interview, municipal official, December 1 2009).
22   Interviews with users conducted between December 2009 and February 2010. At the time of writing, more than three years later, the same observations could still be made.
23   The death of a young schoolboy in February 2011, a victim of police violence, triggered three months of strong popular mobilization against the government.
24   See Chapter 4.
25   On the idea of entangled modernities, see Note 3.
26   In South Asia, 'wet' markets sell fresh food, while 'dry' markets sell clothes or machines.
27   The first shopping mall in Hanoi, Tang Trien Plaza, was built in 2000 in a very central location.
28   Big C is more like a US shopping mall, with a large department store and a series of other smaller outlets around it, whereas Vincom is closer to the Asian model comprising a variety of different shops approximately equal in size.
29   Interviews with 28 users in September 2009 undertaken by Vietnamese researchers.
30   Interviews with 12 shop-workers in September 2009.
31   Interview with a shopkeeper, June 19 2009.
32   Ibid.
33   This part is based on 15 interviews with users, and six short interviews with shopkeepers.
34   This atmospheric dimension of places has been theorized in interesting ways by Peter Sloterdijk (2004).
35   The successful mobilisation of Hanoi's civil society against the construction of a Disneyesque entertainment park in the large and centrally situated Thong Nhat Park in 2007 shows, however, that some sectors of the population are progressively becoming more critical and more vocal. On this controversy and more generally on issues of public space in Hanoi, see Chapter 4 and Söderström and Geertman (2013).

Conclusion
For a Politics of Urban Relatedness

This book claims that urban development is increasingly shaped by transnational and translocal relations. Its aim has not been to measure their role in comparison with the role of local and regional factors. It has rather been to investigate and compare different processes of change generated by these relations taking into consideration different dimensions of cities' *mondialisation* (i.e. not restricted to economic globalization). In doing this, I have tried to advance urban studies empirically and analytically. In this general conclusion I first briefly return to the specificities of my relational urban analysis. I then summarize my main empirical results and discuss what we can learn analytically about the role of relationality from the studies gathered in this monograph. Finally, on this basis I propose, extending a suggestion by John Friedmann (Friedmann, 2007), the development of an assets-based politics of urban relatedness.

The idea of studying relational geographies has turned mainstream in recent years, but remains at the same time an underdeveloped research program as it mostly takes the form of abstract theorizing, except in specific research domains such as policy mobility studies. Understandably in this context, relational thinking in geography has been attacked for being too vague about what entities are precisely related across space and for paying too little attention to how relations have historically developed, how connections and flows depend on and create material

Cities in Relations: Trajectories of Urban Development in Hanoi and Ouagadougou,
First Edition. Ola Söderström.
© 2014 John Wiley & Sons, Ltd. Published 2014 by John Wiley & Sons, Ltd.

places, and how they are infused with power. Arguing that geography is necessarily relational but that this critique is also to a large extent legitimate, I have proposed an analysis that looks at how relations between cities have historically evolved, how they are moored in specific built environments, and how their effects on urban social practice are both constraining and enabling. Moreover, drawing on Deleuze's search for novelty through relations and proposing to move beyond a too-narrow focus on urban neoliberalization and the specific domain of policy mobilities, I have explored the generative power of transnational relations in shaping *urban policies*, *urban forms*, and *urban practices*.

My second contribution to the development of urban relational geographies lies in an effort to develop relational urban comparisons. Like relational geographies, relational comparisons have as their premise that spatial entities cannot be studied as discrete knowledge objects. To what type of analysis this premise precisely leads is however as yet rather unclear. I have therefore proposed to consider relational urban comparisons as composed of two different dimensions: first the comparison of the worlds of relations of the cities' considered (i.e. more than the relations between them) in terms of their *type*, *intensity*, and *orientation*; and second, the comparison of the effects that these relations generate in different domains of urban life and development. The third way this book takes urban studies into new terrains is by analyzing the trajectories of two cities at the margins of global flows of exchange until the early 1990s. Throughout the book I have shown that *mondialisation does* matter in many ways even in cities at the very bottom of the globalization ladder and very relation-poor 20 years ago. Such cities therefore should no longer be considered as "unfortunate footnote[s] to the phenomenon of globalization" (Shatkin, 1998: 378) but as sites to be researched in order to widen our understanding of how globalization and urban change are mutually constructed. In the empirical chapters of the book, I show how Hanoi and Ouagadougou have negotiated economic transition and more broadly an intensifying globalization. The results of their relational comparison to which I now turn bring a nuanced understanding of this process. It is also through comparison that their trajectories of change become more distinctly perceptible.

Comparing Processes, Worlds of Relations, and Relational Effects

The most obvious element in the comparison of Vietnam's and Burkina Faso's capitals is the economic transition process. Hanoi and Ouagadougo have been on parallel tracks with an initial phase in the late 1980s, corresponding to the Compaoré coup against Sankara in Burkina Faso and the *Doi Moi* in Vietnam; in the early 1990s, new national constitutions leading to the (re)privatization of land, enterprises, and housing; and through successive waves in the 1990s and 2000s, the liberalization of trade and foreign investments. In both capital cities, this process has led to the rise of non-state actors (private development companies, partially privatized state-owned ones, consultants, civil society), increasing levels of corruption, informal constructions, and urban sprawl. The differences between the trajectories followed by both cities become more perceptible when considering the evolution of their worlds of relations. The *type* of relations clearly differs as Ouagadougou has mainly globalized by establishing political connections (through national development agencies, NGOs, city networks, regional conferences) and Hanoi has done so by capturing global economic flows (through remittances and FDIs). The *intensity* of relations, with much higher investment and tourist flows in Hanoi, and *orientation* – Hanoi being now clearly oriented towards the rest of Asia and Ouagadougou still mainly following the old colonial route with France – clearly differ as well. This difference in trajectory illustrates the necessity to look systematically at the different dimensions and geographies of *mondialisation* to characterize contemporary urban change instead of talking about an unspecified "urban globalization."

I also argue in this book that transnational or translocal relations should not only be compared as such, although this provides necessary background information, but in their territorializing effects. Some relations have little territorial consequence and others are more performative because of local institutional strategies and forms of agency. The economic interests of governing parties' *nomenklatura* or the role of popular mobilization against certain developments play for instance a crucial role in the articulation between relationality and territoriality. This is why the main part of *Cities in Relations* (Chapters 3–6) is devoted to comparing the generative effects of transnational connections.

Using the distinction between market- and social-centered policies, I have shown that there are substantial differences in terms of policy relations between and within the two cities. In general terms, both cities have witnessed, under the pressure and influence of World Bank and other foreign consultants, a turn towards more market-centered policies, notably characterized by a strong decrease in the provision of affordable public housing. However, at a closer look a more variegated situation appears. In Burkina Faso's capital city, different policy connections are used to support competing strategies of different parts of the state apparatus. The national state, on the one hand, uses its diplomatic relations to carve out "spaces of sovereignty" where market-oriented, master-planned neighborhoods are developed (leading to increasing levels of socio-spatial polarization). In contrast, although some of its projects are "image" oriented, the municipality uses its strong implication in city networks to sustain a more social-centered urban development agenda around issues of environment, health, and culture.

In Hanoi, where the municipality has little effective power, such contradictions within the state apparatus are less important. Striking is rather the discrepancy between cosmetic collaborations and effective ones: relations with European countries in the form of social-centered master-plans are usually of the first type, while market-centered connections with Asian partners are of the second type and get translated into residential or commercial enclaves for the elite.

The analysis of policy relations in terms of master-planning (Chapter 3) also points to the emergence of a new geopolitical urban development order. Since 1990, the horizon of policy relations has widened far beyond the connections with the former metropole to include the US, Asia, and the Middle East. Moreover, Ouagadougou has become a regional model city and an active exporter of "good practices" to other cities in the South. If Hanoi is very rarely mentioned as a model in South–South exchanges, it has witnessed a clear shift in its policy relations where South Korea, Indonesia, and Japan tend to supplant Europe and the US. This geopolitical shift is accompanied by a transformation of priorities as these inter-Asian relations are much more market-centered than the waning European relations.

The comparison of the two cities also allows an observation of different moments in the development of specific urban policies (Chapter 4). In Hanoi, the analysis of the making of a post-socialist public space policy made visible the different ontologies of and strategies for public space specific to different relations with elsewhere, from green belts to street design. Looking at a relational policy in the making also highlights the potential of certain relations and the presence of alternative policies, as well as the instrumental use of certain policy connections by local actors. Ouagadougou is ahead in this respect, as the city started to develop a public space policy in collaboration with the city of Lyon in 1996 and more recently with other African cities in order to develop more context-relevant strategies. This book also provides insights into how city relations increasingly shape architectural forms (Chapter 5) and user practices (Chapter 6): dimensions that are less frequently explored in contemporary urban studies. I showed that even ordinary cities like Hanoi and Ouagadougou increasingly participate in spatially stretched processes of design. However, they are clearly not involved in the same circuits of architectural conception: while, because of its economic attractiveness, Hanoi is "becoming iconic" and a target for private-driven master-planning, Ouagadougou is not. I also showed that transnational design does not simply connect a place of architectural production – the office of a large London design firm for instance – to a place of consumption in the Global South, but takes place "in between" these places involving processes of mutual learning and co-produced design (what I called "design in the wild"). Finally, I showed that the state responds to this cosmopolitanization of architecture by promoting national narratives (through aesthetic control and architectural education) in the design of public buildings. In contrast with most existing literature in the domain, I therefore argued that transnational design in the cities considered cannot be reduced to logics of branding and capital accumulation.

This is one of the ways in which my comparative analysis of these cities in the South "speaks back" to mainstream critical urban studies. My last chapter, dealing with what traveling types do (and what people do with them) also speaks back in the sense that it shows that the conceptual couple discipline/resistance, often used to capture the relation between forms and practices, is insufficient. Forms with their embedded norms – such as the road interchange and shopping malls I investigated – are means through which users are governed, but they are also occasions of self-government and learning. In the words of Osborne and Rose (1999: 740), the liberal city, which Ouagadougou and Hanoi are becoming, is "the milieu for the regulation of a carefully modulated freedom" and not simply of a discipline/resistance dialectic. If new urban types can be seen as instruments for the making of neoliberal selves, they also provide urbanites with new affordances and possibilities for autonomous action and self-reflection.

In summary then, the relational geography and comparison of these two cities proposed by this book goes beyond narratives of economic transition and neoliberalization. It invites scholars in urban studies to be specific about cities' multiple relations with elsewhere and what they produce. However, I would also like to move beyond this call for an attention to specificity and propose a more general conclusion to be drawn from this comparison. It has to do first with cities' relational worlds and second with a politics of relatedness.

The Evolving Relational Worlds of Cities

The latest visit I made to Ouagadougou was with a Swiss friend who has been visiting the city very regularly for over 20 years. During his first visit in 1992 he met Michel, a Burkinabè living in the city. Together they founded an association aimed at providing poor children living in the sprawling periphery with the possibility of going to school or getting vocational training. Through this NGO, Swiss families sponsor the most disadvantaged children by paying for the schooling fees. It all started with a class of 25 children; 20 years later the school had over 2,000 children. What was, at the start, one of a myriad of transnational connections between Ouagadougou and elsewhere thus became by chance (and through friendship) a relation with quite substantial consequences.

This story is emblematic of the relational worlds that this book has been exploring. It contains the three analytical conclusions I want to tease out of my relational comparison concerning the imagination of relations in urban studies, their specificity and power. First, this book shows that while city relations are often reduced to financial flows or policy connections, our understanding of urban development would gain both from vastly enlarging our imagination of urban relatedness and focusing on "relations that matter." Cities are caught in and constantly weave anew vast worlds of relations. Some of these connections are ephemeral and without important impact. Others generate important changes in cities. To define this world of city relations, Latour's (2005) notion of "plasma" is helpful. Plasma for Latour (2005: 244) is made of elements that are not yet formatted and mobilized within actor-networks: "It resembles a vast hinterland providing the resources for every single course of action to be fulfilled, much like the countryside for an urban dweller, much like the missing masses for a cosmologist trying to balance out the weight of the universe." It is made of virtual components in other words.[1] Cities' worlds of relations can be seen as such a plasma or a reservoir out of which generative relations are made through human action and non-human effects. To further build on this metaphor, I suggest distinguishing between connections and relations, two terms that are generally used interchangeably (as I have done so far in this book) in urban studies. Etymologically, a connection is a "binding together" (*co* and *nectere* in Latin), while the word "relation" leads us back to an account, a narrative (the meaning of the Latin *relatio*). So if we (playfully) use this distinction, we can say that relations are connections about which a story can be told, connections that matter. Relations can thus be defined as strong and generative connections. Lausanne and Ouagadougou were connected in many different ways in the early 1990s. But, throughout the 1990s and 2000s my two friends in Switzerland and Burkina Faso have established one of the significant relations of Ouagadougou with elsewhere, now involving many other persons, flights, affective bonds, financial transfers, shipped goods, exchanged messages, and so on. A connection within a plasma of different connections became a relation.[2]

Second, attention to specificity and to the articulation of relations is important to better understand urban relationality. Tracing all relations of cities with elsewhere (not to talk about connections) – in the above defined sense – is of course an impossible task, even in the cases of rather marginal cities like Ouagadougou or Hanoi. To investigate cities' relations we therefore need to select specific relations as I have done in this book by focusing on policies, forms, and practices. The relevance of these three relational registers is of course open to debate, but they are helpful in order to explore the various *modi operandi* of relations in different domains of urban life. Recent work has improved our understanding of urban *policy* relations. We can now study policy relations using a repertoire corresponding to different and often complementary relational processes: policy mobility, topological relations, and inter-referencing. But more work is needed to investigate how other types of relations are established and affect urban development. This book provides some elements in that direction, showing that relations in the domain of architecture can, on the one hand, be described using the same repertoire but, on the other, are quite specific because characterized by the greater importance of hierarchically organized circuits of design, the fact that design takes place increasingly "in between sites," and the role of urban and architectural types. I have also shown that policy and design relations are closely articulated with transnational relations in terms of urban practices and imaginaries because norms of conduct and images of modernity travel with new urban types and policies. However, specific to city relations in terms of practice are the unpredictable tactics of users and the shifting geographies of modernity that inspire them. Urban studies should therefore not only extend the purview of urban relatedness but also attend to the specificity and articulations of different registers of relations. Obviously, these different registers are partially connected by the common grammar of neoliberalization as privatization, competition, profit, and commodification are recurrent motifs within these worlds of relations. But, as my short story of the Ouagadougou school shows, cities relational lexicon and syntax exceeds the process of neoliberalization.

The third analytical point is power through urban relations. Power of course pervades city relations: it is present in the land grabs making possible FDI-financed upper-class edge-cities, or in the eviction of street vendors to create the image of a city center attractive for foreign real estate companies or organizers of international conferences. This is important but not new, of course. The added insight provided by an analysis of the evolving relational worlds of cities lies elsewhere. It lies first in the fact of highlighting that power through relations involves a wider range of processes than those previously mentioned, such as "governing at a long distance" through the introduction of new urban types. In terms of theoretical approaches this means that political economy is not sufficient but that it should be combined in relational urban studies with other resources such as governmentality studies or Actor-Network Theory. Second, relations themselves, as we saw for instance apropos the different strategies of the national government and the Municipality of Ouagadougou, form a battleground. In a situation of abundance, where the plasma of connections is expanding through the acceleration of *mondialisation*, struggles over what should be a city's privileged transnational urban relations are increasing. The third and last point is tightly correlated to the previous one as it consists of stressing the importance today of shifting geographies of power. Following relations through times and in two different cities shows how their orientation varies in different domains: from FDIs and ODAs to imaginations of modernity. Here also, more work deserves to be done to more systematically analyze the changing geopolitics of city relations. Notions such as "Chinafrica" capture the shift in power in Africa caused by China's massive investments in the continent over recent decades. However, behind such wide regional transformations, cities display more subtle and sometimes contradictory movements, including the development of South–South relations.

These different analytical points – imagination, specificity, and power – coalesce in the question of a politics of urban relatedness. I have striven throughout this book to avoid a normative stance. But I want to conclude by breaking that self-imposed rule in order to briefly suggest how cities could use a broader imagination of city relations.

An Assets-based Politics of Relatedness

"Which of the two cities is doing better?" is the question I have often been asked by non-academics (academics generally have more quirky ones) or by media people when discussing this work. I have often answered: "Hanoi is trying to climb up the ladder of world-city ranking, mimicking cities at the top and destroying its assets instead of using them to conceive a sustainable and context-sensitive development strategy. Ouagadougou, on the other hand, uses intelligently city networks to find the resources for its own development agenda." This is a caricature but it also says something about the ways these two cities manage their transnational relations.

This contrast also resonates with a paper by John Friedmann (2007), given as a UN-Habitat Award Lecture, where he pleads for an "assets based development of newly urbanizing regions." In the paper,

Friedmann criticizes the idea that the future of cities mainly depends on their capacity to attract outside capital. To that he opposes "the long-term endogenous development of seven clusters of regional assets that will generate what I consider to be the true wealth of city-regions" (Friedmann, 2007: 988), and suggests ways in which governments may promote such a development.[3] Investments, he argues, should build on assets existing in a city-region "rather than soliciting investments from global firms into an underdeveloped asset base subject to further degradation" (ibid.: 996); "it also calls," he adds, "for enlightened political leadership that has embraced a vision not geared to an imaginary that comes straight out of Hollywood movies and television" (ibid.: 997)

The political elite of Vietnam and Burkina Faso both have Hollywoodian urban imaginaries. They dream of Hanoi as a top world-city and promote edge-cities resembling Dubai's "palm" or "world" islands. They project Ouagadougou as an African Geneva and try to construct a mega-conference center. In the process, Hanoi's unique social assets, such as public life in the historic center, its unique cultural assets, such as the extraordinary shophouse morphology, and its unique environmental assets – the very specific mix of agriculture and urbanity, the lake landscape – are carelessly destroyed.[4] At work in Hanoi we have for the time being a narrow imagination of relatedness that leads its elite to follow the routes leading to the usual urban role models instead of trying out less beaten tracks. Ouagadougou is comparatively more protected from these footloose dreams because of its weak economy, the counter-power of the municipality, and hopefully also by recent moves, with the national development plan launched in 2006, towards a more coherent territorial development policy. However, Friedmann does not simply oppose endogenous strategies to foreign investments, arguing, for instance, that the former can trigger the latter. As a conclusive thought, I would like to push this argument further.

In this study I have shown how pervasive, diverse, and often contradictory relations with elsewhere are, even in cities way down in the various globalization indexes. This makes it difficult to disentangle today the endogenous from the exogenous: are the Vincom towers (Chapter 6) financed by a member of the Vietnamese diaspora exogenous? Is the Reemdoogo musical garden (Chapter 5) co-conceived by Grenoble and Ouagadougou endogenous? This is rather difficult to say and therefore today the contrast between endogenous and exogenous development strategies does not seem very useful. It is important rather to conceive urban development strategies that are both rooted in a specific context, based on a city's assets *and* mobilize relations that can support the development of these assets. This requires an attention and careful study of specificity as well as a carefully crafted politics of urban relatedness.

By that term I am not simply referring to the international relations of cities through which they try to promote their image, their solutions or, alternatively, try to attract foreign investment and learn from elsewhere. By politics of relatedness I mean two things. The first is a politics of learning: a strategic reflection on the models of urban development that could be inspirational given the specific situation and asset base of a city. A reflection aimed at looking beyond the main avenues of city relations, beyond the automatic will to emulate the usual suspects of world-city literature and rankings, from London to Vancouver. The second is – because models are always partial – to develop a multilateral strategy of relations where different partnerships would respond to specific aims and needs of urban development. In this respect, the strategy of the city of Ouagadougou is quite exemplary. My hope is that on these two issues – an asset-based evaluation of urban models and the design of a multilateral strategy of relatedness – the type of relational comparative urbanism that I have tried to promote with this book can be thought-provoking and … maybe even useful.

Notes

1   For a critique of this notion from a Deleuzian point of view, see Anderson et al. (2012: 179).

2   I am consciously pushing Latour's argument a bit here since plasma for him is what is unconnected by socio-technical networks. But what can be totally unconnected? Therefore I think the distinction connection/relation is useful.

3   The seven assets are: human, social, cultural, intellectual, natural, environment, and urban.

4   Describing assets as place-specific does not imply that they are such in their historical making. The "Asian" shophouse typology is for instance the result of transnational relations between Europe and Asia, much as the "European" bungalow is the result of relations between India and Great Britain (King, 1990).

References

Abaza, M. (2001). Shopping malls, consumer culture and the reshaping of public space in Egypt. *Theory, Culture and Society*, 18(5), 97–122.

Adey, P. (2006). If mobility is everything then it is nothing: towards a relational politics of (im) mobilities. *Mobilities*, 1(1), 75–94.

Akrich, M. (1992). The de-scription of technical objects. In Bijker, W. and Law, J., *Shaping Technology/Building Society*. Cambridge: MIT Press, 205–224.

Allen, J. (2003). *Lost Geographies of Power*. Oxford: Wiley-Blackwell.

Allen, J. (2008). Powerful geographies: spatial shifts in the architecture of globalization. In Clegg, S. and Haugaard, M., *The Handbook of Power*. Los Angeles: Sage, 157–173.

Allen, J. and Cochrane, A. (2007). Beyond the territorial fix: regional assemblages, politics and power. *Regional Studies*, 41(9), 1161–1175.

Allen, J. and Cochrane, A. (2010). Assemblages of state power: topological shifts in the organization of government and politics. *Antipode*, 42(5), 1071–1089.

Amati, M. (2008). Green Belts: a twentieth-century planning experiment. In Amati, M., *Urban Green Belts in the Twenty-First Century*. London: Ashgate, 1–18.

Amin, A. (2002). Spatialities of globalisation. *Environment and Planning A*, 34(3), 385–400.

Amin, A. (2004). Regions unbound: towards a new politics of place. *Geografiska Annaler: Series B, Human Geography*, 86(1), 33–44.

Anderson, B., Kearnes, M., McFarlane, C. and Swanton, D. (2012). On assemblages and geography. *Dialogues in Human Geography*, 2(2), 171–189.

Cities in Relations: Trajectories of Urban Development in Hanoi and Ouagadougou, First Edition. Ola Söderström.

© 2014 John Wiley & Sons, Ltd. Published 2014 by John Wiley & Sons, Ltd.

Appadurai, A. (1986). *The Social Life of Things.* Cambridge: Cambridge University Press.

Appadurai, A. (1996). *Modernity at Large.* Minneapolis: University of Minnesota Press.

Arabindoo, P. (2011). "City of sand": stately re-Imagination of Marina Beach in Chennai. *International Journal of Urban and Regional Research,* 35(2), 379–401.

Audier, S. (2012). *Néolibéralisme(s).* Paris: Grasset.

Balima, S.-T. and Frère, M.-S. (2003). *Médias et communications sociales au Burkina Faso. Approche socio-économique de la circulation de l'information.* Paris: L'Harmattan.

Barnett, C., Robinson, J. and Rose, G. (2008). *Geographies of Globalisation: a demanding world.* London: Sage.

Barnett, C., Cloke, P., Clarke, N. and Malpass, A. (2010). *Globalizing Responsibility: the political rationalities of ethical consumption.* Oxford: Wiley-Blackwell.

Beall, J. and Fox, S. (2009). *Cities and development.* London: Routledge.

Berney, R. (2011). Pedagogical urbanism: creating citizen space in Bogotá, Colombia. *Planning Theory,* 10(1), 16–34.

Biehler, A. (2010). *Enjeux et modes de constitution des espaces publics à Ouagadougou (Burkina Faso).* Paris: U.F.R de Géographie, Université Paris 1 Panthéon-Sorbonne.

Biehler, A. and Le Bris, E. (2010). Les formes d'opposition aux politiques de la ville à Ouagadougou. In Hilgers, M. and Mazzocchetti, J., *Révoltes et oppositions dans un régime semi-autoritaire: le cas du Burkina Faso.* Paris: Karthala, 133–150.

Binger, C. (1892). Du Niger au golfe de Guinée par les pays de Kong et le Mossi. Paris: Musée de l'Homme.

Bishop, R., Phillips, J. and Yeo, W. (2003). *Postcolonial Urbanism: Southeast Asian cities and global processes.* London: Routledge.

Blunt, A. (2005). Cultural Geography: cultural geographies of home. *Progress in Human Geography,* 29(4), 505–515.

Blunt, A. (2008). The "skyscraper settlement": home and residence at Christodora House. *Environment and Planning A,* 40, 550–571.

Bondi, L. (1998). Gender, class, and urban space: public and private space in contemporary urban landscapes. *Urban Geography,* 19(2), 160–185.

Borden, I. (2001). *Skateboarding, Space and the City: architecture and the body.* Oxford: Berg.

Bouaniche, A. (2007). *Gilles Deleuze, une introduction.* Paris: Agora.

Boudreau, J. A., Hamel, P., Jouve, B. and Keil, R. (2007). New state spaces in Canada: metropolitanization in Montreal and Toronto compared. *Urban Geography,* 28(1), 30–53.

Boyer, F. and Delaunay, D. (2009). « *OUAGA, 2009* ». *Peuplement de Ouagadougou et Développement urbain, Rapport provisoire.* Ouagadougou: Ambassade de France.

Brenner, N. (2001). World city theory, globalization and the comparative-historical method: reflections on Janet Abu-Lughod's interpretation of contemporary urban restructuring. *Urban Affairs Review,* 36(6), 124–147.

Brenner, N. and Keil, R. (2006). *The Global Cities Reader.* London: Routledge.

Brenner, N., Peck, J. and Theodore, N. (2010). Variegated neoliberalization: geographies, modalities, pathways. *Global Networks,* 10(2), 182–222.

Bunnell, T. and Das, D. (2010). Urban Pulse – a geography of serial seduction: urban policy transfer from Kuala Lumpur to Hyderabad. *Urban Geography*, 31(3), 277–284.

Bunnell, T. and Maringanti, A. (2010). Practising urban and regional research beyond metrocentricity. *International Journal of Urban and Regional Research*, 34(2), 415–420.

Burawoy, M. (2000). *Global Ethnography: forces, connections, and imaginations in a postmodern world*. Los Angeles: University of California Press.

Callon, M. (1996). Le travail de la conception en architecture. *Cahiers de la Recherche architecturale*, 37, 25–35.

Callon, M. and Rabeharisoa, V. (2003). Research "in the wild" and the shaping of new social identities. *Technology in Society*, 25(2), 193–204.

Chakrabarty, D. (2000). *Provincialising Europe: post-colonial thought and colonial difference*. Princeton: Princeton University Press.

Clarke, N. (2012a). Actually existing comparative urbanism: imitation and cosmopolitanism in North–South partnerships. *Urban Geography*, 33(6), 796–815.

Clarke, N. (2012b). Urban policy mobility, anti-politics, and histories of the transnational municipal movement. *Progress in Human Geography*, 36(1), 25–43.

Cochrane, A. and Ward, K. (2012). Guest editorial: Researching the geographies of policy mobilities: confronting methdological challenges. *Environment and Planning A*, 44(1), 5–12.

Collier, S. J. (2012). Neoliberalism as big Leviathan, or...? A response to Wacquant and Hilgers. *Social Anthropology*, 20(2), 186–195.

Collier, S. J., Lakoff, A. and Rabinow, P. (2007). What is a laboratory in the human sciences? *ARC Working Paper*.

Cook, I. (2004). Follow the thing: papaya. *Antipode*, 36(4), 642–664.

Cormier, J. (1993). *L'Etat, les cités de la Révolution burkinabè et les bailleurs de fonds*. Paris: Institut Français d'Urbanisme, Université Paris VIII.

Crang, P., Dwyer, C. and Jackson, P. (2003). Transnationalism and the spaces of commodity culture. *Progress in Human Geography*, 27(4), 438–456.

Crot, L. (2006). "Scenographic" and "cosmetic" planning: globalization and territorial restructuring in Buenos Aires. *Journal of Urban Affairs*, 8(3), 227–251.

Darling, J. (2010). A city of sanctuary: the relational re-imagining of Sheffield's asylum politics. *Transactions of the Institute of British Geographers*, 35(1), 125–140.

Dekeyser, C. (1998). *Caractéristiques et évolution de la périphérie d'une ville sud-saharienne: le cas de Ouagadougou, Burkina Faso*. Utrecht: Universiteit Utrecht Faculteit Ruimtelijke Wetenschappen.

Deleuze, G. and Guattari, F. (1986). *Kafka: toward a minor literature*. Minneapolis: University of Minnesota Press.

Deleuze, G. and Guattari, F. (1987). *A Thousand Plateaus: capitalism and schizophrenia*. Minneapolis: University of Minnesota Press.

Deleuze, G. and Guattari, F. (1991). *Qu'est-ce que la philosophie?* Paris: Editions de Minuit.

Derudder, B., Hoyler, M., Taylor, P. and Witlox, F. (2011). *International Handbook of Globalization and World Cities*. Cheltenham: Edward Elgar.

Dévérin-Kouanda, Y. (1990). Gestion des espaces collectifs: pratiques ouagalaises. *Espaces et sociétés* (62–63), 93–105.

Diasso-Yameogo, C. and Ouedraogo, S. (2005). *Etude préliminaire sur la migration et les transfert d'argent des migrants burkinabè*. Ouagadougou: Centre d'Innovation Financières.

Dolowitz, D. and Marsh, D. (1996). Who learns what from whom: a review of the policy transfer literature. *Political Studies*, 44(2), 343–357.

Douglass, M. (2008). Civil society for itself and in the public sphere: comparative research on globalization, cities and civic space in Pacific Asia. In Douglass, M. and Ho, K. C., *Globalization, the City and Civil Society in Pacific Asia*. London: Routledge, 27–49.

Douglass, M. and Daniere, A. (2008). *The Politics of Civic Space in Asia: building urban communities*. London: Routledge.

Douglass, M. and Ho, K. C. (2008). *Globalization, the City and Civil Society in Pacific Asia: the social production of civic spaces*. London: Routledge.

Drabo, I. (1993). Influences des styles de l'habitat traditionnel burkinabè sur l'urbanisation moderne de Ouagadougou. In *Centre Culturel Français, Découvertes du Burkina, tome II*. Paris – Ouagadougou: SÉPIA-A.D.D.B, 185–213.

Driver, F. (1993). *Power and Pauperism: the workhouse system, 1834–1884*. Cambridge: Cambridge University Press.

Drummond, L. (2000). Street scenes: practices of public and private space in urban Vietnam. *Urban Studies*, 37, 2377–2391.

Drummond, L. (2003). Popular television and images of urban life. In Drummond, L. and Thomas, M., *Consuming Urban Culture in Contemporary Vietnam*. London Routledge, 155–169.

Drummond, L. and Lien, N. T. (2008). Uses and understandings of public space among young people in Hanoi, Vietnam. In Douglass, M. and Daniere, A., *The Politics of Civic Space in Asia: building urban communities*. London: Routledge, 175–196.

Drummond, L. and Thomas, M. (2003). *Consuming Urban Culture in Contemporary Vietnam*. London: Routledge

Edensor, T. (2002). *National Identity: popular culture and everyday life*. Oxford: Berg.

Edensor, T. (2005). *Industrial Ruins: aesthetics, materiality and memory*. Oxford: Berg.

Edensor, T. J. and Jayne, M. (2011). *Urban Theory Beyond the West: a world of cities*. London: Routledge.

Eisenstadt, S. (2000). Multiple modernities. *Daedalus*, 129(1), 1–29.

Ewen, S. (2012). Le long XXe siècle, ou les villes à l'âge des réseaux municipaux transnationaux. *Urbanisme* (383), 46–49.

Farías, I. and Bender, T. (2010). *Urban Assemblages: how actor-network theory changes urban studies*. London: Routledge.

Faulconbridge, J. (2009). The regulation of design in global architecture firms: embedding and emplacing buildings. *Urban Studies*, 46(12), 2537–2554.

Faulconbridge, J. (2010). Global architects: learning and innovation through communities and constellations of practice. *Environment and Planning A*, 42, 2842–2858.

Faulconbridge, J. and McNeill, D. (2010). Guest editorial: Geographies of space design. *Environment and Planning A*, 42, 2820–2823.

Ferguson, J. (2006). *Global Shadows: Africa in the neoliberal world order*. Durham: Duke University Press.

Flint, J. (2003). Housing and ethopolitics: constructing identities of active consumption and responsible community. *Economy and Society*, 32(4), 611–629.

Foucault, M. (2004). *Cours au Collège de France 1978–1979: Naissance de la biopolitique*. Paris: Seuil.

Fourchard, L. (2001). *De la ville coloniale à la cour africaine. Espaces, pouvoirs et sociétés à Ouagadougou et à Bobo-Dioulasso (Haute-Volta) fin XIXᵉ siècle–1960.* Paris: L'Harmattan.

Fournet, F., Meunier-Nihiema, A. and Salem, G. (2009). *Ouagadougou (1850–2004). Une urbanisation différenciée*. Marseille: IRD.

Freidberg, S. (2004). *French Beans and Food Scares: culture and commerce in an anxious age*. Oxford: Oxford University Press.

Friedmann, J. (1986). The world city hypothesis. *Development and Change*, 17(1), 69–83.

Friedmann, J. (2007). The wealth of cities: towards an assets-based development of newly urbanizing regions. *Development and Change*, 38(6), 987–998.

Geertman, S. (2001). The image of a dreamhouse in Vietnam: globalisation and changing urban life in Hanoi. Paper given at the World Planning Conference in Shanghai, July 2001.

Geertman, S. (2007). *The Self-organizing City in Vietnam: processes of change and transformation in housing in Hanoi*. Eindhoven: Bouwstenen Publicatieburo.

Geertman, S. (2010). Fresh markets, a way of life and public health under threat. Healthbridge Livable Cities Programme – Presented as Key-Note lecture at Public Forum "Public Markets in the Corporate City" in Hanoi.

Geertman, S., Söderström, O., Chi, L., Thong, N. and Loan, P. (2014). *Globalizing Hanoi*. forthcoming.

Gehl, J. (2010). *Cities for People*. Washington: Island Press.

Genuit, C. and Rijksen, A. (1994). *Policies and Legislation for the Houses in the Ancient Quarter of Hanoi*. Delft: University Printing House.

Ghertner, D. A. (2011). Rule by aesthetics: world-class city making in Delhi. In Roy, A. and Ong, A., *Worlding Cities: Asian experiments and the art of being global*. Oxford: Wiley-Blackwell, 279–306.

Gibson, J. (1979). *The Ecological Approach to Visual Perception*. Boston: Houghton Mifflin.

Gieryn, T. (2002). What buildings do. *Theory and Society*, 31(1), 35–74.

Guggenheim, M. and Söderström, O. (2010a). Introduction: Mobility and the transformation of built form. In Guggenheim, M. and Söderström, O., *Re-shaping Cities: how global mobility transforms architecture and urban form*. London: Routledge, 3–19.

Guggenheim, M. and Söderström, O. (2010b). *Re-shaping Cities: how global mobility transforms architecture and urban form*. London: Routledge.

Gugler, J. (2004a). Introduction. In Gugler, J., *World Cities Beyond the West: globalization, development and inequality*. Cambridge: Cambridge University Press, 1–26.

Gugler, J. (2004b). *World Cities Beyond the West: globalization, development and inequality*. Cambridge: Cambridge University Press.

Gusfield, J. R. (1984). *The Culture of Public Problems: drinking-driving and the symbolic order*. Chicago: University of Chicago Press.

Habermas, J. (1962). *Strukturwandel der Öffentlichkeit. Untersuchungen zu einer Kategorie der bürgerlichen Gesellschaft*. Darmstadt: Neuwied.

Hannerz, U. (1996). *Transnational Connections: culture, people, places*. London: Routledge.

Harris, R. (2008). Development and hybridity made concrete in the colonies. *Environment and Planning A*, 40(1), 15–36.

Hart, G. (2002). *Disabling Globalization: places of power in post-apartheid South Africa*. Pietermaritzburg: University of Natal Press.

Hart, G. (2004). Geography and development: critical ethnographies. *Progress in Human Geography*, 28(1), 91–100.

Harvey, D. (1989). From managerialism to entrepreneurialism: the transformation in urban governance in late capitalism. *Geografiska Annaler. Series B. Human Geography*, 3–17.

Harvey, D. (2001). Globalization and the "spatial fix". *Geographische Revue*, 3(2), 23–30.

Harvey, D. (2006a). The political economy of public space. In Low, S. M. and Smith, N., *The Politics of Public Space*. London: Routledge, 17–34.

Harvey, D. (2006b). *Spaces of Global Capitalism*. New York: Verso Books.

Harvey, D. (2007). *A Brief History of Neoliberalism*. Oxford: Oxford University Press.

Healey, P. (1997). *Collaborative Planning: shaping places in fragmented societies*. London: Macmillan.

Healey, P. (2012). The universal and the contingent: some reflections on the transnational flow of planning ideas and practices. *Planning Theory*, 11(2), 188–207.

Healey, P. and Upton, R. (2010). *Crossing Borders: international exchanges and planning practices*. London: Routledge.

Hilgers, M. (2009). *Une ethnographie à l'échelle de la ville. Urbanité, histoire et reconnaissance à Koudougou (Burkina-Faso)*. Paris: Karthala.

Hoa, T. (2011). Community participation in urban planning for sustainable development in Vietnam – prospect and challenges. Unpublished manuscript, Faculty of Architecture and Urban Planning, National University of Civil Engineering, Hanoi.

Hosagrahar, J. (2005). *Indigenous Modernities: negotiating architecture and urbanism*. London: Routledge.

Huxley, M. (2007). Geographies of governmentality. In Crampton, J. and Elden, S., *Space, Knowledge and Power: Foucault and geography*. Aldershot: Ashgate, 185–204.

Imrie, R. and Street, E. (2009). Regulating design: the practices of architecture, governance and control. *Urban Studies*, 46(12), 2507–2518.

Jacob, C. (1991). *Géographie et ethnographie en Grèce ancienne.* Paris: Armand Colin.

Jacobs, J. M. (2006). A geography of big things. *Cultural Geographies*, 13(1), 1–27.

Jacobs, J. M. (2012). Urban geographies I: Still thinking cities relationally. *Progress in Human Geography*, 36(3), 412–422.

Jacobs, J. M. and Cairns, S. (2008). The modern touch: interior design and modernisation in post-independence Singapore. *Environment and Planning A*, 40, 572–595.

Jacobs, J. M. and Cairns, S. (2011). Ecologies of dwelling: maintaining high-rise housing in Singapore. In Watson, S. and Bridge, G., *The New Companion to the City*. Oxford: Blackwell, 79–95.

Jacobs, J. M. and Lees, L. (2013). Defensible space on the move: revisiting the urban geography of Alice Coleman. *International Journal of Urban and Regional Research*, 1559–1583.

Jacobs, J. M. and Merriman, P. (2011). Practising architectures. *Social and Cultural Geography*, 12(3), 211–222.

Jacobs, J. M., Cairns, S. and Strebel, I. (2007). 'A tall storey ... but, a fact just the same': The Red Road high-rise as a black box. *Urban Studies*, 44, 609–629.

Jaglin, S. (1995). *Gestion urbaine partagée à Ouagadougou: pouvoirs et périphéries (1983–1991).* Paris: Karthala – ORSTOM.

Jessop, B., Brenner, N. and Jones, M. (2008). Theorizing sociospatial relations. *Environment and Planning D: Society and Space*, 26(3), 389–401.

Jones, M. (2009). Phase space: geography, relational thinking, and beyond. *Progress in Human Geography*, 33(4), 487–506.

Kaika, M. (2011). Autistic architecture: the fall of the icon and the rise of the serial object of architecture. *Environment and Planning D: Society and Space*, 29(6), 968–992.

Kantor, P. and Savitch, H. V. (2005). How to study comparative urban development politics: a research note. *International Journal of Urban and Regional Research*, 29(1), 135–151.

Kaviraj, S. (1997). Filth and the public sphere: concepts and practices about space in Calcutta. *Public Culture*, 10(1), 83–113.

Kerkvliet, B. J. T. (2004). Surveying local government and authority in contemporary Vietnam. In Kerkvliet, B. J. T. and Marr, D. G., *Beyond Hanoi: local government in Vietnam.* Copenhagen: NIAS, 1–27.

Kim, J. and Kim, T. (2008). Issues with green belt reform in the Seoul metropolitan area. In Amati, M., *Urban Green Belts in the Twenty-First Century.* London: Ashgate, 37–57.

King, A. (1990). *Urbanism, Colonialism, and the World-economy: cultural and spatial foundations of the world urban system.* London: Routledge.

King, A. (2004). *Spaces of Global Cultures: architecture, urbanism, identity.* London: Routledge.

Klauser, F. (2012). Thinking through territoriality: introducing Claude Raffestin to Anglophone sociospatial theory. *Environment and Planning D: Society and Space*, 30(1), 106–120.

Kloosterman, R. C. (2008). Walls and bridges: knowledge spillover between 'superDutch' architectural firms. *Journal of Economic Geography*, 8(4), 545–563.

Knox, P. and Taylor, P. (2005). Toward a geography of the globalization of architecture office networks. *Journal of Architectural Education*, 58, 23–32.

Koh, D. (2004). Illegal construction in Hanoi and Hanoi's wards. *European Journal of East Asian Studies*, 3(2), 337–369.

Koh, D. (2006). *Wards of Hanoi*. Singapore: Institute of Southeast Asian Studies.

Koperdraat, A. and Schenk, H. (2000). Living in a colonial environment transition: residents in Hanoi's "French Quarter". In Luan, T. and Schenk, H., *Shelter and Living in Hanoi*. Hanoi: Cultural Publishing House, 57–84.

Labbé, D. (2010). *Facing the Urban Transition in Hanoi: recent urban planning issues and initiatives*. Montréal: INRS.

Labbé, D. and Boudreau, J. A. (2011). Understanding the causes of urban fragmentation in Hanoi: the case of new urban areas. *International Development Planning Review*, 33(3), 273–291.

Labbé, D. and Musil, C. (2011). L'extension des limites administratives de Hanoi: un exercice de recomposition territoriale en tension. *Cybergeo: European Journal of Geography*.

Latour, B. (2005). *Reassembling the Social: an introduction to Actor-Network-Theory*. Oxford: Oxford University Press.

Latour, B. (2009). Spheres and Networks: two ways to reinterpret globalization. *Harvard Design Magazine*, 30, 138–144.

Leaf, M. (1999). Vietnam's urban edge: the administration of urban development in Hanoi. *Third World Planning Review*, 21(3), 297–315.

Legg, S. (2006). Governmentality, congestion and calculation in colonial Delhi. *Social and Cultural Geography*, 7(5), 709–729.

Lévy, J. (2008). *L'invention du monde: une géographie de la mondialisation*. Presses de Sciences Po.

Logan, W. (1995). Heritage planning in post-Doi Moi Hanoi: the national and international contributions. *Journal of the American Planning Association*, 61(3), 328–343.

Logan, W. (2000). *Hanoi: biography of a city*. Washington: University of Washington Press.

Logan, W. (2009). Hanoi, Vietnam: representing power in and of the nation. *City*, 13(1), 87–94.

Lorrain, D. (2002). Capitalismes urbains. Des modèles européens en compétition. *L'Année de la régulation*, 6, 195–239.

Luan, T. (1997). Hanoi: balancing market and ideology. In Douglass, M. et al., *Culture and the City in East Asia*. Oxford: Clarendon Press, 124–145.

Luan, T. (2002). Transformation des modes de vie et de la morphologie urbaine à Hanoi. In Charbonneau, F. and Hau, D., *Enjeux modernes d'une ville millénaire*. Montreal: Trames, 88–96.

Malpas, J. (2012). Putting space in place: philosophical topography and relational geography. *Environment and Planning D: Society and Space*, 30, 226–242.

Malpass, A., Cloke, P., Barnett, C. and Clarke, N. (2007). Fairtrade urbanism? The politics of place beyond place in the Bristol Fairtrade City campaign. *International Journal of Urban and Regional Research*, 31(3), 633–645.

Marr, D. (2003). A passion for modernity: intellectuals and the media. In Luong, H., *Postwar Vietnamese Society: an overview of transformational dynamics.* New York: Rowman and Littlefield 226–257.

Marston, S., Paul Jones III, J. and Woodward, K. (2005). Human geography without scale. *Transactions of the Institute of British Geographers,* 30, 416–432.

Masima, P. (2006). *Vietnam's Development Strategies.* London: Routledge.

Massey, D. (1991). A global sense of place. *Marxism Today,* 35(6), 24–29.

Massey, D. (2004). Geographies of responsibility. *Geografiska Annaler: Series B, Human Geography,* 86(1), 5–18.

Massey, D. (2005). *For Space.* London: Sage.

Massey, D. (2007). *World City.* Cambridge: Polity Press.

Massey, D. (2011). A counterhegemonic relationality of place. In McCann, E. and Ward, K., *Mobile Urbanism: cities and policymaking in the global age.* Minneapolis: University of Minnesota Press, 1–14.

Mattelart, A. (2005). *Diversité culturelle et mondialisation.* Paris: La Découverte.

Mayaram, S. (2009). *The other global city.* London: Routledge.

McCann, E. (2011). Urban policy mobilities and global circuits of knowledge: toward a research agenda. *Annals of the Association of American Geographers,* 101(1), 107–130.

McCann, E. and Ward, K. (2010). Relationality/territoriality: toward a conceptualization of cities in the world. *Geoforum,* 41(2), 175–184.

McCann, E. and Ward, K. (2011a). *Mobile Urbanism: cities and policymaking in the global age.* Minneapolis: University of Minnesota Press.

McCann, E. and Ward, K. (2011b). Urban assemblages: territories, relations, practices, power. In McCann, E. and Ward, K., *Mobile Urbanism: cities and policymaking in the global age.* Minneapolis: University of Minnesota Press, xiii–xxxv.

McCann, E. and Ward, K. (2012). Assembling urbanism: following policies and "studying through" the sites and situations of policy making. *Environment and Planning A,* 44(1), 52–67.

McCann, E. J. (2008). Expertise, truth, and urban policy mobilities: global circuits of knowledge in the development of Vancouver, Canada's "four pillar" drug strategy. *Environment and Planning A,* 40(4), 885–904.

McFarlane, C. (2009). Translocal assemblages: space, power and social movements. *Geoforum,* 40(4), 561–567.

McFarlane, C. (2010). The comparative city: knowledge, learning, urbanism. *International Journal of Urban and Regional Research,* 34(4), 725–742.

McFarlane, C. (2011). *Learning the City: knowledge and translocal assemblage.* Oxford: Wiley-Blackwell.

McGee, T. G. (2009). Interrogating the production of urban space in China and Vietnam under market socialism. *Asia Pacific Viewpoint,* 50(2), 228–246.

McNally, S. (2003). Bia om and Karaoke: HIV and everyday live in urban Vietnam. In Drummond, L. and Thomas, M., *Consuming Urban Culture in Contemporary Vietnam.* London Routledge, 110–122.

McNeill, D. (2009). *The Global Architect: firms, fame and urban form.* London: Routledge.

McNeill, D. and Tewdwr-Jones, M. (2003). Architecture, banal nationalism and re-territorialization. *International Journal of Urban and Regional Research*, 27(3), 738–743.

Meyer, J., Boli, J., Thomas, G. and Ramirez, F. (1997). World society and the nation-state. *American Journal of Sociology*, 103(1), 144–181.

Miller, P. and Rose, N. (2008). *Governing the Present: administering economic, social and personal life*. Cambridge: Polity Press.

Minh, N. and Thuy, P. (2003). Representations of Doi Moi society in contemporary Vietnamese cinema. In Drummond, L. and Thomas, M., *Consuming Urban Culture in Contemporary Vietnam*. London Routledge, 191–201.

Myers, G. (2003). *Verandahs of Power: colonialism and space in urban Africa*. Syracuse: Syracuse University Press.

Nasr, J. and Volait, M. (2003). *Urbanism – Imported or Exported? Native aspirations and foreign plans*. London: John Wiley & Sons, Ltd.

Nijman, J. (2007). Introduction – comparative urbanism. *Urban Geography*, 28(1), 1–6.

Ong, A. (2011). Introduction: worlding cities, or the art of being global. In Roy, A. and Ong, A., *Worlding Cities: Asian experiments and the art of being global*. Oxford: Wiley-Blackwell, 1–26.

Osborne, T. and Rose, N. (1999). Governing cities: notes on the spatialisation of virtue. *Environment and Planning D: Society and Space*, 17(6), 737–760.

Osborne, T. and Rose, N. (2004). Spatial phenomenotechnics: making space with Charles Booth and Patrick Geddes. *Environment and Planning D: Society and Space*, 22(2), 209–228.

Parnell, S. and Robinson, J. (2012). (Re)theorizing cities from the Global South: looking beyond neoliberalism. *Urban Geography*, 33(4), 593–617.

Peck, J. (2011a). Creative moments: working culture, through municipal socialism and neoliberal urbanism. In McCann, E. and Ward, K., *Mobile Urbanism: cities and policymaking in the global age*. Minneapolis: The University of Minnesota Press, 41–70.

Peck, J. (2011b). Geographies of policy: from transfer-diffusion to mobility-mutation. *Progress in Human Geography*, 35, 773–797.

Peck, J. and Theodore, N. (2001). Exporting workfare/importing welfare-to-work: exploring the politics of Third Way policy transfer. *Political Geography*, 20(4), 427–460.

Peck, J. and Theodore, N. (2010a). Mobilizing policy: models, methods, and mutations. *Geoforum*, 41(2), 169–174.

Peck, J. and Theodore, N. (2010b). Recombinant workfare, across the Americas: transnationalizing "fast" social policy. *Geoforum*, 41(2), 195–208.

Peck, J. and Theodore, N. (2012). Follow the policy: a distended case approach. *Environment and Planning A*, 44(1), 21.

Peck, J. and Tickell, A. (2002). Neoliberalizing space. *Antipode*, 34(3), 380–404.

Peck, J., Theodore, N. and Brenner, N. (2013). Neoliberal urbanism redux? *International Journal of Urban and Regional Research*, 37(3), 1091–1099.

Phe, H. (2002). Investment in residential property: taxonomy of home improvers in Central Hanoi. *Habitat International*, 26, 471–486.

Philo, C. (1989). Enough to drive one mad: the organisation of space in nineteenth-century lunatic asylums. In Wolch, J. R. and Dear, M. J., *The Power of Geography: how territory shapes social life*. Boston: Unwin Hyman, 258–290.

Pierre-Louis, L., Philifert, P. and Biehler, A. (2007). *Le développement durable: un concept planétaire au risque de dynamqiues territoriales maghrébine et sahélienne (Maroc–Burkina Faso)*. Paris: Ministère de l'équipement – PUCA, Ministère de l'écologie et du développement durable – UMR LOUEST.

Pieterse, E. A. (2008). *City Futures: confronting the crisis of urban development*. London: Zed Books.

Piveteau, A. (2004). *Evaluer les ONG*. Paris: Karthala.

Prince, R. (2010). Policy transfer as policy assemblage: making policy for the creative industries in New Zealand. *Environment and Planning A*, 42(1), 169–186.

Prince, R. (2012). Policy transfer, consultants and the geographies of governance. *Progress in Human Geography*, 36(2), 188–203.

Quénot, H. (2007). Construction du champ politique local et politique de propreté à Accra et Ouagadougou. In Fourchard, L., *Gouverner les villes d'Afrique. État, gouvernement local et acteurs privés*. Paris: Karthala, 69–88.

Rabinow, P. (1989). *French Modern: norms and forms of the social environment*. Chicago: University of Chicago Press.

Raffestin, C. (1986). Territorialité: concept ou paradigme en géographie sociale? *Geographica Helvetica* (2), 91–96.

Randeria, S. (2006). Entangled histories: civil society, caste solidarities and legal pluralism in post-colonial India. In Keane, J., *Civil Society: Berlin perspectives*. Oxford: Berghahn, 213–241.

Randeria, S. (2007). Global designs and local lifeworlds. *Interventions: international journal of postcolonial studies*, 9(1), 12–30.

Ren, X. (2011). *Building Globalization: transnational architecture production in urban China*. Chicago: University of Chicago Press.

Rentetzi, M. (2008). Configuring identities through industrial architecture and urban planning: Greek tobacco warehouses. *Science Studies*, 21(1), 64–81.

Robinson, J. (2002). Global and World Cities: a view from off the map. *International Journal of Urban and Regional Research*, 26(3), 531–554.

Robinson, J. (2004). In the tracks of comparative urbanism: difference, urban modernity and the primitive. *Urban Geography*, 25(8), 709–723.

Robinson, J. (2006). *Ordinary Cities: between modernity and development*. London: Routledge.

Robinson, J. (2011a). Cities in a world of cities: the comparative gesture. *International Journal of Urban and Regional Research*, 35(1), 1–23.

Robinson, J. (2011b). Comparisons: colonial or cosmopolitan? *Singapore Journal of Tropical Geography*, 32(2), 125–140.

Robinson, J. (2011c). The spaces of circulating knowledge: city strategies and global urban governmentality. In McCann, E. and Ward, K., *Mobile Urbanism: cities and policymaking in the global age*. Minneapolis: University of Minnesota Press, 15–40.

Robinson, J. (2013). "Arriving at" urban policies/the urban: traces of elsewhere in making city futures. In Söderström, O. et al., *Critical Mobilities*. London: Routledge, 1–28.

Ros, L. (2001). Typologies de l'habitat dans leur rapport à l'espace urbain et péri-urbain. In Clément, P. and Lancret, N., *Hanoï, le cycle des métamorphoses: formes architecturales et urbaines.* Paris: Ed. recherches/Ipraus, 243–277.

Roy, A. (2011). Urbanisms, worlding practices and the theory of planning. *Planning Theory*, 10(1), 6.

Roy, A. and Ong, A. (2011). *Worlding Cities: Asian experiments and the art of being global.* Oxford: Wiley-Blackwell.

Sassen, S. (1991). *The Global City: New York, London, Tokyo.* Princeton: Princeton University Press.

Sassen, S. (2002). *Global Networks, Linked Cities.* London: Routledge.

Saunier, P.-Y. (2001). Sketches from the Urban Internationale, 1910–1950: voluntary associations, international institutions and US philanthropic foundations. *International Journal of Urban and Regional Research*, 25(2), 380–403.

Saunier, P.-Y. (2002). Taking up the bet on connections: a municipal contribution. *Contemporary European History*, 11(4), 507–527.

Saunier, P.-Y. and Ewen, S. (2008). *Another Global City: historical explorations into the transnational municipal moment, 1850–2000.* New York: Palgrave Macmillan.

Savitch, H. V. and Kantor, P. (2002). *Cities in the International Marketplace: the political economy of urban development in North America and Western Europe.* Princeton and Oxford: Princeton University Press.

Schmidt, V. H. (2006). Multiple modernities or varieties of modernity? *Current Sociology*, 54(1), 77–97.

Segbers, K., Raiser, S. and Volkmann, K. (2007). *The Making of Global City Regions: Johannesburg, Mumbai/Bombay, Sao Paulo, and Shanghai.* Baltimore: Johns Hopkins University Press.

Shatkin, G. (1998). "Fourth world" cities in the global economy: the case of Phnom Penh, Cambodia. *International Journal of Urban and Regional Research*, 22(3), 378–393.

Simone, A. M. (2004a). *For the City Yet to Come: changing African life in four cities.* Durham: Duke University Press.

Simone, A. M. (2004b). People as infrastructure: intersecting fragments in Johannesburg. *Public Culture*, 16(3), 407–429.

Simone, A. M. (2010). *City Life from Jakarta to Dakar: movements at the crossroads.* London: Routledge.

Simpson, T. (2011). "Neoliberalism with Chinese Characteristics": consumer pedagogy in Macao. In Schmid, H. et al., *Cities and Fascination: beyond the surplus of meaning.* London: Ashgate, 187–205.

Sion, J. (1929). *Asie des moussons.* Paris: Armand Colin.

Sissao, C. (1989). Ouagadougou et les centres urbains du Burkina-Faso. In Dulucq, S. and Goerg, O., *Les investissements publics dans les villes africaines 1930–1985 – habitat et transport.* Paris: L'Harmattan, 70–86.

Sloterdijk, P. (2004). *Schäume.* Berlin: Suhrkamp.

Smith, M. P. (2003). *Transnational Urbanism: locating globalization.* Oxford: Blackwell.

Söderström, O. (1992). *Les métamorphoses du patrimoine: formes de conservation du construit et urbanité.* Lausanne: Presses Centrales.

Söderström, O. (1996). Paper cities: visual thinking in urban planning. *Cultural Geographies*, 3(3), 249–281.

Söderström, O. (1997). *L'Industriel, l'architecte et le phalanstère: discours, formes et pratiques du logement ouvrier à Ugine*. Paris: L'Harmattan.

Söderström, O. (2000). *Des images pour agir: le visuel en urbanisme*. Lausanne: Payot.

Söderström, O. (2010). Forms and flows in the contemporary transformations of Palermo's city centre. In Guggenheim, M. and Söderström, O., *Re-shaping Cities: how global mobility transforms architecture and urban form*. London: Routledge, 189–209.

Söderström, O. and de Dardel, J. (forthcoming). Carceral connections: the US prison and penal policy in Columbia.

Söderström, O. and Geertman, S. (2013). Loose Threads: the translocal making of public space policy in Hanoi. *Singapore Journal of Tropical Geography*, 34, 244–260.

Söderström, O., Dupuis, B. and Leu, P. (2013). Translocal urbanism: how Ouagadougou strategically uses decentralised cooperation. In Obrist, B., et al. (eds.) *Living the City in Africa*. Basel: SGAS (with Lit Verlag), 99–117.

Söderström, O., Cogato Lanza, E., Lawrence, R. and Barbey, G. (2000). *L'usage du projet: pratiques sociales et conception du projet urbain et architectural*. Lausanne: Payot.

Söderström, O., Dupuis, B., Geertman, S. and Leu, P. (2010). *La mondialisation des formes urbaine à Hanoi et Ouagadougou*. Neuchâtel: Institut de Géographie, Université de Neuchâtel et Fonds National Suisse de la Recherche Scientifique.

Söderström, O., Fimiani, D., Giambalvo, M. and Lucido, S. (2009). *Urban Cosmographies*. Roma: Meltemi.

Söderström, O., Randeria, S., D'Amato, G., Ruedin, D. and Panese, F. (2013). On mobilities and moorings. In Söderström, O. et al., *Critical Mobilities*. London: Routledge, V–XXXV.

Springer, S. (2009). Violence, democracy, and the neoliberal "order": the contestation of public space in post-transitional Cambodia. *Annals of the Association of American Geographers*, 99(1), 138–162.

Springer, S. (2011). Public space as emancipation: meditations on anarchism, radical democracy, neoliberalism and violence. *Antipode*, 43(2), 525–562.

Staeheli, L. A. and Mitchell, D. (2007). Locating the public in research and practice. *Progress in Human Geography*, 31(6), 792–811.

Staeheli, L. A. and Mitchell, D. (2008). *The People's Property?: power, politics, and the public*. London: Routledge.

Steck, J.-F. (2006–2007). La rue africaine, territoire de l'informel? *Métropolis* (66/67), 73–86.

Stone, C. N. (1989). *Regime Politics: governing Atlanta, 1946–1988*. Lawrence, KS: University Press of Kansas.

Stone, D. (2004). Transfer agents and global networks in the "transnationalization" of policy. *Journal of European Public Policy*, 11(3), 545–566.

Strebel, I. (2011). The living building: towards a geography of maintenance work. *Social and Cultural Geography*, 12(3), 243–262.

Taylor, C. (1995). Two theories of modernity. *The Hastings Center Report*, 25(2), 24–33.

Taylor, P. J. (2004). *World City Network: a global urban analysis*. London: Routledge.

Therborn, G. (2003). Entangled modernities. *European Journal of Social Theory*, 6(3), 293–305.

Thomas, F. (2001). L'espace public, un espace moribond ou en expansion? *Géocarrefour*, 76(1), 75–84.

Thomas, M. (2002). Out of control: emergent cultural landscapes and political change in urban Vietnam. *Urban Studies*, 39(9), 1611–1624.

Thong, N. (2001). Histoire de Hanoi: la ville en ses quarties. In Clément, P. and Lancret, N., *Hanoi; Le cycle des métamorphoses. Formes architecturales et urbaines*. Paris: Cahiers de l'IPRAUS, 17–30.

Thrift, N. (2006). Space. *Theory, Culture and Society*, 23, 139–146.

Thrift, N. (2008). *Non-Representational Theory: space, politics, affect*. London: Routledge.

Tilly, C. (1984). *Big Structures*. New York: Russell Sage Foundation.

Tolia-Kelly, D. P. (2004). Materializing post-colonial geographies: examining the textural landscapes of migration in the South Asian home. *Geoforum*, 35(6), 675–688.

Toussaint, J. Y. and Vareilles, S. (2009). A qui profite la concertation? *Geographica Helvetica*, 2009, 235–243.

Turco, A. (2010). *Configurazioni della territorialità*. Milan: Franco Angeli.

UN-Habitat (2007). *Profil urbain de Ouagadougou*. Nairobi: UNPD.

UN-Habitat (2008). *Country Programme Document 2008–2009*. Nairobi: UN-Habitat.

UN-Habitat (2009). *Planning Sustainable Cities: global report on human settlements 2009*. London: Earthscan/James & James.

Urry, J. (2007). *Mobilities*. Cambridge: Polity Press.

Vasudevan, A. (2011). Dramaturgies of dissent: the spatial politics of squatting in Berlin, 1968–. *Social and Cultural Geography*, 12(3), 283–303.

Vertovec, S. (2009). *Transnationalism*. London: Routledge.

Vu Tuan, A. (1994). *Vietnam's Economic Reform: results and problems*. Hanoi: Social Science Publishing House.

Ward, K. (2006). "Policies in Motion", urban management and state restructuring: the translocal expansion of business improvement districts. *International Journal of Urban and Regional Research*, 30(1), 54–75.

Ward, K. (2007). Business improvement districts: policy origins, mobile policies and urban liveability. *Geography Compass*, 1(3), 657–672.

Ward, K. (2008). Editorial – Toward a comparative (re) turn in urban studies? Some reflections. *Urban Geography*, 29(5), 405–410.

Ward, K. (2010). Towards a relational comparative approach to the study of cities. *Progress in Human Geography*, 34(4), 471–487.

Ward, S. (1999). The international diffusion of planning: a review and a Canadian case study. *International Planning Studies*, 4(1), 53–77.

Watson, V. (2009). Seeing from the South: refocusing urban planning on the globe's central urban issues. *Urban Studies*, 46(11), 2259–2275.

Wells-Dang, A. (2010). Political space in Vietnam: a view from the "rice-roots". *The Pacific Review*, 23(1), 93–112.

Wells-Dang, A. (2011). Informal pathbreakers: civil society networks in China and Vietnam. Birmingham: Department of Politics and International Studies University of Birmingham.

Wetzstein, S. and Le Heron, R. (2010). Regional economic policy "in-the-making": imaginaries, political projects and institutions for Auckland's economic transformation. *Environment and Planning A*, 42, 1902–1924.

Woolgar, S. (1991). Configuring the user: the case of usability trials. In Law, J., *A Sociology of Monsters: essays on power technology and domination*. London: Routledge, 58–99.

World Bank (2010). *Silencieuse et fatale: la corruption discrète entrave les efforts de développement de l'Afrique*. Washington: Banque internationale pour la reconstruction et le développement/Banque mondiale.

Wright, G. (1991). *The Politics of Design in French Colonial Urbanism*. Chicago: University of Chicago Press.

Wright, G. and Rabinow, P. (1982). Savoir et pouvoir dans l'urbanisme moderne colonial d'Ernest Hébrard. *Les cahiers de la recherche architecturale* (9), 25–43.

Yaneva, A. (2009). *Made by the Office for Metropolitan Architecture: an ethnography of design*. Rotterdam: 010 Publishers.

Young, R. J. C. (1998). Ideologies of the postcolonial. *Interventions*, 1(1), 4–8.

Zuppinger, B. (2005). De la marge urbaine à la ville: régularisation des périphéries informelles de Ouagadougou et enjeux locaux. In Reynard, E. and Dambo, L., *Vivre dans les milieux fragiles: Alpes et Sahel: hommage au Professeur Jörg Winistörfer*. Lausanne: Travaux et Recherches de l'Institut de Géographie de l'Université de Lausanne, 193–210.

Index

Note: Page numbers in *italics* refer to Figures; those in **bold** to Tables

Cities in Relations: Trajectories of Urban Development in Hanoi and Ouagadougou,
First Edition. Ola Söderström.